Understanding Islamist Terrorism

Understanding Islamist Terrorism
The Islamic Doctrine of War
Patrick Sookhdeo Ph.D., D.D.

Published in the United States by Isaac Publishing
6729 Curran Street, McLean VA 22101

ISBN 978-0-9787141-6-1
Printed in the United States of America

Contents

Foreword

Many books have been published in the past two years purporting to explain the roots of Muslim fundamentalism. Some, like Noam Chomsky, say it is simply a response to American imperialism. Others, following the lead of Samuel Huntington, see it as the result of an inevitable clash between faith-based civilisations. Others again see it as a "pathological response" to the spread of liberal democratic values – having much in common with the mid-20th century aberrations of communism, fascism and nihilism. On this view the blame lies with the failure of liberal civilisation to live up to its own ideals. Hence the Islamist solution is to sweep away the existing order and replace it with God's rule on earth. But all such reductionist explanations miss the mark unless they cast light on the Muslim tradition of jihad, to which Christianity has no counterpart. Is this to be understood as a holy war of conquest to be pursued until the whole world embraces the Muslim faith, or at least submits to Muslim rule? Or is it more correctly seen as a spiritual struggle against temptation and sin to improve and purify oneself – jihad of the heart? Is it true that Mr. bin Laden's 1998 *fatwa* against "the Jews and the Crusaders" is regarded by many if not most Muslims as a travesty of their faith? More particularly is suicide bombing rightly seen as a sure route to holy martyrdom or a grotesque distortion of Islam?

Few people are better qualified to interpret the Islamic doctrine of war than the author of this short book. Patrick Sookhdeo comes from a Guyanese background and his knowledge of Islam is derived not only from academic study but also from personal experience. He holds a Ph.D. from London University's School of Oriental and African Studies, and is a Visiting Fellow at Cranfield University, Royal Military College of Science. There are few people to be found anywhere in the world with a better understanding in practice of how Islam works. So while this book relies, as it must, on extensive quotations from the Qur'an and other sources (*hadith*, Shari'ah) it is far from being an academic thesis. On the contrary it focuses, quite precisely, on how those sources have led, by means of a logical reasoning process, into an enormously detailed set of rules to regulate every aspect of devotional, family, social, economic, military and political life.

This book falls into four main parts. The first, having introduced the sources and the way in which they are interpreted, sets out the resulting theology of war, peace and the creation of empire. The second deals, in summary outline, with the dramatic expansion and subsequent slow decline of the Muslim world from the seventh century to the present day. The third part deals with the violent sects within Islam, both past and present, the motivation of terrorists and how they are recruited, trained and sent on their deadly missions. The last part deals with the contemporary Muslim debate and offers ten options for dealing with the problem of Islamist terrorism.

This book offers no easy solutions. One has to grapple with the texts, whose meaning is by no means always obvious; and where they oppose each other either reconcile them or live with the contradiction. One has to face the facts of faith and practice which are sometimes ugly and often very alien to our own. One has to admit to glaring mistakes made by the West in trying to cope with Islam over the past thirteen hundred years. Above all one has to think clearly and dispassionately how best to cope with Islamic fundamentalism as we find it today. As Patrick Sookhdeo says "A spider weaves its web in secret in a dark corner, and cannot be tackled until a light is shone upon it". This book shines a clear light into many corners of this convoluted subject. It is an indispensable primer for all who seek to respond to the Islamic doctrine of war – or even simply to understand it better.

General Sir Hugh Beach GBE, KCB, MC

Hugh Beach spent forty years in the Royal Engineers. His last appointment was as Master General of the Ordnance (Army Board Member for Procurement). After leaving active service he was Warden of St George's House in Windsor Castle for five years, and in later years he chaired the Boards of Management of both Church Army and SPCK.

The jihad is the Islamic *bellum justum* and may be regarded as the very basis of Islam's relationships with other nations.

– Majid Khadduri[1]

Jihad is the signature tune of Islamic history.

– M.J. Akbar[2]

Introduction:
The Interpretation of Sources

Is the cup half full of water, or is it half empty? Human interpretation of basic data can be influenced by many different factors, exterior and interior, conscious and subconscious. This is particularly true in the religious arena, where basic sources are liable to be given a whole spectrum of interpretations, for ultimately there is no way of proving or disproving any particular believer's understanding of a religious text.

There is also plenty of scope for contrasting interpretations in many other areas of life. America's "war on terror", following the tragic events of September 11th 2001, is considered a "war on Islam" by many Muslims despite repeated denials by western leaders.

The theme of this book is the doctrine of war in Islam, a subject which is surrounded by much confusion. What we can be sure of is that a discussion of war features overtly in Islamic theology and thought from its earliest days until now. We can also be sure that there are a multitude of different interpretations which are sincerely held and practised by different individual Muslims.

An example of difference in interpretation can be clearly seen in the varying understandings of the word "jihad" (literally "striving"). For some Muslims this means military war to spread Islam as a religious and political system – jihad of the sword. For others it is a spiritual struggle against temptation and sin to improve and purify oneself – jihad of the heart. Intermediate are two other possibilities – jihad of the tongue[3] and of the hands, aimed at correcting wrongs and supporting what is right.

It is worth noting here that the term "holy war", so often used as an English translation of "jihad", did not exist in classical Arabic usage. There is a word for war [*harb*] and a word for holy [*muqaddas*] which are sometimes put together in modern Arabic, but were never combined in classical Arabic. However, the use of the term "holy war" in the sense of "war ordained by God" can be supported by the fact that the word "jihad" in the Islamic source texts is commonly followed by the phrase "in the way [i.e. path] of God" and by the fact that the military meaning of jihad was predominant in the understanding of the classical Islamic theologians and jurists.[4]

Although Islamist terrorists – who are included in those who consider jihad to be military war – are few in number, they should not necessarily be considered a marginalized fringe group rejected by the mainstream of Islamic society as "not real Muslims". Their guiding principles are not a modern aberration of some undeniably peaceful true Islam but have deep roots in Islamic history and theology. Such terrorists are simply following a particular interpretation of the sources of Islam. They have selected and prioritised certain aspects and texts of Islamic source material. Other interpretations take the same source material and come to a different conclusion. Those who deny the validity of the terrorists' interpretation are usually very liberal Muslims, whose own interpretations of Islam are unacceptable to the majority. One such example is Bassam Tibi, Professor of International Relations at the University of Göttingen, Germany and formerly Bosch Fellow and Research Associate at Harvard University, who states categorically: "The terrorism of Islamic fundamentalists is not a jihad in the authentic tradition – even though they conceive of their actions as a jihad."[5] It should be noted that others may make similar public denials not through conviction but for tactical reasons.

Contemporary Islam has also produced a range of newer perspectives on war, making a discussion of the subject more complex than it would have been in an earlier age. In the past there was much more of a consensus (albeit always with some dissident variations) on what a Muslim should believe about war. This classical historic understanding has now been challenged by many alternative interpretations. The following chapters of this book will seek to set out the classical Islamic doctrine of war, for this is still the interpretation with which all other interpretations are compared and contrasted by their respective proponents. It is also the doctrine still followed closely by many modern Muslims as will be seen in the latter part of the book.

Some modern arguments against the classical Islamic doctrine of war

Before embarking on a description of the classical Islamic doctrine of war, it is helpful to consider briefly some of the main threads of argument offered by contemporary Muslims who have a more pacific faith than historical Islam. A useful discussion from this viewpoint can be found in the chapter "War and Peace in Islamic Law" by Harfiyah Haleem and Abdul Haleem in *The Crescent and the Cross*.[6] Like other Muslims with a peaceable perspective, the authors tackle a range of points found in the classical Islamic scholars' doctrine of war and offer alternative interpretations. Clearly it is sometimes a struggle to maintain respect for the revered scholars of the past whose classical interpretations are now being so radically revised. Shafi'i (768-820)[7] is described as confused, and opinions are attributed to him with phrases like "as Shafi'i himself probably realised" or "this does not necessarily mean that Shafi'i thought non-combatants could be killed".[8]

1. *War is only justified for self-defence*[9] *or pre-empting an imminent attack.* The first Muslims suffered ten years of persecution in Mecca before they fought back.[10] When self-
   defence is required, war becomes not only justifiable but
   an obligation, as the Qur'an commands, "Fight in the
   cause of God those who fight you." (Q 2:190).[11] One of
   the great exponents of the defensive nature of jihad was
   Mahmud Shaltut (1893-1963) the Sheikh of Cairo's prestigious Al-Azhar University.[12] Another was Sir Syed Ahmed

Khan (1817-1898) who tried to persuade his fellow Indian Muslims that they were only justified in fighting the British powers if the British *actively* prevented them from exercising their Islamic faith.[13] A contemporary exponent is Dr Abdel Mo'ti Bayoumi, a member of the Islamic Research Institute at Al-Azhar University.[14] This is the line of argument in Fatoohi's book *Jihad in the Qur'an* which he wrote after September 11th 2001 for Muslims, for those considering converting to Islam, and to convince other non-Muslims of the peaceful nature of Islam. Fatoohi holds that armed jihad is a temporary measure for self-defence but peaceful jihad, in the sense of self-improvement and preaching Islam and working for good, is permanent.[15]

2. *War is only justified if the aim is to stop evil and oppression.* Haleem et al. quote from the Qur'an in support of this, to indicate that God has set one group of people against another in order to prevent the earth from becoming "full of mischief" (Q 2:251).[16] Dr Kamal Boraiq'a Abd es-Salam of Al-Azhar University, using another Qur'anic verse for support (Q 2:193),[17] states that:

> The purpose of war in Islam is to suppress tyranny, ensure the right of man to his home and freedom within his nation, prevent persecution in religion and guarantee freedom of belief to all people.[18]

Interestingly both Haleem et al. and Abd es-Salam confound the two justifications – self-defence and the elimination of oppression – and treat these two ideas as if they were one. Perhaps this is indicative of a preferential concern for oppressed Muslims rather than for oppressed people in general.[19] (See also the comments of Mohammed al-Asi quoted on page 146.)

Another important contemporary voice who takes the line that jihad is primarily to rescue the weak from persecution is Ali Asghar Engineer.[20]

3. *Qur'anic commands to make war were applicable only in their specific contexts.* Classical doctrine taught that Jews and Christians should be fought until they submitted and paid a special tax (Q 9:29, quoted on page 30) but Shaltut asserts that this referred to a particular group of treacherous, oath-breaking non-Muslims described in Q 9:7-13 and was not a general command.[21] Haleem et al. use the same Qur'anic passage and the same argument to deny the classical teaching that Muslims should fight pagans (i.e. polytheists) until the pagans are either killed or have converted to Islam.[22]

   A different kind of contextual argument is used by Shaltut with reference to the Qur'anic command "Fight the unbelievers who gird you about, and let them find firmness in you" (Q 9:123). This Shaltut interprets as a tactical directive for application once legitimate fighting has broken out; it is a war plan which tells the Muslims that "when enemies are manifold, it is imperative to fight the nearest first of all, then the nearest but one and so on, in order to clear the road from enemies and to facilitate the victory."[23]

   The same reasoning is applied by some scholars to sections of other Islamic teaching on war, not found in the Qur'an. In the words of Dr Bayoumi such legislation is "situation-related" or "time-related"[24] and therefore not universally applicable.

4. *Some of the early Muslim scholars were misguided in the deductions they made from the Qur'an and the* hadith.[25] For example, the normal concept of *Dar al-Harb*[26] is erroneous,[27] and Shaybani's pivotal work on Siyar is mostly his personal opinion based on expediency rather than the *hadith*.[28] A particularly important aspect of this argument concerns the traditional method of weighting the relative importance of individual Qur'anic verses.[29] This is what produced the aggressive stance of classical Islamic doctrine, but some modern scholars have rejected the method, including the eminent Mahmud Shaltut.[30]

5. *Fresh interpretation of Arabic terminology.* Some arguments under this heading include the following. (i) The Arabic word "jihad" should not be taken to include "fighting" for which there is another term, *qital,* in the Qur'an. It should only mean the striving for personal improvement.[31] (ii) The Qur'anic command "Fighting [*qital*] is prescribed for you" (Q 2:216) comes soon after a verse about enduring trials and adversity (Q 2:214). It is argued that the Arabic could just as well mean "Being fought against is prescribed for you" i.e. a statement that the Muslims would have to endure the affliction of being attacked.[32] (iii) Although jihad is an obligation [*fard*], an obligation is not the same as a compulsion.[33]

Scholars who argue as above are also usually at pains to emphasise that when war becomes necessary it should be fought justly and without recourse to excessive violence. For example, non-combatants should not be harmed, neither should crops, animals or the environment.[34] There is also an emphasis on the fact that those who go to war should have the right motives – not for personal glory or for personal gain but what the Qur'an calls *fi sabil illah* [in the way of God].[35]

Such scholars may also assert that early Muslims who took a more aggressive stance on war were merely heterodox sects like the Khariji,[36] who they argue were not part of mainstream Islam. Nevertheless the scholars' own efforts to counter and argue away the classical Islamic teaching on war do seem by implication to acknowledge how widely accepted this doctrine has been for many centuries. It is still the benchmark against which all other teaching on war is compared. This is the doctrine which will be outlined in the following chapters.

The development of the classical doctrine

The Islamic doctrine of war was developed over a period of time by the same processes which Islamic scholars used to develop other areas of Islamic doctrine and law. The primary source of Islamic teaching is the Qur'an, revered by Muslims as the word of God, the original being engraved in Arabic on a stone tablet in heaven. Muslims believe that the text of the Qur'an was revealed piece-meal to Muhammad during the last twenty-three years of his life (610-632). Various collections of the revelations were put together, differing slightly from each other, but between 650 and 656 efforts were made to suppress all but one of these.

Second in importance and authority as a source is the *hadith*, that is traditional accounts of what Muhammad said and did. They gain their authority from Muhammad's own command in his farewell sermon to hold on to two things he was leaving them that would prevent them going astray – the Qur'an and the *hadith*.[37] Further authority is given by a verse in the Qur'an which urges Muslims to follow Muhammad's example:

Ye have indeed in the Apostle of God a beautiful pattern (of conduct)
Q 33:21

The stories are numerous, and different scholars have made their own collections, the largest ones dating from two or three centuries after Muhammad. Much scholarly effort has been put into ascertaining which of the many stories are the most reliable. Validity is usually judged by the chain of transmission i.e. the list of people by whom the story was passed down. The most reliable collections are recognisable by the word *sahih* [true] before the name of the compiler.

From these two sources Islamic jurists gradually evolved a detailed body of legislation called the Shari'ah. Five main versions of this exist today – four different Sunni schools of law and one Shi'a school – each being favoured in different parts of the world. The Sunni schools were founded by Hanifa, Malik, Shafi'i and Hanbal, the Shi'a school by Imam Ja'far. Although differing on minor points, the five schools agree on basic issues. These enormously detailed sets of rules to regulate every aspect of devotional, family, social, economic, military and political life were derived from the Qur'an and *hadith* by a logical reasoning process known as *ijtihad*. It is worth taking some time to look at the main types of problems facing those engaged in *ijtihad*.

Firstly, despite the fact that the Qur'an and Muhammad's own words and actions were all held to be divinely inspired, there often appeared to be a conflict of opinion between these various sources. Even within the Qur'an itself there were many verses which seemed to contradict each other. Furthermore the Qur'anic text is often remarkably vague and ambiguous; many individual verses are open to a multitude of interpretations, some examples of which have been given above. So although the Qur'an was more authoritative, the *hadith* was often easier to understand. Then there was the problem of how to legislate on issues not actually mentioned in either the Qur'an or the *hadith*.

Some rules and tools were devised to guide the scholars in their perplexity. Firstly there was the concept of *naskh*. This term is most often translated into English as "abrogation" and describes a simple rule of Qur'anic interpretation whereby in any case of self-contradiction within the Qur'an the later-dated verse (*nasikh*, that which abrogates) is assumed to take precedence over the earlier verse (*mansukh*, that which is abrogated). Some scholars emphasise that this does not mean the earlier verse is actually untrue and cancelled out, but that it has been subordinated to and modified by the later verse. The application of this simple rule is made complex in practice by the fact that the Qur'an is not arranged in chronological order so considerable scholarship is needed to know the relative dates of any two verses, and in some cases scholars differ. The huge impact of *naskh* on the classical Islamic doctrine of war is explained in chapter 2.

Other tools of *ijtihad* included *ijma'* [the consensus of Muslim scholars on any given subject] and *qiyas* [analogical reasoning, helpful when trying to derive laws on subjects not covered in the sources]. Other factors taken into consideration, but carrying less weight, included the prevailing customs of pre-Islamic Arabia and various general principles such as the public good, a harm must not be removed by means of a greater harm etc.[38]

The founders of the five schools of Islamic law lived in the eighth century and the first half of the ninth century. In the eleventh century the Islamic state began to disintegrate and one of the Sunni caliphs, seeking to prevent the development of too many new groupings, announced that "the door of *ijtihad*" had closed i.e. that no further law-making was necessary. The existing Sunni schools were sufficient. This has created a great reluctance amongst the majority of Sunni Muslims to indulge in *ijtihad* even to this day. The belief that the door of *ijtihad* has yet to be re-opened (if ever), is reinforced by a belief that *ijtihad* can only be practised by scholars of unusual personal piety as well as unusual learning.[39] Hence it is that the majority of today's Sunni Muslims see it as heresy to consider altering or updating the Shari'a.[40]

Nevertheless, since the closing of the door of *ijtihad*, there have been many individual Muslims who have departed from the standard teaching. Two of the best known in medieval times were al-Ghazali (d.1111) who promoted Sufism (Islamic mysticism) and Ibn Rushd (also known as Averroes, 1126-98) who took a rationalist approach.

Modern calls to return to the original sources and make a new *ijtihad* may seek to reform Islam in one or other of two directions. Some seek a modernisation and liberalisation to keep Islam in step with other contemporary civilisations, others seek to create a stricter and more puritanical faith completely unblemished by any outside influence. With regard to the Islamic doctrine of war, we have already looked briefly at some examples of the former (see pages 13-16). Some examples of the latter will be considered in chapter 5. Other aspects of the debate are mentioned in chapter 8.

Other sources

Non-Muslim scholars have identified some non-Islamic sources of the Islamic doctrine of war. The influence of these external sources would be denied by devout Muslims, who would not wish to acknowledge that uninspired human input had played any part in the development of their faith. But for the sake of completeness it may be helpful to outline the main factors.[41]

Pre-Islamic factors include:

1. *Pre-Islamic traditions of northern Arabia*

In this lawless tribal society, hostility to all other tribes was presumed, unless a specific agreement had been made with a particular tribe. The inter-tribal raid (*ghazwa* or razzia) was a frequent and normal part of life. In many ways the raids were more like sport than war. The result was generally a redistribution of wealth (e.g. livestock) or women from the losing tribe to the winning tribe, and loss of life was rare. There appear to have been at least some rules governing the conduct of razzias, including a prohibition on attacking non-combatants with lethal intent. Harming women and children was probably considered dishonourable. (See also pages 75-76.)

There was also another kind of tribal conflict called *manakh*, which was rarer and more bloody. These were generally disputes over resources like grazing ground or wells and only arose in exceptional circumstances such as severe drought. *Manakh* was effectively a battle for the survival of the tribe.

2. *Byzantium*

Byzantine culture had an ideology of imperial victory (derived from Roman ideas) and divine aid (derived from Judaism). Muslim rulers would most likely have felt the need to affirm the same two concepts in respect of the Islamic state. Byzantine culture can also be seen as having had an influence on the development of the Islamic concept of the unity of the Islamic state under a single ruler (caliph or imam). Only the state, under its head, can launch a jihad (see page 42). The Byzantines viewed war as a great evil and had some notion of the possibility of a just war, for example, against external enemies in self-defence. Justice and mercy were supposed to characterise the emperor's dealings with his own people.

3. *Sassanian Persians*

The Sassanians had an ideology of imperial victory and divine support similar to that of the Byzantines. They appear to have held that only defensive war was justified, but that included defence of their religion (Zoroastrianism) as well as of their territory. Sometimes there seems to have been a requirement for the emperor to act justly, as in Byzantine culture, though there does not appear to have been a similar requirement for him to act mercifully, at least not in the context of keeping order within his empire. External enemies could be dealt with severely.

4. *The ever-present reality of war*

The daily reality of war must have shaped popular attitudes. For example the Byzantine emperor was not, despite the ideology, always victorious in battle, which would surely have created some question marks in the minds of his subjects.

5. *Apocalyptic traditions*

Traditions concerning the imminent end of the world were very widespread. With Jewish, Christian or Hellenistic roots, these prophecies often foretold war – even defeat – as a precursor to the Last Days and ultimate victory. Apocalyptic thought appears to have been particularly popular in the Christian kingdom of Axum (Ethiopia). It must also have brought comfort to the beleaguered Byzantines, who lost huge areas of territory to the Persians in the early seventh century and then again to the Muslims a few years later. Islam has a full and detailed eschatology in which war is a key portent. Possibly Muhammad and his followers saw themselves as instruments of God, cleaning up the world by eliminating false belief, in preparation for the Day of Judgement.

Later influences on the Islamic doctrine of war include:

1. *The Crusades*

   While the Crusades had no effect on the theory or conduct of jihad[42] they are worth mentioning as they appear to have produced a heightened religious fervour because the Muslims were once more fighting Christians (albeit Europeans). This reminded them of the golden age of early Islam when their ancestors had swept to victory against the Byzantine Christians.

2. *Eurasian steppe traditions*

   This influence came from the Turkish and Mongol tribes of central Asia who were introduced to the Islamic world as slaves, troops or migrants from the ninth century onwards. They eventually established a number of Muslim regimes in different parts of the world lasting from the eleventh to the twentieth centuries. The main departure from classical Islamic doctrine was the concept that a ruler had absolute authority to make "secular" state law, independent of any religious law. This created a tension between two parallel law systems, as was seen markedly in the Ottoman Empire.

Sources:
Qur'an, *hadith*, Shari'ah

While many Muslims would condemn the use of war or terrorism in the name of Islam, the source texts of Islam do contain some passages which can without difficulty be interpreted to permit, even to command, violence of this kind. This violence is targeted primarily against polytheists, but also against Jews and Christians, and against erring Muslims.

During his early years of prophethood in Mecca (610-622), Muhammad focused on prayer and meditation. His approach to Jews, Christians and other non-Muslims was peaceful, cooperative and non-violent. After opposition and persecution forced him to flee to Medina in 622, he became the spiritual, political and military leader of an Islamic state. While in Medina he believed that God gave him permission to fight those who were persecuting the Muslims.[1] As he gained power, he became much more aggressive in his pronouncements and his actions[2] against all opponents and non-Muslims, including his Meccan adversaries, massacring many, enslaving others and expelling them from their lands. He made a particular point of attacking trade caravans.

Qur'an

Because of Muhammad's change of attitude when he moved from Mecca to Medina, the Qur'an is a contradictory mixture of the peaceable and the bellicose. The nineteenth century Islamic jurist Ibn Abidin highlighted the gradual stages by which the transition was made:

Know thou that the command of fighting was revealed by degrees, for the Prophet was at first commanded to deliver his message, then to discuss and dispute and endeavour to convince the unbelievers by arguments, then the believers were permitted to fight, then they were commanded to fight at first at any time, except the sacred months, then absolutely, without any exception.[3]

According to the rule of abrogation (*naskh*, see page 18), it is the harsher and more violent Medinan passages that apply today because they are later, while the earlier conciliatory passages dating from Muhammad's days in Mecca are not applicable. Mahmoud Mohamed Taha summarised the situation in classical Islam: "All the verses of persuasion, though they constitute the primary or original principle, were abrogated or repealed by the verses of compulsion (jihad)."[4]

There are a considerable number of verses which speak of love, peace and forgiveness towards non-Muslims. Many of these are in *sura* (chapter) 2. For example:

Quite a number of the People of the Book[5] wish they could turn you (people) back to infidelity after ye have believed, from selfish envy, after the Truth hath become manifest unto them: but forgive and overlook, till God accomplish his purpose: for God hath power over all things. Q 2:109

Those who believe (in the Qur'an) and those who follow the Jewish (scriptures), and the Christians and the Sabians, – any who believe in God and the Last Day, and work righteousness, shall have their reward with their Lord: on them shall be no fear, nor shall they grieve. Q 2:62

But a number of Muslim scholars assert that all such verses are abrogated by the so-called "Sword Verse", Q 9:5, which commands Muslims to fight anyone who refuses to convert to Islam.[6] This verse is a favourite of modern Islamist militants.[7]

But when the forbidden months are past, then fight them and slay the Pagans wherever ye find them, and seize them, beleaguer them, and lie in wait for them in every stratagem (of war); but if they repent, and establish regular prayers and practise regular charity, then open the way for them: for God is oft-forgiving, most merciful. Q 9:5

In addition to the Sword Verse, there are a plethora of other apparent Qur'anic injunctions to make war, particularly war against non-Muslims with the aim of converting them to Islam.

Some occur even in *sura* 2, where so many peaceable verses are found.

> Fight in the cause of God those that fight you, but do not transgress the limits; for God loveth not transgressors. And slay them wherever ye catch them, and turn them out from where they have turned you out; Q 2:190-191

> And fight them on until there is no more tumult or oppression, and there prevail justice and faith in God; but if they cease, let there be no hostility except to those who practise oppression. Q 2:193

> Fighting is prescribed for you, and ye dislike it. But it is possible that ye dislike a thing which is good for you, and that ye love a thing which is bad for you. Q 2:216

> And fight them on until there is no more tumult or oppression, and there prevail justice and faith in God altogether and everywhere; but if they cease, verily God doth see all that they do. Q 8:39

> Let not the unbelievers think that they can get the better (of the godly): They will never frustrate (them). Against them make ready your strength to the utmost of your power, including steeds of war, to strike terror into (the hearts of) the enemies, of God and your enemies, and others besides, whom ye may no know, but whom God doth know. Q 8:59-60

> Fight those who believe not in God nor the Last day, nor hold that forbidden which hath been forbidden by God and His Apostle, nor acknowledge the Religion of Truth, (even if they are) of the People of the

Book, until they pay the *jizya* with willing submission, and feel themselves subdued. Q 9:29

Many other examples could be given of verses which can easily be understood to command or commend warfare (and especially to convince Muslims who were reluctant to fight).[8] There are also other verses which speak of non-Muslims as the enemies of Muslims,[9] and about Islam's ultimate goal to establish Islamic authority over the whole world.[10]

Reuven Firestone distinguishes four kinds of war verses and concludes that the transition from pre-Islamic ideas about war to the fully-fledged Islamic doctrine of jihad was far from smooth, and that there must have been many early Muslims who were opposed to militancy and had to be persuaded to overcome their reluctance to fight.[11]

Hadith

The *hadith* traditions recording the words and deeds of Muhammad, although secondary in comparison with the Qur'an, are of huge significance as a source because Muslims must model their lives on Muhammad's in every detail. It is clear from the *hadith* that Muhammad and the first Muslims understood jihad to include physical warfare and literal killing.[12] Recorded in the *hadith* are many statements commanding or commending violence. One of the most often quoted (though less clear than many) is:

> Allah's Apostle said, "Know that Paradise is under the shades of swords."
> *Sahih Bukhari Volume 4, Book 52, Number 73: Narrated 'Abdullah bin Abi Aufa*[13]

Others are more specific about the enemy and the aim of jihad, apparently indicating that Muslims must fight non-Muslims until they are willing to convert to Islam.

> Allah's Apostle said, "I have been ordered to fight with the people till they say, 'None has the right to be worshipped but Allah,' and whoever says, 'None has the right to be worshipped but Allah,' his life and

property will be saved by me except for Islamic law, and his accounts will be with Allah, (either to punish him or to forgive him.)" *Sahih Bukhari Volume 4, Book 52, Number 196: Narrated Abu Huraira*

The Prophet (peace_be_upon_him) said: "I am commanded to fight with men till they testify that there is no god but Allah, and that Muhammad is His servant and His Apostle, face our *qibla*, eat what we slaughter, and pray like us. When they do that, their life and property are unlawful for us except what is due to them. They will have the same rights as the Muslims have, and have the same responsibilities as the Muslims have." *Sunan Abu Dawud Book 14, Number 2635: Narrated Anas ibn Malik*

Some are concerned with fighting particular named categories of non-Muslims, for example polytheists.

The Apostle of Allah (peace_be_upon_him) appointed Abu Bakr our commander and we fought with some people who were polytheists, and we attacked them at night, killing them. Our warcry that night was "put to death; put to death". Salamah said: "I killed that night with my hand polytheists belonging to seven houses." *Sunan Abu Dawud Book 14, Number 2632: Narrated Salamah ibn al-Akwa'*

Some very chilling *hadith*, which describe inanimate nature rising up to betray the Jews, are quoted in the literature of certain radical Islamist groups today. For example:

Allah's Apostle said, "You (i.e. Muslims) will fight with the Jews till some of them will hide behind stones. The stones will (betray them) saying, 'O 'Abdullah (i.e. slave of Allah)! There is a Jew hiding behind me; so kill him." *Sahih Bukhari Volume 4, Book 52, Number 176: Narrated 'Abdullah bin 'Umar*

Examples of the assassination of individuals also occur in the *hadith*.

Allah's Apostle sent a group of the Ansar to Abu Rafi. Abdullah bin Atik entered his house at night and killed him while he was sleeping. *Sahih Bukhari Volume 4, Book 52, Number 265: Narrated Al-Bara bin Azib*

The Prophet said, "Who is ready to kill Ka'b bin Al-Ashraf who has really hurt Allah and His Apostle?" Muhammad bin Maslama said, "O Allah's Apostle! Do you like me to kill him?" He replied in the affirmative. So, Muhammad bin Maslama went to him (i.e. Ka'b) and said, "This person (i.e. the Prophet) has put us to task and asked us for charity." Ka'b replied, "By Allah, you will get tired of him." Muhammad said to him, "We have followed him, so we dislike to leave him till we see the end of his affair." Muhammad bin Maslama went on talking to him in this way till he got the chance to kill him. *Sahih Bukhari Volume 4, Book 52, Number 270: Narrated Jabir bin 'Abdullah*

Ka'b bin al-Ashraf, who was Jewish on his mother's side, was a poet who wrote verse satirising and lampooning Muhammad and some of his close companions. This incident was the result – the hurt which Muhammad refers to had been inflicted by Ka'b's pen. There are also accounts of Muhammad ordering torture.

A group of eight men from the tribe of 'Ukil came to the Prophet and then they found the climate of Medina unsuitable for them. So, they said, "O Allah's Apostle! Provide us with some milk." Allah's Apostle said, "I recommend that you should join the herd of camels." So they went and drank the urine and the milk of the camels (as a medicine) till they became healthy and fat. Then they killed the shepherd and drove away the camels, and they became unbelievers after they were Muslims. When the Prophet was informed by a shouter for help, he sent some men in their pursuit, and before the sun rose high, they were brought, and he had their hands and feet cut off. Then he ordered for nails which were heated and passed over their eyes, and they were left in the Harra (i.e. rocky land in Medina). They asked for water, and nobody provided them with water till they died. (Abu Qilaba, a sub-narrator said, "They committed murder and theft and fought against Allah and His Apostle, and spread evil in the land.") *Sahih Bukhari Volume 4, Book 52, Number 261: Narrated Anas bin Malik*

Muhammad's decision to ethnically cleanse all non-Muslims from the Arabian peninsula is recorded in the *hadith*.

Umar heard the Messenger of Allah (may peace be upon him) say: "I will expel the Jews and Christians from the Arabian Peninsula and will not leave any but Muslims." *Sahih Muslim, Book 19, Number 4366: Narrated by Umar ibn al-Khattab*

The *hadith* also records Muhammad's famous statement that jihad will be performed continuously until the Antichrist comes.

The Prophet (peace_be_upon_him) said: "A section of my community will continue to fight for the right and overcome their opponents till the last of them fights with the Antichrist." *Sunan Abu Dawud Book 14, Number 2478: Narrated Imran ibn Husayn*

The Prophet (peace_be_upon_him) said: "Three things are the roots of faith: to refrain from (killing) a person who utters, 'There is no god but Allah' and not to declare him unbeliever whatever sin he commits, and not to excommunicate him from Islam for his any action; and jihad will be performed continuously since the day Allah sent me as a prophet until the day the last member of my community will fight with the Dajjal (Antichrist). The tyranny of any tyrant and the justice of any just (ruler) will not invalidate it. One must have faith in Divine decree." *Sunan Abu Dawud Book 14, Number 2526: Narrated Anas ibn Malik*

Shari'ah[14]

Not only does the Shari'ah cover the personal, family and devotional life of an individual Muslim but also it lays down how an Islamic state should be governed. Reflecting the political and military ascendancy of Islam in the eighth and ninth centuries when it was compiled, the Shari'ah assumes that power lies in the hands of Muslims.

It is natural, given the sources used and the context in which it was created, that the Shari'ah should contain a set of rules specifically governing the manner in which Muslims are to wage war. These very practical, earthy and militarily relevant instructions leave no doubt that the writers of the Shari'ah believed jihad to encompass actual warfare. There is little difference between Sunni and Shi'a law concerning war.

A number of practical handbooks and other forms of written guidance on the conduct of war were produced by scholars from the various schools of law. The general consensus was that the participants must be adult male Muslims, able-bodied and free (not slaves). They should also be without debt, have spiritual motives and their parents' permission. Opinion on other aspects of the conduct of the war varied, for example, whether non-combatants should be spared, whether crops and animals should be destroyed.[15]

The Hanafi school of Shari'ah[16] has a standard text known as the *Hedaya*, which is available in English translation, albeit eighteenth century English. Book IX contains chapters called "On the Manner of waging War", "Of making Peace, and concerning the Persons to whom it is lawful to grant Protection", "Of Plunder, and the Division thereof", "Of the Conquests of Infidels".

Some examples may indicate the level of detail involved in the *Hedaya's* instructions. The important question of dividing the plunder takes six pages. One fifth must go to the state and the remaining four-fifths is allocated to the troops, with cavalry getting more than the infantry. After this principle is laid down, things become complicated. Should the cavalryman get double or triple what the foot soldier has? What if he has more than one horse? Is his share affected by the quality of his horse? What if he mainly goes into battle on horseback but occasionally on foot? What if his horse was killed or he sold it at the end of the campaign? Then there is the question of what to give slaves, women, children and non-Muslims, and what to do with the fifth that was set aside for the state. All these issues are argued in detail, referring to historical precedent, the example of Muhammad and the opinions of other Muslim scholars.[17]

A fascinating paragraph on the role of women in war is worth quoting in full:

> It is lawful for aged women to accompany an army, for the performance of such business as suits them, such as dressing victuals, administering water, and preparing medicines for the sick and wounded; – but with respect to *young* women, it is better that they stay at home, as this

may prevent perplexity or disturbance. The women, however, must not engage in fight, as this argues *weakness* in the *Mussulmans* [Muslims]; women, therefore must not take any personal concern in battle unless in a case of *absolute necessity*: and it is not laudable to carry *young* women along with the army, either for the purpose of carnal gratification, or for service: if, however, the necessity be *very urgent, female slaves* may be taken, but not *wives*.[18]

With respect to the question of whether women can fight or not, it is interesting to note that Ayesha, one of Muhammad's wives, led troops into battle at the Battle of the Camel (656), but her army was defeated. In the Battle of Jabiya-Yarmuk (636), Muslim women in the camp played an important role by shaming any Muslims who fled the battlefield, sometimes even fighting against them.[19]

Another important work of the same era which is also available in English translation is Shaybani's *Siyar*.[20] Shaybani (750-804) lived during the days of the 'Abbasid dynasty, centred on Baghdad. Born in Iraq, Shaybani was only fourteen when he joined the circle of Abu Hanifa, the founder of the Hanafi school of Shari'ah. Although Abu Hanifa himself died some three years later in 767, Shaybani continued as a follower of Abu Hanifa's disciple Abu Yousuf, and went on to become a teacher, a judge and an adviser to the caliph as well as a prolific author.

Siyar is the branch of Islamic law concerned with international relations, and Shaybani's was the first major work on this subject. Literally "motion", *siyar* had come to mean by Shaybani's time the conduct of the Islamic state in its relationships with non-Muslim communities. Interestingly, the early Muslim jurists used to deal with *siyar* under the general heading of jihad. Shaybani's *Siyar* begins with a citation of *hadiths* about war and then goes on to a systematic study (in the form of a dialogue) on how Muslims should relate to non-Muslims, including chapters on the following subjects: the conduct of the army in enemy territory, the spoils of war, relationships between Muslim territories and non-Muslim territories, peace treaties, and safe-conducts.

The detail which Shaybani covers is fascinating. In the following extract he considers what to do when confronted with a human shield as well as the issue of killing non-combatants.

> I asked: If the Muslims besieged a city, and its people [in their defence] from behind the walls shielded themselves with Muslim children, would it be permissible for the Muslim [warriors] to attack them with arrows and mangonels?
>
> He replied: Yes, but the warriors should aim at the inhabitants of the territory of war and not the Muslim children.
>
> I asked: Would it be permissible for the Muslims to attack them with swords and lances if the children were not intentionally aimed at?
>
> He replied: Yes.
>
> I asked: If the Muslim [warriors] attack [a place] with mangonels and arrows, flood it with water, and burn it with fire, thereby killing or wounding Muslim children or men, or enemy women, old men, blind, crippled or lunatic persons, would the [Muslim warriors] be liable for the *diya* [blood money] or the *kaffara* [atonement]?
>
> He replied: They would be liable neither for the *diya* nor for the *kaffara*.[21]

The fact that Shaybani permits an attack on a place known to have Muslims within it is pertinent to the suicide plane attack on the World Trade Centre on September 11th 2001; it negates the argument that the attack could not have been the work of Islamic terrorists since there were Muslims in the building who were killed in the attack. Other jurists take a range of positions on this issue, some agreeing with Shaybani, others advising that only limited violence should be used if Muslims might be endangered. Al-Awza'i advised that no attack should be made at all, unless individual enemy soldiers showed themselves and could be picked off.[22]

Abu'l-Hasan al-Mawardi (972-1058), a jurist of the Shafi'i school of Shari'a, wrote what is in effect an instruction manual for Islamic rulers entitled *al-Ahkam al-sultaniyya* [*The Ordinances of government*] with detailed instructions on the ruler's duties and obligations in time of war. He defines the enemy in a jihad as those who refuse to convert to Islam:

> The idolators in enemy territory are of two classes. One, those who have received the call to Islam but rejected it and turned away from it... The other are those whom the call to Islam has not yet reached, who would be very few today on account of the victory the Almighty has accorded His Prophet's mission, unless there be nations unknown to us beyond the Turks and Greeks we meet in eastern deserts and remote western areas. We are forbidden to launch surprise attacks on such people and kill them or burn their property, for we may not initiate action against them before inviting them first to Islam, making the Prophet's miracles known to them, and informing them of such arguments as would make them respond favourably. Should they persist in their unbelief after such evidence is shown them, he [the commander] should fight them, for they are from his standpoint in the same class as those who have received the call.[23]

Al-Mawardi is uncertain as to whether old men can be killed in battle, but forbids the killing of women, children or young slaves.

Another important Shafi'i text was written by Ibn Naqib (d.1368) and is called *'Umdat al-Salik* [*Reliance of the Traveller*]. His short section on the rules of warfare forbids the killing of women and children unless they are fighting against the Muslims. He allows the killing of old men (i.e. over 40) and monks, but not the killing of animals (unless they are being ridden into battle "or if killing them will help defeat the enemy") or the cutting down of trees or the destruction of the enemy's houses. He says it is unlawful to kill a non-Muslim to whom a Muslim has given his guarantee of protection, but then adds various conditions.[24] His comments on prisoners of war are quoted on pages 51-2.

A famous Maliki scholar, the Spanish-born Ibn Rushd, included the subject of jihad in his primer for Islamic jurists *Bidayat al-Mujtahid wa Nihayat al-Muqtasid*,[25] which quotes the opinions of a range of other scholars from various different schools. His book is intended as a starting point for *ijtihad* and he refrains from assessing the validity of the opinions he quotes. It covers a similar range of practical detail to other works, including for example the treatment of prisoners of war (whether or not they can be killed or only ransomed, enslaved or freed), whether or not monks and hermits may be killed, whether fire is a legitimate weapon, whether buildings, trees and cattle can be attacked, and facing what odds a Muslim soldier would be permitted to retreat rather than fight.

Ibn Taymiyya (1263-1328) was a scholar of the Hanbali school whose extremist religious stance resulted in him spending several years in prison. Although he was not a mainstream scholar, it is useful to consider what he says of jihad as his teaching continues to be influential in certain sections of the Muslim world today (see chapter 5). He was not only a prolific author but also himself participated in several military expeditions against heretics. His treatment of jihad in his *al-Siyasa al-Shar'iyya fi Islah al-Ra'i wa-al-Ra'iyya* [*Governance according to God's Law in reforming both the Ruler and His Flock*] has less to say about the practical aspects of war than the other works described, but instead emphasises the religious justification for jihad by quoting from the Qur'an and *hadith* including war against rebellious Muslims.[26] He exalts military jihad as the best religious act a man can perform, better than pilgrimage, prayer or fasting, and as implying "all kinds of worship, both in its inner and outer forms. More than any other act it implies love and devotion for God."[27] He says that women, children, monks, the elderly, disabled etc. are not to be killed unless they offer active help to the enemy's war effort such as by propaganda or espionage.[28]

The North African philosopher-historian Ibn Khaldun (1332-1406) defined jihad as "a religious duty, because of the universalism of the

(Muslim) mission and (the obligation to) convert everybody to Islam either by persuasion or force". He contrasts this with the doctrine of Christians and Jews, asserting that "the other religious groups did not have a universal mission, and the holy war was not a religious duty to them, save only for purposes of defence". He recognized also that Christians and Jews were not "under obligation to gain power over other nations, as is the case with Islam".[29]

For Shi'a Muslims the law on war was mainly laid down at the time of Abu Ja'far Muhammad ibn Hasan al-Tusi (995-1067) who wrote an influential treatise called *al-Nihaya* [*The Conclusion*]. It is very similar to Sunni doctrines of war,[30] except for the requirement that jihad must be led by a divinely inspired imam (supreme Shi'a leader).[31]

The Theology of War, Peace and Empire-Building

Classical Islam divides the world into two: the part where Muslims are in power (*Dar al-Islam*, the house of Islam) and the part where Muslims are not in power (*Dar al-Harb*, the house of war). Muslims have an obligation to try to change *Dar al-Harb* into *Dar al-Islam*. Modern Muslims may use many methods to try to achieve this, but Muhammad's way was by military conquest, jihad.[1] Hence there is a theological justification for the use of violence against the non-Muslim world.[2]

Islamic scholars debate how to define what is or is not *Dar al-Islam*,[3] a question which is far from academic as *Dar al-Islam* is exempt from war, while *Dar al-Harb* is not. The sacred space of *Dar al-Islam* is further subdivided into three kinds with varying degrees of sanctity, which are reflected in rules of varying strictness concerning the presence of non-Muslims (dead or alive).[4]

The classical teaching was practised for many centuries. In the words of Kenneth Cragg:

> Historically, Islam has made good its capacity to belong with wide diversities of humankind. But always, traditionally, this universality was on the basis of surrender.[5]

It was to the revival of this essentially imperialist strand within traditional Islam in the world today that Samuel Huntington was pointing in his 1996 book *The Clash of Civilizations*[6] in which he described the Islamic world as having "bloody borders". A map in the 1999 edition of *The Times History of the World* depicting the revival of religious conflicts in the world highlights virtually every country in the Islamic world whilst only Northern Ireland and Myanmar (Burma) can be found as modern illustrations of religious conflicts in non-Islamic contexts.[7] Of course most Muslims would respond that these are mainly liberation struggles and argue, quite rightly, that Muslims have faced varying degrees of discrimination and hostility in many of these contexts.

Islam has an inbuilt theological urge at its very core towards empire-building i.e. the continual expansion of its political dominion. This is seen as obedience to the divine duty imposed on Muslims to spread Allah's rule and religion to the whole world. While this does not mean the forced conversion of individuals, it does mean Islamic domination of all political structures and the imposition of Shari'ah.

Islam therefore accepts as natural that Muslims should rule non-Muslims, and considers it unnatural that non-Muslims should rule Muslims. The latter arrangement is regarded as akin to blasphemy, and likely to lead to corruption of religion and morality. This is the great affront of the non-Muslim world against Islam. Richard Chartres, the Anglican Bishop of London, describes Islam's unwavering belief in its own superiority:

> There is an immense sense in Islam of the superiority of Islam to every-thing else – and this is in terrible full-frontal collision with the evident inferiority of Muslim societies, technically, politically, economically, militarily... The crisis in Islam (it's not so much a battle between East and West, Christians and Muslims, it's a battle in Islam) comes from the terrible collision of this sense of superiority with the evident inferiority in so many other ways, which causes bewilderment and fierce debate on how we are going to get out of this bind.[8]

Zaki Badawi, president of the Muslim College in London, affirms the Islamic requirement for political power, and Islam's inability to function as a minority:

As we know the history of Islam as a faith is also the history of a state and a community of believers living by Divine law. The Muslims, jurists and theologians, have always expounded Islam as both a Government and a faith. This reflects the historical fact that Muslims, from the start, lived under their own law. Muslim theologians naturally produced a theology with this in view – it is a theology of the majority. Being a minority was not seriously considered or even contemplated. The theologians were divided in their attitude to minority status. Some declared that it should not take place; that is to say that a Muslim is forbidden to live for any lengthy period under non-Muslim rule. Others suggested that a Muslim living under non-Muslim rule is under no obligation to follow the law of Islam in matters of public law. Neither of these two extremes is satisfactory. Throughout the history of Islam some pockets of Muslims lived under the sway of non-Muslim rulers, often without an alternative. They nonetheless felt sufficiently committed to their faith to attempt to regulate their lives in accordance with its rules and regulations in so far as their circumstances permitted. In other words, the practice of the community rather than the theories of the theologians provided a solution. Nevertheless Muslim theology offers, up to the present, no systematic formulation of the status of being a minority. The question is being examined. It is hoped that the matter will be brought into focus and that Muslim theologians from all over the world will delve into this thorny subject to allay the conscience of the many Muslims living in the West and also to chart a course for Islamic survival, even revival, in a secular society.[9]

The extension of the Islamic empire is very much an aim of radical Muslims today. For example, it was preached by Sheikh Ibrahim Mahdi (an employee of the Palestinian Authority) at the Sheikh ‘Ijilin Mosque in Gaza City on 12 April 2002.

"But the rock and the tree will say: ‘O Muslim, O servant of Allah, a Jew hides behind me, come and kill him.’ Except for the Gharqad tree, which is the tree of the Jews." We believe in this *hadith*. We are convinced also that this *hadith* heralds the spread of Islam and its rule over all the land...

O beloved, look to the east of the earth, find Japan and the ocean; look to the west of the earth, find [some] country and the ocean. Be assured that these will be owned by the Muslim nation, as the *hadith* says, "from the ocean to the ocean..."[10]

The Islamic concept of war

We have already seen how holy war – jihad – is the means of spreading Islamic hegemony throughout the world. In the early days of Islam it was also an indirect means of spreading the Islamic faith, for conversion ensured protection from attack. Because the whole world has not yet been turned into *Dar al-Islam*, the need for jihad logically remains. Two *hadiths* that speaks of continuous jihad have already been quoted (see page 29). A modern comment comes from Dr Ali Othman, for some years adviser on education to the United Nations Relief and Works Agency:

> The spread of Islam was military. There is a tendency to apologise for this and we should not. It is one of the injunctions of the Koran that you must fight for the spreading of Islam.[11]

Some Muslims hold jihad to be a sixth "pillar of Islam" along with the other compulsory duties of affirming the faith, praying, fasting, giving alms, and going on pilgrimage to Mecca. Amongst those who take or took this line were the fierce, austere and fanatical Khariji sect,[12] of whom more later. Another was 'Abd al'Salam Faraj (1952-1982), the founder of the Egyptian militant group al-Jihad, who wrote a popular book called *The Neglected Duty*. Osama bin Laden takes the same line, asserting:

> There are people who say, and it is no secret, that the jihad does not require the [participation] of the entire nation; these words are true, but their intent is not. It is true that jihad cannot include the entire nation today, and that repelling the aggressive enemy is done by means of a very small part of this nation; but jihad continues to be a commandment incumbent personally upon every Muslim.[13]

However most Muslims consider jihad a collective obligation laid on the Muslim community as a whole, and hence not a pillar,[14] the five standard pillars being duties required of each individual believer. According to Ibn Abi Zayd al-Qayrawani (922-966), a leading jurist of the Maliki school of Shari'ah, the fact that some Muslims are performing jihad excuses others from participation: "Jihad is a precept of Divine institution. Its performance by certain individuals may release others from the obligation."[15] Generally jihad is considered the responsibility of the state; individual Muslims cannot wage their own jihads though they should be willing to participate in the communal jihad.[16] Furthermore, a time may come when jihad is no longer necessary i.e. if the whole world is under Islamic rule.[17]

According to Khadduri, when Muslim power began to decline in the tenth century AD, there was a tacit understanding that the obligation for permanent jihad was to be suspended or made dormant for a time. He quotes in his support Ibn Khaldun, asserting that Ibn Khaldun considered this was a process of evolution of the Muslim community from a warlike stage to a civilised stage.[18] However, it is important to realise that Ibn Khaldun viewed the evolution of desert-dwelling "savage groups" to people who "settle in the fertile plains and amass luxuries" as an undesirable development. The savage groups, says Ibn Khaldun, were braver and "therefore better able to achieve superiority and to take away the things that are in the hands of other nations". He praises the first Muslims because "their fortitude ... was not corroded by education or authority".[19]

Examples of jihad from the modern era are more numerous than might be supposed. From 1804 to 1808 Usuman dan Fodio, leader of the Fulani tribe in West Africa, led a jihad against the rulers who were of the Hausa tribe. Some Hausa Muslims protested that a jihad against other Muslims was illegal, but his son, Sultan Bello, justified the jihad on the grounds that the Hausas had mixed their Islam with local pagan practices. The jihad spread south, converting many pagans to Islam and creating a Muslim society in what is now northern Nigeria.[20]

At the beginning of the First World War, the Ottoman Empire declared a jihad against Russia, France and Britain. During November 1914 five *fatwas* issued by the highest religious authority in Istanbul called on Muslims everywhere to join in the war; they were immediately followed by a *beyanname-i cihad* [declaration of holy war] issued by Sultan Mehmed V Reşad.[21] After the war when Mustafa Kemel Ataturk was fighting to remove Greek and Allied forces from Anatolia, this too was seen as a jihad. On 19 September 1921 Atatürk was voted the title of *ghazi* [fighter for the faith, literally "one who takes part in a razzia"] by the Grand National Assembly for his victory over the Greeks at the Battle of Sakarya.[22]

The defence of Afghanistan from Soviet invasion (1979-1989) was known in Pakistan as the Jihad-e-Afghanistan. The Palestinian cause is seen as a jihad, and a recorded message purporting to come from ousted Iraqi president Saddam Hussein in July 2003 described the Iraqi resistance to American forces as a jihad.[23]

Declarations of war

According to Shari'ah the Muslim aggressors must first invite the enemy to convert to Islam before attacking them. If the invitation is accepted there is no attack. This principle of giving an opportunity to avoid attack (on certain terms) is also to be found in antiquity.[24] Ibn Abi Zayd al-Qayrawani wrote:

> We Malikis maintain that it is preferable not to begin hostilities with the enemy before having invited the latter to embrace the religion of Allah except where the enemy attacks first. They have the alternative of either converting to Islam or paying the *jizya*, short of which war will be declared against them.[25]

The majority view is that only the lawful caliph can declare war,[26] giving the enemy the opportunity to convert to Islam (and perhaps a three day period in which to decide) before opening hostilities.[27] Al-Mawardi has already been quoted making it very plain that no attack must be launched until the enemy had been offered the opportunity to convert to Islam in as clear and attractive a way as possible (see page 33). Ibn Rushd attributes the necessity to invite the enemy to convert to Islam before attacking to God's own example recorded in the Qur'an.[28]

> Nor would We visit with Our Wrath until We had sent an apostle (to give warning). Q 17:15

There is also a clear instruction by Muhammad recorded in the *hadith*.

> It has been reported from Sulaiman b. Buraid through his father that when the Messenger of Allah appointed anyone as leader of any army or detachment he would exhort him to fear Allah and to be good to the Muslims who were with him. He would say: "… When you meet your enemies who are polytheists, invite them to three courses of action. If they respond to any one of these, you also accept it and withhold yourself from doing them any harm. Invite them to (accept) Islam; if they respond to you accept it from them and desist from fighting them …If they refuse to accept Islam, demand from them the *jizya*. If they agree to pay, accept it from them and hold off your hands. If they refuse to pay the tax, seek Allah's help and fight them... *Sahih Muslim Book 19, Number 4294*

A number of early texts provide us with examples of the actual words used to issue these ultimatums. Usually couched in diplomatic language rather than overtly threatening, it is important to recognise the true message within them. The following example was supposedly sent by Muhammad to the Byzantine Emperor Heraclius.[29]

> In the name of Allah, the Gracious, the Merciful. From Muhammad the servant of Allah and Apostle to Heraqle [Heraclius], the Grand Chief of Byzantines: Peace be unto those who followed the right path. Thence I call upon you with the call of Islam, submit [to Islam] and you will be safe, [if you do] God will reward you twice, if you decline, then you will be liable to the sins of peasants. 'O people of the book! Come to common terms as between us and you, that we worship none but God, that

we associate no partner with Him; that we erect not, from among ourselves, lords and patrons other than God. If they turn back, say ye: Bear
witness that we are Muslims [they who have surrendered].[30]

To another Christian leader, the Patriarch of the Egyptian Copts,
Muhammad wrote in similar vein, inviting him to embrace Islam
and promising him a two-fold reward by God for his acceptance
and for those who would follow in his footsteps but warning him, if
he declined, of being accountable for himself and for all the Copts.
The letter continued:

> O people of the Book, come to the common terms between us and you,
> that we shall worship none but Allah, and that we shall ascribe no part-
> ner unto Him, and that none of us shall take others for lords beside
> Allah. And if they turn away, then say: Bear witness that we are they who
> have surrendered unto Him.[31]

In a letter to Muqavgas, the leader of the Coptic tribe, Muhammad
invites Muqavgas to accept Islam. If not, he warns that the "sin of
calamity" will be on him. If Muqavgas fails to respond to this invitation, Muhammad says, "bear witness that we are Muslims."[32]

A slightly less subtle example was sent by one of Muhammad's
commanders to the Persians. The phrase about "loving to be killed"
is a typical Islamic warning of imminent attack. Often it is expressed
as saying that Muslims love death.[33]

> Peace be to those who follow the guidance. To proceed: We summon
> you to Islam, but if you refuse then pay the *jizya* in submission feeling
> humbled. If you refuse to do that, I have with me people who love being
> killed in God's path as the Persians love wine. Peace to those who fol-
> low the guidance.

Shi'a Muslims face a difficulty over the need for the imam (the Shi'a
prefer this term for the supreme leader of the Muslim community –
the *umma* – while Sunnis use "caliph") to declare war. The majority
of them believe that their last imam disappeared in 873 and they are
still waiting for his return as the Mahdi (the "God-ordained rightly

guided one" who will renew Muslim glory).[34] Ayatollah Khomeini, who overthrew the Shah of Iran in 1979, managed to get around this by his doctrine of *velayat-e faqih*[35] which overcame Shi'a resistance to political action in the absence of the rightful imam.

Modern Muslims still declare jihad. While in Mecca in 1978 Yasser Arafat declared a jihad to liberate Palestine.[36]

Osama bin Laden's "Declaration of war against the Americans occupying the land of the two holy places",[37] dated 23 August 1996, runs to 22 pages.[38] It uses the traditional language of "loving death" to make its threat.

> I say to you William[39] that: These youths love death as you love life. They
> inherit dignity, pride, courage, generosity, truthfulness and sacrifice from
> father to father. They are most delivering and steadfast at war.[40]

He followed this up on 23 February 1998 with a *fatwa* entitled "Jihad Against Jews and Crusaders" issued jointly with four other Islamist leaders.[41] Beginning by quoting the Sword Verse (Q 9:5) it went on to set out the Muslim grievances and then told all Muslims:

> The ruling to kill all Americans and their allies – civilians and military
> – is an individual duty for every Muslim who can do it in any country
> where it is possible to do it...[42]

Other texts were then quoted to prove that this was God's command.

The leader of the Laskar Jihad, an Islamist terrorist group active in Indonesia, particularly in Maluku and Sulawesi, issued a declaration of war which, like many modern Islamic declarations of war, gloated over American military failures. The first part was addressed to Muslims, urging them to prepare for war. The second part was addressed to the enemy:

> You listen to this. Woe to the pawns of America. You listen to this.
> Woe to the pawns of the World Council of Churches. You listen to
> this. Woe to the pawns of the Zionist Crusaders. You listen to this.
> Woe to the Jews and the Christians. We the Muslim people invite

the army of America to prove their strength here in Maluku. Let us fight to the bitter end. Let us prove for the umpteenth time that the Muslim people cannot be defeated by the physical strength which is always boasted about. The events of the second Afghanistan will take place in Maluku when you are determined to carry out your threats. Woe to America. Now you! Woe to America who is now suffering various defeats, various awesome beatings in Afghanistan. Let us meet like men on the battlefield...[43]

An Indonesian jihad manual, published in 2001, states as a "military doctrine of Islam" that before attacking the enemy it is necessary to give them give warning and teaching so that they wake up and accept Islam as their religion and submit to Islamic power.[44]

Invitations to embrace Islam or face the consequences, closely modelled on the early examples quoted above, are announced annually by the British-based Islamist group Al-Muhajiroun in London's Trafalgar Square. These statements could be interpreted (and probably are by those issuing them) as a traditional Islamic declaration of war on non-Muslims.

Types of jihad

Muslim scholars have analysed jihad in different ways. One analysis is given by Khadduri as follows:[45]

1. *Jihad against polytheists*

Polytheists must be fought until they are willing to convert to Islam. The term refers to pagans who have no concept of a single supreme deity, of whom there were many in the Arabian peninsula in the early days of Islam. Even larger numbers were encountered in later centuries when Islam expanded into Africa and Asia.

2. *Jihad against Muslims*

   (i) *Against apostasy*

   This jihad applies to groups of Muslims who renounced Islam and joined *Dar al-Harb* e.g. some of the Arab tribes who rebelled soon after Muhammad's death. Because of their treason against the Islamic state they were given no chance to make peace on any terms except their return to Islam. Apart from this, rules of engagement were similar to a war against *Dar al-Harb*.

(ii) *Against dissension and rebellion*

Dissenters were those who had unorthodox religious ideas but still submitted to the authority of the imam or those who had a grievance unrelated to beliefs. If they moved on to disobedience to the imam they were to be fought. The rules of engagement in such a war were more generous than in wars against unbelievers, for example prisoners of war could not be killed and their property could not be appropriated. The more destructive methods of attack were only permitted as a last resort. This type of jihad is found only in Shi'a Islam.

3. *Jihad against the People of the Book*

Ahl al-Kitab [the People of the Book][46] had a threefold choice: conversion to Islam (and then full citizenship in the Islamic state), *dhimmi* status i.e. second-class citizenship as non-Muslims within the Islamic state in return for submission and payment of *jizya* tax, or war with the Muslims.

4. *Strengthening the frontiers* (ribat)

This was a defensive type of jihad with the purpose of safeguarding the frontiers of *Dar al-Islam*. It was of particular significance in Islamic Spain when it was under attack by Christian European forces. The concept of ribat is supported by Q 8:60[47] and various *hadiths*.[48]

An alternative, modern analysis of jihad has been made by Sheikh 'Abdullah 'Azzam, the spiritual mentor of Osama bin Laden. He divides the worldwide jihad into the following three categories:

1. Within Muslim countries, with the goal of reinstating rule by Shari'a.
2. In countries with Muslim minorities, situated on the "fault lines" with other cultures e.g. the Balkans, Chechnya, Kashmir.
3. The international cultural struggle, in which Islam takes on Western – especially American – civilisation. [49]

Rules of engagement

The conduct of war was governed by detailed rules, which generally forbade the killing of women, children and other non-combatants and the unnecessary destruction of property. This principle is derived from Caliph Abu Bakr's address to the first expedition sent to the Syrian border.[50] The requirement to declare war and give the enemy a chance to convert to Islam and thus avoid battle has been discussed above. Variations on the rules occur amongst the different Islamic jurists.

Variations on the rules also occurred during the jurisdiction of Muhammad himself. For example, treachery and mutilation[51] were prohibited by Muhammad until the Muslims found themselves on the receiving end of such behaviour at the hands of the Meccans. He then changed his ruling and ordered his followers to retaliate in a similar way.[52]

Non-combatants

The Sunni jurists are agreed that in general non-combatants who did not participate in the fighting should be unharmed. This included women, children, monks, the elderly, blind and insane. However, a certain branch of the Kharijis did permit the killing of women and children.[53]

Some Hanafi and Shafi'i Sunni jurists held that peasants and merchants who did not participate in the fighting should be unharmed.[54] If the elderly or monks did anything to assist the enemy they were no longer exempt from attack.[55]

A comment by Shaybani permitting attack on a city by mangonels, flooding or fire, despite the risk to enemy non-combatants has already been quoted (see page 32).[56] He also allowed the cutting of water supplies, the poisoning of water supplies, and the use of poisoned or burning arrows.[57] (Some jurists specifically banned the use of poisoned arrows.)[58]

The issue of human shields has already been dealt with (see page 32).

Destruction of property

Abu Bakr's principle of no unnecessary destruction was supported fully by al-Awza'i (d. 774) and al-Thawri (d. 778) but greatly limited by many other jurists, including the founders of the four schools of Sunni law.[59] For example Malik, who compiled the first collection of *hadiths* under the title *Muwatta'* [*Way Made Smooth*], permits the destruction of everything except the flock and beehives. Hanifa requires the destruction of everything that cannot be brought under the control of the Islamic forces; this includes houses, churches, trees, flocks and herds. Shafi'i allows the destruction of trees and all inanimate objects, but animals can only be killed if leaving them alive would strengthen the enemy.[60] Shaybani also permits the killing of animals, destruction of towns and cutting down of trees. Interestingly his reasons include not only the practical (preventing the enemy from using the destroyed items) but also the psychological (to humiliate and anger the enemy).

> I asked: If the believers in the territory of war capture spoil in which there are [animals such as] sheep, riding animals, cows which resist them and they are unable to drive them to the territory of Islam, or weapons which they are unable to carry away, what should they do [with them]?
>
> He replied: As to weapons and goods, they should be burned, but riding animals and sheep should be slaughtered and then burned.
>
> I asked: Why should not [the animals] be hamstrung?

He replied: Because that is mutilation, which they should not do because it was prohibited by the Apostle of God. However, they should not leave anything that the inhabitants of the territory of war could make use of.

I asked: Do you think that they should do the same with whatever [other] animals refuse to be driven away or with whatever weapons and goods are too heavy to carry?

He replied: Yes.

I asked: Do you think that it is objectionable for the believers to destroy whatever towns of the territory of war that they may encounter?

He replied: No. Rather do I hold that this would be commendable. For do you not think that it is in accordance with God's saying, in His Book: "Whatever palm trees you have cut down or left standing upon their roots, has been by God's permission, in order that the ungodly ones might be humiliated." So, I am in favour of whatever they did to deceive and anger the enemy.[61]

Prisoners of war

The taking of prisoners of war (generally regarded in pre-Islamic times as part of the booty and very cruelly treated) is a subject on which the Qur'an gives some guidance:

It is not fitting for an Apostle that he should have prisoners of war until he hath thoroughly subdued the land. Ye look for the temporal goods of this world; but God looketh to the Hereafter: And God is exalted in might, Wise. Had it not been for a previous ordainment from God, a severe penalty would have reached you for the (ransom) that ye took. But (now) enjoy what ye took in war, lawful and good. Q 8:67-9

According to A. Yusuf Ali's comment[62] this means that the motive of worldly gain (by demanding a ransom) was not normally approved so prisoners should not normally be taken. If, however, many lives had already been lost in battle it might be better to take prisoners.

On this principle, 70 prisoners were taken at the Battle of Badr (624) and ransomed, with divine approval.

The first part of the above verse appears to indicate that prisoners should not be taken in the early stages of a war, but when the enemy is defeated the loss of life can be reduced and prisoners taken. Another verse backs this up:

> When ye have finally subdued them, bind a bond firmly (on them): thereafter (is the time for) either generosity or ransom: until the war lays down its burdens. Q 47:4

With such a variety of possibilities, it is small wonder that the issue of prisoners of war is one on which the various schools of Shari'a differ considerably. Some jurists, following Q 47:4, completely forbid the execution of prisoners and permit them only to be ransomed or freed. Others permit the execution of prisoners, but often hedge this with provisos, for example, that they should be given the opportunity to convert to Islam instead, or that there should be a military need to reduce the strength of the enemy. Other options include not only ransoming or setting free for nothing, but also enslaving them or exchanging them for Muslim prisoners. There was general agreement that women and children prisoners should not be killed but enslaved. The following is the guidance given by Ibn Naqib in *Reliance of the Traveller*:

> Whoever enters Islam before being captured may not be killed or his property confiscated, or his young children taken captive.

> When a child or a woman is taken captive, they become slaves by the fact of capture, and the woman's previous marriage is immediately annulled.

> When an adult male is taken captive, the caliph considers the interests (of Islam and the Muslims) and decides between the prisoner's death, slavery, release without paying anything, or ransoming himself in exchange for money or for a Muslim captive held by the enemy. If the prisoner becomes a Muslim (before the caliph chooses any of the four

alternatives) then he may not be killed, and one of the other three alternatives is chosen.[63]

Abu Yusuf also held that the fate of the prisoners (death or ransom) should be decided on the basis of the interests of the Muslims.[64] Shaybani also affirmed this, clearly stating that male prisoners of war should be killed if that would be advantageous to the Muslims, unless they were willing to convert to Islam (in which case they would be enslaved) or had previously been granted a safe-conduct (in which case they would be freed).[65] Any blind, disabled or insane prisoners of war should not be killed.[66] However, elsewhere Shaybani says that male prisoners unable to walk were to be killed, whereas transport had to be hired for women and children prisoners unable to walk.[67] The Kharijis generally held that prisoners should be killed, but only extremist Kharijis such as the followers of Nafi' ibn al-Azraq always adhered to this rule.[68]

Muslim prisoners captured by the enemy were under no obligation to submit to or obey their captors; they could escape (unless they had promised not to) or destroy enemy property if they had opportunity.[69] Muslim prisoners were not to give any valuable information to the enemy, must refuse to fight against Islam, and must not renounce their faith unless forced to do so.[70]

Espionage and propaganda

There is a phrase in the famous Sword Verse (Q 9:5) which is interpreted by some Muslims as encouragement to use espionage. "… Slay the Pagans wherever ye find them, and seize them, beleaguer them, and *lie in wait for them in every stratagem (of war)*" [emphasis added].[71]

Muhammad himself made good use of spies. Hamidullah describes Muhammad's use of a "network of intelligence service, espionage and counter-espionage" and asserts that this played a large part in his successful conquest of the Arabian peninsula.[72] He reviews Muhammad's use of spies during the battles of Badr, Uhud and the *Khandaq*, the war of Khaibar, the conquest of Mecca and various other military expeditions.[73] It was also thanks to intelligence reports that Muhammad was able to thwart various assassination conspiracies and to facilitate assassination plans of his own. For example on hearing that Ka'b bin al-Ashraf, a chief of the Jewish tribe of Banu an-Nadir, had come to Mecca to use his poetry to instigate the Meccans to take revenge on Muhammad for the Muslim victory at the Battle of Badr, Muhammad "sent a small detachment who succeeded in assassinating the chief in his own castle nipping the evil in the bud".[74]

One particular intelligence-gathering expedition is described by Kandhalvi in his popular compilation of *hadiths* under the title "Huzaifah Goes For Spying".[75] Huzaifah was ordered by Muhammad: "Go to the enemy camp and bring us their news. Return immediately after observing what they are doing." Huzaifah duly went to the camp of the enemy, who in this case were the Jews of Banu Qurayza in Medina. The Jews became aware of his presence and shouted, "There is a spy among us. Every one of us should catch the hand of the person next to him." With great presence of mind Huzaifah caught hold of a nearby hand and demanded loudly, "Who are you?" Thus he managed to escape detection. When he reported back to Muhammad, Huzaifah could "see his beautiful teeth shining" on hearing of his spy's narrow escape.

Propaganda was also a tactic used by Muhammad with great success in order to create suspicion and dissension amongst his enemies. Hamidullah describes in detail how Muhammad sent a new convert to Islam to plant doubts in the minds of two groups of his enemies – the Meccans and a Jewish tribe in Medina.[76] This convert first warned the Banu Qurayza Jews in Medina not to trust the Meccans and suggested they asked the Meccans for some hostages to ensure their loyalty. Then he told the Meccans that the Jews were conspiring with the Muslims and wanted to hand over the Meccan leaders to the Muslims. He also recommended that the Meccans should ask the Jews to attack on the Sabbath when the Muslims would not be expecting it – an idea that was sacrilegious to the Jews. The resulting hostility between the Jews and the Meccans can be imagined.

Punishment for foreign spies caught by the Muslims was severe. If a non-Muslim who had been granted a safe-conduct to enter Islamic territory was later discovered to be a spy, he was to be killed. Crucifixion could be used, in order to deter others, unless the spy were a woman.[77] In the case of child spies, they are not to be killed but would become *fay'* [property taken from non-Muslims without fighting, which went to the state treasury].[78]

The punishment for a Muslim caught spying for the enemy seems to have been less clear cut. According to the Shafi'i and Maliki schools of Shari'a this can be left to the discretion of the commanding officer. The Hanafi school says he should be imprisoned until he repents. Al-Awza'i suggests exile.[79]

The early Muslims continued to practise espionage and propaganda. Infiltration was a particular speciality of the Isma'ilis (see pages 91-2). Mention must be made of a medieval Shi'a group, the Fatimids, who were one of the first political powers to develop a sophisticated ministry of propaganda employing secret agents in order to establish their reign in Sunni Egypt. Information was disseminated through mosque prayers, by pre-arranged "spontaneous" arguments in public libraries, by declaration from minarets, government communiqués on stone tablets and paper placed at strategic public places, hired poets who eulogised the Fatimids, bribery, and neutralising potential dissidents by appointing them to high office.[80] There is a long tradition within Islamic societies of the deliberate use of propaganda to promote favoured interpretations of Islam to Muslim societies and the wider non-Muslim world which survives until today.

Naval warfare

The early Muslims, being desert-dwelling Arabs, were reluctant to go to sea (a fact which helped the Byzantine Empire to hold out against continued Muslim aggression). The most that Muhammad himself did in terms of naval warfare was, firstly, to send some auxiliary forces by sea to Aqaba to lend support to Muslims engaged in a land battle[81] and, secondly, to send 300 troops in pursuit of some Africans sighted in boats off the Arabian coast near Mecca. The Muslim troops reached an island, the Africans fled, and the Muslims returned to the mainland.[82]

Eventually the Muslim forces became more active at sea, occupying Cyprus in 648.[83] Many churches of the Byzantine era on Cyprus became mosques. By the tenth century Muslims had gained control of much of the Mediterranean, and their pirates were becoming a serious menace to Europeans. They became a major sea-power again in the fifteenth century when the Ottoman Turks controlled much of the eastern Mediterranean and African coasts, though they suffered a crushing defeat off Lepanto in 1571.

It is striking how little is written by Islamic jurists about the conduct of a war at sea, in contrast to the vast amounts of literature dealing with land-based warfare. So great was the general antipathy towards the sea that various *hadiths* report Muhammad promising that anyone who died in jihad at sea would have double the reward of a martyr who died on land.[84] One *hadith* records that Muhammad said, "Paradise is granted to the first batch of my followers who will undertake a naval expedition."[85] Shaybani states that as soon as a jihad fighter sets foot on a ship all his sins will be forgiven.[86]

Most of the rules of maritime warfare were derived by analogy with land warfare, a ship being seen as equivalent to a castle. Thus a ship could be attacked by hurling stones at it, by cutting it off from outside support, by fire or by sinking. Other tactics were designed to create panic, for example, throwing on to the ship such things as snakes, scorpions and harmful powders.[87] If the enemy tried to protect themselves by taking Muslims on board as human shields, their ship could still be attacked.[88]

The division of spoils – always an important topic in classical Islamic writings about war – was as on land.[89] However, there were special rules about prisoners of war which related to the fact that ships overloaded with booty and prisoners might sink. If the Muslims feared they would sink, they were permitted to throw into the sea not only the property they had taken but also the prisoners they had taken including women and children.[90] They were not, however, allowed to throw overboard any Muslim women or children who might happen to be on the ship,[91] nor any *dhimmis* on board, nor any non-Muslims who had been granted a safe-conduct.[92]

Putting the theory into practice

How were these rules put into practice by the first Muslims? The answer would seem to be that their practice was variable, and even Muhammad himself did not always follow the rules. As has already been explained, Muhammad is seen as the model for all other Muslims to follow, and therefore any lapses from the established norm set a particularly significant precedent.

As has been seen, Caliph Abu Bakr (632-4) gave strict orders that the civilian population and the livestock were to be spared, when the Muslims conquered new territory.[93] The aim of putting all Arabs under Muslim control drove Caliph 'Umar (634-644) to demand the return of some Arabs[94] who had fled to Byzantine-controlled areas. He threatened that if they were not returned to him he would retaliate against the Christians within his territory, breaking the treaties made with them for their protection. According to the Muslim historian al-Tabari, 'Umar's threat ran as follows:

> It has come to my notice that a certain group of Arab tribesmen has left our territory and has sought residence in your territory; by God, if you do not drive them back, we will surely dissolve our covenants with the Christians living under Arab sovereignty, and expel them.[95]

The Banu Taghlib, a Christian tribe, were unwilling to pay the demeaning *jizya* and insisted on paying the *sadaqa* tax like Muslim Arabs. According to the rules they could not do this and remain Christians. Caliph 'Umar, afraid that they too might defect to the Byzantines, made a treaty with them whereby the Taghlib were charged *sadaqa* at double the rate paid by Muslims and forbidden to baptize their children. It appears, however, that the Taghlib continued to baptize their children regardless, for Caliph 'Ali (656-661) later said that he would have killed their fighting men and taken captive the children because they had broken the treaty by baptizing their children and thus forfeited their right to protection.[96]

While Christians were supposed to be allowed to keep both their faith and their lives under Islamic rule, the 60-strong garrison of Gaza were killed in 637 for refusing to convert to Islam.[97] This appears to have been an exceptional event. Some reports say that this may have been as a result of the anger of the Muslim commander 'Amr whom the Byzantines had treacherously tried to murder during negotiations. The wives and children of the garrison were spared, as were the civilian inhabitants of Gaza.[98]

Another apparent case of Muslims breaking their rules of engagement to get revenge for treachery was the murder of one Sergios who had spoiled the Arabs' trade. He is reported to have been killed by being suffocated in a drying camel stomach.[99]

Despite their rules of engagement the Muslim Arabs gained a reputation for ferocity, possibly indicating that they may not always have followed them closely. There are however few documented cases of mutilation, so it may have been chiefly their ferocity in battle that was feared, as indicated by Patriarch Sophronius of Jerusalem, writing in 634.[100] But the Oath of Justus for Jacob in the *Doctrina Iacobi nuper baptizati* (an anti-Jewish document written in c.634) stated that even if Jews and Saracens cut him into pieces piece by piece he would not deny Jesus Christ, which might indicate that the author of this oath thought it a possibility.[101]

At the hard-fought Battle of Jabiya-Yarmuk in 636, in which the Muslims suffered heavy losses but eventually won, they did not take prisoners on the battlefield, though afterwards they captured some of the Byzantine enemy who had fled.[102]

With regard to prisoners of war, Muhammad set an infamous example of brutality in 627 against the Banu Qurayza, a Jewish tribe who lived in Medina. Muhammad besieged them because he feared they would join his enemies. The Qurayza offered to pay tribute, but Muhammad refused. He demanded that they embrace Islam, which the Qurayza refused. Finally Muhammad accepted their unconditional surrender.

The Aws, a Medinan clan who were allies of the Banu Qurayza, pleaded with Muhammad to be lenient with them. Muhammad asked if they would accept a decision from one of their own, which they readily agreed to. Muhammad then sent for Sa'd ibn Mu'adh, a member of the Aws clan who had converted to Islam some time previously. Sa'd was dying from a wound he received fighting in defence of Medina, and his sentence on the Banu Qurayza was that the men should be killed and the women enslaved. Muhammad did not demur – the word of a dying man was considered doubly honourable by Arabs – and indeed responded that Sa'd's judgement was the judgement of God. The next day the men were beheaded one by one, and their bodies thrown into specially dug trenches. The process took all day, the last decapitations being performed by torchlight. The number killed is estimated at 700 by some sources[103] or even up to 900 by others.[104] Women and children were enslaved, and all the possessions of the tribe seized.[105]

Muslims have generally justified this massacre (which sent shock waves throughout Arabia, and after which the tribe ceased to exist) as specially sanctioned by God. This was the view of al-Mawardi (d.1072) who wrote "… it was not permitted [for Muhammad] to forgive [in a case of] God's injunction incumbent upon them; he could merely forgive [transgressions, offences etc.] in matters concerning his own person."[106] Hamidullah defends the massacre in a different way describing it as being "a decision of the arbitrator of [the Banu Qurayza's] own choice who applied to them their own Biblical law" and cites Deuteronomy 20:13-14.[107] But many non-Muslim historians have condemned it as completely unjustified – "a barbarous deed … an act of monstrous cruelty" in the words of Sir William Muir whose biography of Muhammad was based entirely on Muslim sources.[108] The military imperative was certainly clear, in that the Banu Qurayza were the last of three Jewish tribes in Medina to be dealt with by Muhammad. The first had been allowed to leave with all their possessions, while the second just managed to escape with their lives. Unsurprisingly both had become staunch allies of Muhammad's enemies. It would seem Muhammad did not want to make the same mistake again.

The "rightly guided" caliphs had their own preferences on prisoners of war. Abu Bakr was against ransoms,[109] preferring that prisoners taken by the Muslims should either convert to Islam or be killed.[110] Umar liked to kill at least some of the prisoners he had taken,[111] but to buy back Muslims taken prisoner by the enemy.[112]

Adapting jihad for modern times

Various contemporary Muslim authors have tackled the subject of rules for the conduct of jihad in modern times. Many of these works appear to be designed primarily to defend the image of Islam to westerners. They discuss the subject of international relations not only in wartime (as did the classical authors) but also in peacetime (an innovation). Generally the authors select the most humane regulations to be found in the classic Islamic works on jihad and present them as the norm (rather than as one end of the spectrum). In Peters' summary, "The classical doctrine of jihad has been stripped of its militancy and is represented as an adequate legal system for maintaining peace in the domain of international relations." Furthermore the best of Islamic principles are often contrasted with the worst of contemporary international practice. For example, the western practice of surprise attacks is contrasted unfavourably with the classical Islamic requirement to offer the enemy the chance to convert to Islam or pay *jizya* before launching the attack.[113]

Writings perhaps not intended for non-Muslim readers sometimes take a different stance. For example an article in a Kuwaiti Arabic-language newspaper, discussed the issue of killing non-combatants. It argued that "in the modern age" an army is supported by a whole range of complementary activities and all the people engaged in those activities are legitimate targets "especially on occupied Muslim lands such as Palestine"; indeed everyone in Israel who pays taxes or voted Ariel Sharon into power was a legitimate target. It also argued that civilians could be killed "when Muslims must launch a comprehensive attack against their enemies or shoot them from afar" as Muhammad shot at the people of Taif with a catapult when he was besieging their city. Enemy civilians, women and children as well as Muslims could be accidentally killed in such attacks (for example, suicide attacks) without incurring blame. The only exception was that "places that are designated for children and frequented only by them are not to be targeted".[114]

A comment from Mahathir Mohamad, then Malaysian prime minister, is interesting not least because Malaysia is generally thought of as a moderate Muslim country. Mahathir urged an international conference of young Muslims to acquire the skills and technology needed to create modern weapons in order to "strike fear into the hearts of our enemies and defend us". He listed as examples tanks, battleships, fighter planes and rockets, and said that matching western development in these areas would "prevent Islam from being humiliated, looked down upon and regarded as a religion of terrorists".[115]

Weapons of mass destruction

In terms of the conduct of modern warfare, the Islamic rule that non-combatants should not become involved would exclude the use of weapons of mass destruction.[116] One modern Islamic authority,[117] however, considers that nuclear weapons are a legitimate deterrent, reasoning from the following Qur'anic verse:

> Against them make ready your strength to the utmost of your power, including steeds of war, to strike terror into (the hearts of) the enemies of God and your enemies, and others besides, whom ye may not know, but whom God doth know. Q 8:60

Based on another verse from the Qur'an he asserts they could be used in retaliation or defence if the enemy has already used them.

> If then any one transgresses the prohibition against you, transgress ye likewise against him. Q 2:194

Following the Iraq war of March-April 2003, Dr Ahmed Omar Hashim, the president of Al-Azhar, also referred to Q 8:60 and called on Arab nations to obtain weapons of mass destruction so as to have the power God orders them to have in order to combat aggression. He stated that "the notion of ability [in this verse] is absolute. In other words, Muslims should fight their enemies with the same weapons, and even try to exceed them."[118]

Abdul Rahman Bilal, a major in the Pakistani Army, has argued that the Islamic world should acquire nuclear capability to serve as a deterrent "whenever its existence is threatened". He does not permit the use of chemical and biological weapons by Muslim countries, but urges that research should be done to find suitable antidotes.[119] Since Bilal wrote this, Pakistan has proudly declared itself a nuclear power, with its so-called "Islamic bomb".

Pakistan's radical Jamaat ud-Daawa party supports the use of "atomic weapons" in jihad, and their leader has praised the scientist who shared Pakistan's nuclear technology with Libya, Iran and North Korea, calling him a hero and saying: "He shared the technology for the supremacy of Islam and he acted on Allah's command."[120]

Saudi Arabia is considering acquiring nuclear capability as a deterrent,[121] and Iran is alleged to have a nuclear programme already. Certainly, Iran's chairman of the Expediency Council, Akbar Hashemi Rafsanjani, has said that Iran must acquire nuclear technology.[122]

Peter Probst, an expert on terrorism at the Pentagon, has noted that religiously motivated terrorists are generally more willing to cause mass casualties than are secular terrorists, and may even actively seek mass casualties. Marvin Centron, president of the American organization Forecasting International, concurs, stating that that "new groups, such as Osama bin Laden's, have fewer restrictions on the use of weapons of mass destruction".[123] Centron's statement was borne out when evidence came to light in January 2004 that Osama bin Laden's Al-Qa'eda had indeed been seeking to develop chemical and biological weapons in Kandahar, southern Afghanistan, until interrupted by the US-led invasion of Afghanistan in October 2001. The programme was headed by a Malaysian called Yazid Sufaat, who had studied biochemistry in the US and had been an officer in the Malaysian army. He was under the direction of Hambali, an Indonesian accused of heading Al-Qa'eda's operations in south-east Asia and also known as Riduan Isamuddin.[124]

Prisoners of war

Modern authors forbid the killing of prisoners of war. They base all their POW theory on a phrase in Q 47:4[125] which offers the alternatives of freeing the prisoners with or without a ransom.[126] Enslavement they say was only valid when the enemy practised it also, based on Q 16:126

> And if ye do catch them out, catch them out no worse than they catch you out.

Prisoners must be treated well according to Q 76:8

> And they feed, for the love of God, the indigent, the orphan, and the captive.

During the first days of the Iraq war of March-April 2003, the Iraqi Foreign Minister Naji Sabri stated that the Iraqis would treat their coalition prisoners of war in accordance with the teachings of Islam. "We are committed first of all to the teachings of Islam, and second we are committed to the conventions of Geneva in dealing with the prisoners of war." This statement, made in the context of video footage of five American POWs being aired on Al-Jazeera TV in contravention of the Geneva Convention,[127] makes clear the Iraqi intention to be guided by Islam rather than the Geneva Convention in any conflict between the two.[128]

Peace treaties

Another change to the classic doctrine which some mainstream modern scholars promote is the possibility of making *permanent* peace treaties with non-Muslims.[129] Some of these however make permanent peace conditional on non-Muslims submitting to the Islamic state and paying *jizya*, which is really no different from classical Islam.[130] Others hold that the only condition necessary is that Islam may be propagated without hindrance in the other state.[131]

The Islamic concept of peace

Peace is generally dealt with in classical Islam under the heading of "war". Peace is seen as an interlude in the jihad process that must go on until the whole world is *Dar al-Islam*, under the rule of Islam. War, being ordained by God, is viewed as positive. Peace therefore stands in danger of being negative unless it can be justified.

Permanent peace can be justified only within *Dar al-Islam*. The Arabic words for "peace" and "submission" come from the same root, and this is indicative of the nuance which the term "peace" generally carries in Islam, that of peace as a result of submission. Permanent peace in Islam is something like the *pax Romana*, a peace which results from the imposition of Islamic power, thus preventing all dissension. It could be termed the *pax Islamica*.

Peace treaties

Temporary peace can be achieved by making a treaty [*hudna*[132]] with the enemy, but this is only permissible if it is advantageous for the Muslims, and preferably should not last for more than ten years.[133] For example, the Muslims made a three-year peace agreement with Byzantine-ruled Egypt which allowed the Muslims to concentrate on attacking Iraq[134] and northern Syria. When the military situation became more favourable for attacking Egypt they did so (639).[135]

If Muslims were to make a peace treaty that was not in their own interests it would be tantamount to abandoning the war, and so disobeying God's command. Thus peace-making is justifiable only if it is seen as part of the long-term war effort. It is scarcely an exaggeration to say that in classical Islam peace is considered a specialised kind of war.

> Peace, moreover, is *war* in effect, where the interest of the Mussulmans [Muslims] requires it, since the design of war is the removal of evil and this is obtained by means of peace:[136]

When circumstances change so that it becomes advantageous to the Muslims to break the treaty they must do so, having given due notice of their intention to the enemy and allowing time for this news to disseminate throughout the enemy's territory. If the Muslims fail to renew the war when it becomes advantageous to them to do so, they are considered deserters.[137]

The Qur'an is strict about Muslims keeping the terms agreed, as long as the enemy has not violated the treaty.

> (But the treaties are) not dissolved with those pagans with whom ye have entered into alliance and who have not subsequently failed you in aught; nor aided any one against you. So fulfil your engagements with them to the end of their term: for God loveth the righteous. Q 9:4

> … break not your oaths after ye have confirmed them; Q 16:91[138]

However a *hadith* records an instruction by Muhammad to army commanders which appears to indicate that different kinds of promise or guarantee had different levels of sanctity. Some were less binding and could be broken more casually.

> …When you lay siege to a fort and the besieged appeal to you for protection in the name of Allah and His Prophet, do not accord to them the guarantee of Allah and His Prophet, but accord to them your own guarantee and the guarantee of your companions, for it is a lesser sin that the security given by you or your companions be disregarded than that the security granted in the name of Allah and His Prophet be violated…
> *Sahih Muslim Book 19, Number 4294*

According to Sheikh 'Abdul Rahman 'Abdul Khaliq, peace treaties with Jews are made to be broken. In response to a question about the duty of a Muslim with regard to peace treaties with Jews he writes:

> The first duty is to firmly believe in their invalidity and that because they contain invalid conditions they were born dead the very day they were given birth to ...

> The second duty of the Muslim is to believe that these treaties do not bind him and that it is not lawful for him to give effect to any of their contents except under compulsion and necessity ...

> The third duty is to work towards overthrowing these treaties...

Four more duties follow: the duty to detest and fight Jews, the duty to unite the Muslim community in so doing, the duty to believe that the presence of Jews in the Arab world is because Arab governments were not sufficiently Islamic, and the duty to pray for Muslim unity and victory over the Jews.[139]

Saudi Arabia's Grand Mufti, Sheikh Abdul Aziz Ibn Baz, also has made it clear that any cessation of hostilities with Israel could only ever be a temporary measure, pending the time that Muslims became strong enough to gain possession of the whole land for themselves.

> The peace between the leader of the Muslims in Palestine and the Jews does not mean that the Jews will permanently own the lands which they now possess. Rather it only means that they would be in possession of it for a period of time until either the truce comes to an end, or until the Muslims become strong enough to force them out of the Muslim lands – in the case of an unrestricted peace.[140]

Islamic jurists define a treaty as a form of 'aqd (literally, a tie), meaning an agreement on a certain act which has the object of creating legal consequences. It has a broader meaning than the western concept of a contract because it implies a meeting of minds which follows an offer being made by one party and accepted by the other.

This meeting of minds is more important than any legal niceties of signatures, witnesses etc.[141] Muhammad himself made a number of treaties, which his successors considered models to be emulated.[142] Treaties were categorised as either temporary (with *Dar al-Harb*) or perpetual (arrangements with the People of the Book regarding their *dhimmi* status within an Islamic state). Treaties with *Dar al-Harb* could include agreements on the payment of tribute, cessation of fighting, safe travel for civilians and ransoming prisoners of war.

Another kind of agreement, discussed at great length by the traditional Muslim jurists, was the granting of a temporary safe-conduct (*aman*) to a non-Muslim who wanted to spend some time in Islamic territory, often a merchant or trader.[143]

Taqiyya

In the context of peace treaties and negotiations, it is important to note that in classical Islam Muslims are permitted to lie in certain situations, one of which is war.[144] This kind of permitted deception is called *taqiyya*, and is particularly prevalent amongst Shi'a Muslims. Generally translated in English as "dissimulation" or "concealment" the Arabic word derives from a root meaning to "shield" or "guard" oneself. Shi'as are a minority amongst Muslims and have often been persecuted by the majority Sunnis. In this context they have evolved the doctrine of *taqiyya*, which is included in almost every classical work of Shi'a jurisprudence, permitting a person to deny their true beliefs in order to save themselves from harm. However, although supposedly only for emergencies, *taqiyya* has "in practice become the norm of public behaviour whenever there is a conflict between faith and expediency".[145]

The Qur'anic basis of *taqiyya* lies in the following verses.

> Any one who, after accepting faith in God, utters unbelief, - except under compulsion, his heart remaining firm in faith – but such as open their breast to unbelief, - on them is wrath from God, and theirs will be a dreadful penalty. Q 16:106

This verse indicates that the "dreadful penalty" will not be applied to someone who denied their faith *under compulsion*. It is backed up by another verse which occurs in the Qur'anic story of Moses, in which a man who has himself "concealed his faith" questions the wisdom of killing someone for the sake of his faith:

> A believer, a man from among the people of Pharaoh, who had concealed his faith, said: "Will ye slay a man because he says, 'My Lord is God'? Q 40:28

A general warning against friendship with non-Muslims is also seen as lending support to the doctrine of *taqiyya*.

> Let not the believers take for friends or helpers unbelievers rather than believers; if any do that, in nothing will there be help from God: except by way of precaution, that ye may guard yourselves from them. Q 3:28

There is also support from the *hadith* which permits lying in three situations: to one's wife, in war, and for the purpose of reconciliation.

> Allah's Messenger (peace be upon him) said, "Lying is allowed in only three cases: falsehood spoken by a man to his wife to please her, falsehood in war, and falsehood to put things right between people. *Al-Tirmidhi Number 5033: Narrated by Asma', daughter of Yazid.*

Muslim gives a slight variation on this:

> ... Ibn Shihab said he did not hear that exemption was granted in anything what the people speak as lie but in three cases: in battle, for bringing reconciliation amongst persons and the narration of the words of the husband to wife, and the narration of the words of a wife to her husband (in a twisted form in order to bring reconciliation between them). *Sahih Muslim Book 32, Number 6303*

Variations on this *hadith* are also recorded in the collections of Bukhari, Abu Dawud and an-Nasa'i. It is also quoted by the respected Egyptian *hadith* scholar Sheikh Mansur Ali Nasif.[146]

A somewhat different *hadith* reports Muhammad giving permission to lie in order to kill someone. It begins as follows:

Allah's Apostle said, "Who is willing to kill Ka'b bin Al-Ashraf who has hurt Allah and His Apostle?" Thereupon Muhammad bin Maslama got up saying, "O Allah's Apostle! Would you like that I kill him?" The Prophet said, "Yes." Muhammad bin Maslama said, "Then allow me to say a (false) thing (i.e. to deceive Ka'b)." The Prophet said, "You may say it." ... *Sahih Bukhari Volume 5, Book 54, Number 369: Narrated by Jabir bin Abdullah*

The rest of this rather long *hadith* goes on to tell the story of how Muhammad bin Maslama duly lied to Ka'b and thus managed to kill him.

The Shi'a imams also repeatedly affirmed the doctrine of *taqiyya*, the sixth imam Ja'far as-Sadiq (699-765) deeming it the essence of religion with remarks such as "He who has no *taqiyya* has no religion" and "The *taqiyya* is [a mark of] my religion, and that of my forefathers."[147] According to some scholars a further reason for the institution of *taqiyya* was that the Shi'a imams held that religious truths were not to be debased by dissemination to the general public but should be reserved for those capable of understanding them.[148]

Modern Shi'a scholarship has defined four distinct categories of *taqiyya*:

(1) Enforced (*ikrahiyya*): yielding to the instructions of an oppressor in order to save one's life.

(2) Precautionary or apprehensive (*khawfiyya*): Shi'a Muslims performing acts and rituals authorised by the *fatwas* of Sunni religious leaders in Sunni countries.

(3) Arcane (*kitmaniyya*): to conceal one's beliefs as well as the number and strength of one's co-religionists, and to carry out clandestine activities to further religious goals. This is applicable in times of weakness when normal open propagation of one's beliefs (*idha'ah*) cannot be carried out.

(4) Symbiotic (*mudarati*): co-existence with the Sunni majority, participating with them in social and religious congregations in order to maintain Islamic unity and establish a powerful state comprising all Muslims.[149]

Historical treaties

The early sources record many treaties made by the Muslims with those they had threatened or attacked. The following examples are from the period of the "rightly guided caliphs", traditionally seen as a model for later Muslims to emulate.

After their decisive victory over the Byzantines at the Battle of Jabiya-Yarmuk in 636, part of the Muslim army pursued the fleeing Byzantines to Melitene (also called Malatya) which they captured. They made a treaty with its inhabitants requiring them to pay *jizya*, the Islamic tax on conquered Jews and Christians. Heraclius' furious reponse was to send troops to burn Melitene.[150]

After the fall of Damascus in December 636, an agreement was made at Ba'labakk, which gave the Greeks who wanted to evacuate the Ba'labakk area a staged withdrawal.[151] It was apparently a deliberate Muslim strategy to allow non-Muslims to leave conquered territory, because "it was better to allow hard-core non-Arab opponents of the regime to depart, and avoid becoming a disgruntled fifth column behind Muslim lines".[152] This seems to indicate a Muslim expectation that non-Muslims and non-Arabs were unlikely to become contented citizens of an Islamic state.

Either one or two truces were made in 637 at the Syrian stronghold of Chalkis. The first was apparently for one year only, after which Chalkis and its environs were supposed to surrender to the Muslims.[153] The terms of the second were that the Byzantines would make an annual payment of gold to the Muslims in return for which the Muslims would refrain from crossing the Euphrates i.e. would not invade Mesopotamia.[154] These Chalkis truces did not postpone for very long the loss of Syria or Mesopotamia to the Muslims, though Kaegi thinks they may have ensured the survival of the Byzantine empire by giving them time to prepare the defence of the empire's heartland, Anatolia.[155] In 639 the Muslims broke the truce(s) on the pretext that the Byzantines had failed to pay the agreed tribute. However, Kaegi speculates that the real reason was probably the Muslims' fear that the Byzantines were using the time to mobilise more troops for a counter-offensive.[156] If so the Muslims were acting exactly in line with the Islamic teaching when they broke the truce because they feared it was becoming disadvantageous for them.

A later treaty was made with the Byzantine governor of Cyprus in 648 or 649 – peace in exchange for an annual payment of 7,000 dinars and the passing on of information to the Muslims about any Byzantine activities. The unfortunate Cypriots also had to pay tribute to the Byzantines and give them information about the Muslims.[157]

For details of peace treaties in modern times see page 85.

Pacifism

Pacifism is not completely unknown in Islam, though as will be seen there are very few groups whose commitment to pacifism on principle is absolute. Some Shi'as believe that nothing can be done to defend their community until the return of the Twelfth Imam, who went into hiding in 873. When he returns as the Mahdi he will call the community to arm itself in order to restore pristine Islam and establish universal justice. They therefore adopt a quietist posture with almost fatalistic resignation. However, the same theology inspires other Shi'as to respond in the opposite way by taking an activist political posture, calling on their fellow-believers to be alert and ready for revolution.[158]

More often the approach to pacifism is by means of emphasising the spiritual understanding of jihad, that is, the battle with self against sinful habits, desires and actions. Those who take the line of emphasising the spiritual jihad often quote a *hadith* in which Muhammad described physical battle as "the lesser jihad [*jihad-e-asghar*]" i.e. inferior to the struggle for personal purity which he called "the greater jihad [*jihad-e-akbar*]". One version runs:

> A group of Muslim soldiers came to the Holy Prophet [from a battle].
> He said: Welcome, you have come from the lesser jihad to the greater
> jihad. It was said: What is the greater jihad? He said: The striving of a
> servant against his low desires. *Al-Tasharraf, Part I, p.70*

However, these *hadiths* are not included in the most important collections and are not very well attested, for example the first narrator was known to have fabricated some *hadiths*. They are therefore discounted by radicals and militants.

The spiritual understanding of jihad is especially prevalent among Sufis. Thus for example a movement known as Muridism,[159] which developed in Senegal under the leadership of the Sufi Amadu Bamba in the late nineteenth century, responded to French colonialism first by passive resistance and then by compromise and cooperation.[160]

However, not all the mystics of Islam have been inclined towards pacifism. Some have initiated movements of religious and social revolt against non-Muslim powers. Sufi-led rebellions against western colonial powers may be said to have begun in the Caucasus in the late eighteenth century under the Sufi leader Sheikh Mansur Ushurma who led a violent resistance against the Russians.[161] In the 1810s Naqshbandiyya Sufism became established in the region under Sheikh Khalid al-Shahrazuri, who was strongly antagonistic to what he called "the enemies of religion, the cursed Christians".[162] A particular cause of Muslim resentment was the Russian ban on slave trading and raiding; the capture of Christian Armenians and Georgians for sale as slaves in the Middle East had been a significant source of income for the Muslims of the region and they believed the Russian prohibition violated their Islamic legal rights to enslave non-Muslims. Other causes of bitterness towards the Russians were heavy taxes, the introduction of alcohol and gambling, the abuse of Muslim women, and the cruelty of the Russian military.[163] After a particularly brutal punishment raid by the Russians on a Chechen village called Dadi-Yourt in 1819 a militant Sufi movement developed in the 1820s, known as Muridism (confusingly, the same name as the later pacifist Sufi movement in Senegal).[164]

Other examples of Sufi-led rebellions against western colonialism include Sayyid Ahmad Barelwi (d.1831) who resisted British colonisation of the Mughal Empire in India, the Mahdist revolution of Sudan where many of the earliest Muslim missionaries and teachers were Sufis[165] (1882-1898, see page 93), the Sanussiya movement in Libya (1837-1931) and 'Abd al-Qader in the Maghreb (1808-1883). Examples of Sufi-led rebellions against Muslim regimes considered not Islamic enough include Usuman dan Fodio in West Africa (see page 51) and the dervish-led rebellion of Kurds against the newly formed Turkish Republic in 1925.

It is also interesting to note the very close links that had developed between some Sindhi *pirs* (Sufi "saints" – spiritual guides) and the Deobandi[166] by the early twentieth century.[167] Some *pirs* became very committed to the pan-Islamic cause and some were given senior ranks in Maulana Ubaidullah Sindhi's "Army of God" which he set up in 1915 in Afghanistan with the intention of invading India in rebellion against British rule. Others were involved in the Khilafat movement (1919-1924) which tried to preserve the status of the Sultan of Turkey as Caliph.[168]

One very remarkable example of non-violent action occurred amongst the Pathans of north-west India. The Pathans are one of the most warlike peoples of the world, who normally despise the very idea of peace, and no government has yet been able to control them, whether British, Pakistani or Afghan. Yet a Puritan reformer called Abdul Ghaffar Khan[169] (1890-1988) managed to persuade the Pathans of the power of non-violence. In the struggle for a political voice for the Pathans, his party had a uniformed but *unarmed* wing called the *Khudai Khidmatgaran* [Servants of God] whose clothes were dyed a plum colour leading to their nickname the *Surkhposhan* or Red-Shirts. The Red-Shirt movement was at its height in 1930 and by 1932 the North-West Frontier was granted the same political rights and institutions as the rest of the sub-continent had.[170] They held to their policy of non-violence for many years, despite persecution, imprisonment and executions. Well does Abdul Ghaffar Khan deserve his nickname "the Gandhi of the frontier provinces".[171] However, unlike Gandhi, Abdul Ghaffar Khan's non-violence was pragmatic rather than principled – he did not believe that violence against the British could be effective. He managed to find a basis for his ideas of non-violence in both Islam and the traditional Pathan code of *Pukhtunwali*.[172]

A generally non-violent interpretation of jihad is held by the Ahmadiyya sect (considered apostates by other Muslims, and regarded as non-Muslims in Pakistan where they are severely persecuted). Their founder, Mirza Ghulam Ahmad (1835-1908), rejected violent jihad as unnecessary in "a time of peace and security" such as India was enjoying under British rule.[173] However they do permit fighting in self-defence, to punish aggressors, and to ensure freedom to convert to Islam[174] – hence the raising of a volunteer corps of Ahmadis to fight in Kashmir alongside the Pakistani army after Pakistan's independence in 1947.[175]

History:
Muhammad and His Successors

Some liberal Muslim apologists today concede that Muhammad did use violence but claim that this was merely a defensive response in the face of extreme provocation. However, as has been seen above, both the Qur'an and the *hadith* contain texts which, taken at face value, would seem to indicate that Muhammad also took the initiative in engaging in offensive warfare.

Of course it can be argued that Muhammad lived in a very different time from our own and that it is unfair to judge him by modern standards of human rights and military conduct. Similarly the point could be made that Muhammad was merely a man and his belligerent actions and statements are examples of his human failings rather than divine guidance. However, traditionally Islam, whilst understanding Muhammad to be merely human, has also viewed him as effectively perfect, sinless and infallible and a timeless model to guide the Muslim community by example. Thus all but the most liberal or secular of modern Muslims, however uncomfortable they may feel about some of Muhammad's actions, must view them as not only good and just, but divinely sanctioned. In using extreme violence then, Islamist militants are only following the perfect Islamic model of Muhammad. They are simply taking Islamic dogma to its ultimate logical conclusion.

As has already been mentioned, in Muhammad's time there was a great deal of inter-tribal raiding amongst the Arabs, with the aim of stealing camels or sometimes women. Early in 623, the year after the Muslims emigrated to Medina, Muhammad began to send his followers out on razzias, later in the year leading them himself. The targets were always trade caravans from Mecca, the place where he had been rejected and persecuted. Thus in their earliest military efforts the Muslims were taking the offensive. Muhammad forbade Muslims to engage in razzias within the *umma*, but allowed them to attack other tribes so long as their targets were not Muslims. By replacing tribal loyalty with religious loyalty, Muhammad transformed the razzia into the jihad.[1] The final stage of this transformation is described by Reuven Firestone as "the total declaration of war against all groups, whether kin or not, who did not accept the truth or the hegemony of Islam".[2] The result of this was that non-Muslim tribes found themselves facing a choice between converting to Islam or being attacked by the increasing military power of the Muslim community at Medina. As the more local tribes one by one accepted Islam, the Muslims gradually had to move their field of war further away, so as to engage with non-Muslims.[3]

By the time of Muhammad's death in 632 virtually the whole Arabian peninsula had been subjugated to Islamic control. The degree of control varied.[4] Some parts were fully incorporated into the Medinan Islamic state, had converted to Islam and paid tax. In other areas most of the tribes but not all had converted and paid tax, while in areas remote from Medina they paid tax to the Islamic state but had not converted to Islam. Some tribes were politically allied with Medina but never paid taxes or acknowledged Muhammad's religious role.[5]

In considering the implications of the shift from allegiance based on kinship to allegiance based on a shared religion, it is important to understand just how powerful a force tribal loyalty was. Writers have struggled to convey its overriding importance in pre-Islamic Arabia.

> Tribal spirit was no doubt the fountainhead of all cardinal moral ideas
> on which Arab society was built. To respect the bond of kinship by
> blood more than anything else in the world, and to act for the glory of
> the tribe – this was by common consent a sacred duty imposed on every

man i.e. every individual member of the group.[6]

> This limitless and unshakeable attachment … that a pagan Arab feels
> for his fellow-tribesmen, this absolute devotion to the interests, prosper-
> ity, glory and honour of the community into which he was born and in
> which he will die – this is not in any way a sentiment like our patriotism,
> which would appear to a fiery Bedouin too lukewarm. It is a violent and
> terrible passion. It is at the same time the first and most sacred duty of
> all duties; it is the real religion of the desert.[7]

The closest ties were within the clan, the smallest genealogical unit. This kinship has been described as "tantamount to blood soli-darity in a virtually legal sense of the word".[8] While there could be war between brother tribes or even between two branches of the same tribe, the clan was an indivisible unit. Retaliation for the death of any member of a clan is incumbent on all its members. Conversely anyone from the clan of the slayer can be killed in revenge if the slayer himself is not to be found.[9] While loyalty to one's comrades and equals within the kinship group was paramount, there was no equivalent loyalty to one's superiors outside of the kinship group.[10]

It was this allegiance and loyalty which Muhammad redirected from blood relatives to co-religionists, from the tribe or clan to the *umma*. He can also be said to have moderated the more barbarous elements of the razzia by introducing the concept of *dhimma* – a protected status available to Jews Christians and Sabeans (not to pagans) on payment of a tax called *jizya*.[11]

According to Ibn Khaldun, jihad served to promote tribal unity within the *umma* (fighting a common enemy) as well as courage and self-reliance. He distinguished four kinds of warfare: (1) feuding between tribes and families (2) raiding among savage desert peoples i.e. those who earned their livelihood by war (3) jihad against exter-nal enemies (4) dynastic wars against seceders and those who are disobedient, which he considered were wars of "justice". The first two types of war he called wars of rebellion and sedition and consid-ered them unjustifiable. The latter two types of war he called wars of holiness and justice, and considered them justifiable.[12]

The four rightly guided caliphs

Muhammad's immediate successors were the four "rightly guided" caliphs whose rule covered the period 632 to 661. This period is often presented as the golden age of Islam. It was, however, a very violent period. The caliphs expanded Islamic political and military domination into Palestine, Syria, Mesopotamia and Egypt. By no means all of those in the newly conquered territories converted to Islam, but many chose to do so because non-Muslims living under Islam suffered discrimination and various legal disabilities. In addition to the wars of expansion, there were rebellions which had to be put down, frequent rivalries between contenders for the top job, and many assassinations. Three of the first four caliphs – 'Umar, 'Uthman and 'Ali – were assassinated. This period of Islamic history is traditionally regarded by Muslims as a paradigm to which they should aspire, second only in importance to the example of Muhammad himself.

There are many historical sources concerning this period, which have been subjected to painstaking scholarly examination. Some of these were written at the very time the events were taking place, for example a 634 Christmas sermon by Patriarch Sophronius of Jerusalem. Byzantine sources in general are relatively few. The most important are a brief history by Nicephorus (late eighth century) and a chronicle traditionally attributed to the Greek writer Theophanes from the ninth century. One particularly reliable source is that of Eutychius (876-940), a Christian Arab historian from Alexandria.

Muslim Arab histories are more plentiful and usually much lengthier than the other sources. Some of the best sources on the Muslim conquests are Ahmad b.Yahya al-Baladhuri (d.892) who wrote a work entitled *Kitab Futuh al-Buldan* [*Book of the Conquests of the Countries*], al-Tabari (839-923) who wrote *Ta'rikh al-Rusul wa'l-Muluk* [*History of Prophets and Kings*], al-Ya'qubi (d. late ninth or early tenth century) who wrote both a history (*Ta'rikh*) and a geography, Abu Muhammad Amad b. A'tham al-Kufi who wrote his *Kitab al-Futuh* [*Book of Conquests*] around 819, and Ibn Sa'd (ninth century) who wrote *Kitab al-Tabaqat* [*Book of Classes*]. Al-Azdi al-Basri's *Ta'rikh Futuh al-Sham* [*History of the Conquest of Syria*] has details not found elsewhere but needs to be read critically. Various other sources will be mentioned in the following pages.[13]

Rebellion and internal dissension

As soon as Muhammad died various groups of Arabs rebelled against their new Islamic rulers.[14] Some refused to pay tax any more, but were willing to stay Muslims. Others refused to pay tax and gave no commitment that they would continue to adhere to Islam.[15] Certain groups who had always opposed alliance with the Muslims took advantage of the situation to rise against the pro-Muslim factions. The fighting that followed was known as *hurub al-ridda* [the wars of apostasy] although some scholars assert that many of the rebels had never converted to Islam in the first place.[16] It was however a name that stuck, and some Muslim authors describe the rebellion very much in terms of new converts abandoning the faith[17] with a great number of stubborn apostates being burned to death by the renowned general Khalid ibn al-Walid for refusing to return to Islam.[18] Although partly political, there was also a religious character to the rebellions in that four of the six uprisings were led by men who claimed to be prophets.[19] The *Ridda* Wars occupied most of the reign of the first caliph, Abu Bakr (632-4). It was Abu Bakr himself who insisted on dealing ruthlessly with the rebels, following the example of the deceased Muhammad, despite the hesitation of many others in Medina.[20]

The first group to be defeated were the Najd tribes who had asked if they could stop paying tax while remaining Muslims. The Banu Hanifa, a partly pagan, partly Christian tribe who had never paid taxes or converted to Islam, sought independence from Muslim rule under their "prophet" Musaylima; they were similarly defeated in battle and had to submit again to the control of Medina. Likewise, the rebellious tribes in Bahrain, Oman and Yemen were fought in turn until all had renewed their former alliances with Medina. Eventually the whole Arabian peninsula was subdued, and what was effectively a standing army had been created because of the constant warfare and the number of new allies who had joined the victorious Muslims along the way.[21]

The overwhelming Muslim victory in the *Ridda* Wars seems to have been due to the unity and religious fervour of the Muslim forces. The rebels were mainly motivated by a desire for local independence, a love of old traditions, or an antipathy to paying taxes. Only the Banu Hanifa had had a specifically religious objection to Muslim rule. Another important factor was the collapse of the Persian Empire causing its former allies in Bahrain, Oman and Yemen to seek a new powerful ally such as Medina.[22]

The *Ridda* wars were followed by two civil wars (656-661 and 680-692). The first of these resulted in a division of the Muslim community into three main sects following the Battle of Siffin in 657: the Shi'as, the Kharijis and the main body who would later be called Sunnis. The basis of the dispute was the succession to the caliphate. The three sects all had the same attitude to war, but differed over who was a true Muslim i.e. who the enemy was.[23] The puritanical Kharijis took the most extreme stance, deeming that every Muslim who committed a major sin was an apostate and therefore an enemy.

Expansion beyond the Arabian peninsula – "wars of conquest" in the Islamic terminology of the time

Immediately after Muhammad's death, while the Muslims were engaged on the one hand fighting the *Ridda* Wars within the Arabian peninsula, they simultaneously began a campaign to conquer the neighbouring lands of the Byzantine Empire, beginning with Syria. The expedition to Syria had in fact been planned by Muhammad before his death, and Caliph Abu Bakr ensured that it was carried out according to Muhammad's wishes.[24] Some scholars speculate that it may also have served the purpose of keeping happy the peripheral Arab tribes who wanted to go raiding but could not attack their fellow Muslims.[25]

There has been much scholarly debate about why the Byzantine Empire should have succumbed so quickly to the armies of the Muslim Arabs in the 630s despite the fact that the Byzantines had better weapons and more funds. Several contemporary Christian sources saw it as God's judgement on the immorality and debauchery of Christians at the time, and particularly on Emperor Heraclius who had married his niece and supported a compromise theology called Monotheletism which was rejected by both sides (Chalcedonians and Monophysites) in the Christological debate. These sources include Fredegarius in late 650s Gaul, the late seventh century Coptic historian John the Bishop of Nikiu, the late seventh century Armenian historian Sebeos, John Bar Penkaye from north Mesopotamia also in the late seventh century, and various seventh century Monophysite reactions recorded by the twelfth century Syrian Jacobite bishop Michael the Syrian.[26]

In more practical terms, the Byzantines were exhausted from a long but ultimately (in 628) successful war to win back their territory from Sassanian Persian invaders.[27] On the whole they failed to realise the significance of the fact that their Arab enemies – a familiar foe from the past – were now *Muslim* Arabs, strongly motivated by their new faith, which also gave them a loyalty and a cohesion that made them very resistant to Byzantine efforts to get them to betray, desert or change sides.[28] The Christians on the other hand lacked a religious motivation comparable to that of the Muslim invaders and this may have been a factor in the Byzantine losses in the Levant.[29] There was also poor intelligence and poor communication. The Christian population of Syria and Palestine had little inkling of how serious an onslaught they were to face from the Muslims.[30] Sophronius, writing in 634, states that the Muslims attacked "unexpectedly".[31] It seems, however, that the top echelons of Byzantine leadership may have been somewhat less taken by surprise.[32] Emperor Heraclius tried to stir up the people to defend themselves, but in most cases the response was passivity and apathy,[33] perhaps due to the imposition of new military commanders from outside or to the financial cost of defence, which had to be borne by the local people. In addition they were not in the habit of fighting since the imperial government, in an effort to ensure public order, had banned private individuals from owning weapons.[34]

The turning point was the Battle of Jabiya-Yarmuk in Syria in 636, which saw the virtual destruction of the Byzantine army (though not the Byzantine empire). This battle is analysed in detail by Kaegi,[35] whose opinion is that the military dimension was the primary factor in the Muslim conquests of this region.[36] He rejects the hypothesis that Christian sectarianism made many inhabitants of that part of the Byzantine empire disloyal. In fact many Christian Arab tribes of Syria wanted to remain part of the Byzantine Empire, albeit differing from the Emperor in theology, rather than be subject to the Muslim conquerors.[37]

After Mesopotamia and Egypt had also fallen to the Muslims, the next part of the Byzantine Empire to be targeted was Armenia (640-654). In this case – unlike the earlier conquests – the Muslim victory was not primarily due to military causes for the Armenians were better armed and more self-reliant than any other part of the empire. The Armenians' lack of resistance to the Muslim invasion was mainly due to local ethnic antagonisms and to their antipathy towards the Byzantine Empire from whom they differed on some Christological and ecclesiological issues. Some Armenian leaders and their followers defected to the Muslims (though without converting). Nevertheless, the Muslim invasion, which was violent and destructive, was seen by the chroniclers[38] not as liberation but as a catastrophe.[39]

Armenia was also different from Palestine, Syria, Mesopotamia and Egypt in that the general population did not convert to Islam nor become assimilated to Islamic Arabic culture. They remained Christian and distinctively Armenian, and indeed rebelled when the Muslims later pressured them to convert to Islam and imposed higher taxes. On the other hand when Emperor Constans II managed temporarily to restore Byzantine authority over Armenia (652-3), he found Armenians who preferred Muslim rule.[40]

The issue of religious conversions during the expansion of the Islamic empire is a vexed point. According to Kaegi there is no evidence that the Byzantines tried to convert any Muslims to Christianity. Many Muslim soldiers were undoubtedly strongly motivated by their religion, and some Muslim sources record religious polemics that might have been intended to convert. However there is no evidence of the forced conversion of captured Byzantine prisoners.[41] There are *Muslim* reports of the Byzantines killing some of their own number who voluntarily converted to Islam. The earliest of these was Farwa b. 'Amr al-Judhami, governor of Ma'an in southern Palestine, whose conversion appears to have been part of his zealous attempts to develop good personal relations with the Muslims. According to Muslim reports he was executed by the Byzantines.[42] Another early convert from Christianity to Islam, Ziyad b. 'Amr Nuqil, is alleged by Muslim sources to have been unofficially murdered by Christians at Mayfa'a, east of the Dead Sea.[43]

The growth and decline of the Islamic empire

A decisive battle in 642 overthrew the Sassanian Persian dynasty, their provinces being incorporated into the Arabian caliphate. When the power base of the Islamic empire shifted from Medina to Damascus in 661 an immense expansion of territory followed. Under the Damascus-based Umayyads, the first hereditary dynasty of caliphs, Islamic armies conquered east as far as northern India and central Asia (Tashkent 712) and west through North Africa (670), Sicily, Spain (711) and southern France (c.715). The advance across the Straits of Gibraltar was explicitly justified as part of the jihad.[44] In the midst of gaining these new territories, the Muslims continued to hammer away at the Byzantines, repeatedly besieging Constantinople (669, 674-80, 717) and making frequent incursions into Anatolia.

Then in 728-732 the tide turned, and the armies of the Caliphate suffered an unprecedented series of disastrous defeats in several, widely spread, theatres of war.[45] The result was not only a loss of territory but also a loss of morale amongst the Muslim troops. This was exacerbated by the fact that in many battles the senior commander was himself killed. Dramatic failures of this kind were not anticipated in Islamic theology and the resulting demoralisation was that much greater.

These defeats occurred in Sijistan (in modern Afghanistan) where the army was virtually annihilated (728), Ardabil in the Caucasus when only a few hundred Muslim troops survived of an army estimated at 25,000 (730), India where the Indians rebelled and the Muslim troops fled and refused ever to go back (731 or perhaps earlier), and a colossal defeat at the Battle of the Defile near Samarkand in Transoxania (731). Even on the Byzantine front, the Muslims experienced a defeat in 731. Finally, the Muslims were defeated in France at a battle between Poitiers and Tours (732).

Despite all these defeats the Caliphate continued with its policy of expansion on many fronts simultaneously, still suffering frequent – if less disastrous – defeats. This eventually weakened the Damascus-based Umayyad Caliphate so much[46] that it paved the way for the rise of the 'Abbasid Caliphate in Baghdad in 750 which took over from Damascus as the centre of the Islamic state.

The 'Abbasid dynasty continued in Baghdad until 1258 (when Baghdad was conquered by the Mongols), but various other independent caliphates arose in other places during this period, reducing the authority of the 'Abbasid Caliphate. In Spain there was an emirate founded by the Umayyads (after they had been deposed in Damascus by the 'Abbasids) from 755, then in 912 a caliphate which lasted until its capital at Cordova fell to the Christian forces in 1236. Thereafter the centre of Spanish Islam became Granada. An Isma'ili Shi'a Caliphate known as the Fatimids ruled North Africa (910-1171), making their power base in Egypt from 969 onwards. Another Shi'a group, the Buyids, exercised effective control in Baghdad from 945 to 1031 while retaining the nominal Sunni caliph.

Other regional dynasties in the medieval Muslim world included the Arab Hamdanids in Syria and the Persian Samanids in Transoxania. Three Turkish dynasties vied for power, with the Seljuks ultimately triumphing in the early twelfth century. The Seljuks themselves soon divided into independent principalities. The Ottoman dynasty was founded by Osman (pronounced Othman in Arabic, hence the European term Ottoman) who declared his independence of Seljuk rule in Anatolia around 1300. At this time the Ottoman state was simply "a small principality on the borders of the Islamic world, dedicated to Gazâ, the holy war against infidel Christianity".[47] Thus began the long and powerful reign of the Ottoman Caliphate. The Ottomans captured Constantinople from the Byzantines in 1453 and Egypt in 1517. The Ottoman empire continued as the chief Muslim power for about six hundred years.

The Ottomans had an elite fighting force known as the Janissaries (*Yenicheri*). Originally prisoners of war, the Janissaries were later kept up to number by means of a forced levy (*devshirme*) which occurred every few years. In these levies, instituted by Murat II (1421-51), a certain proportion of the Christian boys were taken, forced to become Muslims, and trained for war. There was no justification for this within the Shari'ah but it may have arisen from the concept of Christians paying a tax to their Muslim overlords, in this case making the payment in children rather than in money.[48]

As the military and economic strength of Muslim countries began to decline in comparison with European nations, it became more difficult to adhere to the doctrine of continued expansion into non-Muslim territory and ongoing jihad. Muslim governments had to abandon traditional teaching and, as a matter of sheer practicality, enter into permanent peace treaties with European governments. One such was the Treaty of Zsitivatorok (1606) between the Ottoman sultan and the Holy Roman emperor. A later sultan joined the Concert of Europe by signing the 1856 Paris Peace Treaty, and thus effectively submitted to European international relations.[49]

European colonial expansion resulted in the effective subjugation of much of the Muslim world. But when, in the mid-twentieth century, Muslims were able to shake off the colonial yoke and gain their independence again, they did not on the whole revert to practising the traditional Islamic doctrine of war. Rather, they recognised public international law, for example, joining the United Nations. Even the charter of the Organisation of the Islamic Conference, an international body to which Muslim countries belong, affirms its members' commitment to the UN charter.[50] There have been, however, some very prominent exceptions to this generalisation.[51] Perhaps unsurprisingly Ayatollah Khomeini, the architect of the 1979 Islamic revolution in Iran, stated that he was opposed to treaties that contradicted Islamic law.[52] More surprisingly, Mahmud Shaltut, the Sheikh of Al-Azhar who insisted on a defence-only interpretation of jihad, affirmed the classical teaching that Muslims are free to denounce a treaty that has become disadvantageous to them.[53]

Muslims who have signed international agreements face a painful dilemma when such agreements prevent them from assisting their fellow-Muslims whom they see to be oppressed e.g. in Bosnia and Palestine, for under Islamic law they have an obligation to come to their aid.[54]

Violent Sects and Movements: Past & Present

Once the legitimate use of violence to produce change had been established within the Islamic tradition, certain consequences followed. Violence was not just the prerogative of the Islamic state, but could also be claimed as valid by any Islamic rebel movement which might spring up. Many of these movements held that violence could be directed against civilians as well as against the state's armed forces despite the fact that mainstream teaching tended to forbid attacks on non-combatants.

However, to modern radicals whose aim is to return to the original sources and early model to purify Islam and reclaim its original glory and power, later limiting traditions are not authoritative. As they cast away the restrictions and limits set on jihad by establishment scholars over the centuries, they come face to face with the original texts and models. Sometimes they rediscover early concepts and interpretations which they understand to legitimise indiscriminate violence against diverse enemies.

Early sects

Shi'as

As already seen, the main split in Islam occurred within twenty years of Muhammad's death, when the Shi'as (the name is derived from *Shi'at 'Ali* i.e. the party or faction of 'Ali) separated from the Sunnis in a violent leadership dispute. This period of dispute was called the "great *fitna*" and ran from 656 to 661. The Shi'as believed that only 'Ali and his descendants could hold the position of supreme leader. In 656 the third caliph, 'Uthman, was assassinated and 'Ali ibn Abi-Talib, nephew and son-in-law of Muhammad, installed as the fourth caliph. 'Uthman's cousin, Mu'awiya ibn Abu Sufyan, who was governor of Syria, rebelled against 'Ali, demanding vengeance for 'Uthman's murder.

The dispute continued until 'Ali himself was assassinated (by a Khariji) after which it was then continued by his sons, Hassan and Hussein. Shi'as believe that the elder son Hassan was poisoned on the orders of Mu'awiya. (It seems that actually he renounced his claim to the caliphate in return for a handsome stipend.) The younger son, Hussein, called the "Lord of Martyrs", was killed along with most of his family at the Battle of Karbala (10 October 680). This shocking event rallied many to the Shi'a cause, including Persian Muslims who welcomed an alternative to the Arab arrogance which gave Persian converts to Islam a subordinate position amongst the Arab tribes.

The Shi'a initiated many bloody rebellions which ravaged large regions of the early Islamic empire. Although the first such uprisings were put down by the Sunni majority, the Shi'as eventually played an important part in the downfall of the Umayyad dynasty, only to find power taken not by a descendant of 'Ali but by the descendants of 'Abbas, Muhammad's uncle. Under the 'Abbasid dynasty the Shi'as became a vast secret community, who rebelled from time to time, but were gradually weakened by their own internal divisions, mainly on the vexed question of the succession to the position of supreme leader, whom they called the imam (rather than the caliph). Most of the Shi'a sub-sects believed that the imam was infused with a kind of divine light-substance which made him sinless and infallible. Most sub-sects also believed in the Mahdi, i.e. that one or other of the Imams (sub-sects would differ as to which particular Imam) would return one day, since he had not actually died but merely gone into hiding.

Shi'a Islam, which is predominant in Iran today and whose adherents also form the majority in Iraq, has a strongly developed theology of death and in particular martyrdom. This derives from the martyrdom of Hussein, the role model for Shi'a Muslims, which is the great paradigm for Shi'as. His martyrdom is commemorated annually by Shi'as on its anniversary, the tenth day of the Muslim month of Muharram.

Kharijis[1]

At the same time that the Shi'as split away from the main body of Islam, so did another group – the Kharijis. Their most significant distinguishing feature was that they declared other Muslims to be apostates (and therefore deserving of the death sentence), and thus legitimized jihad against them. Indeed, they held that any Muslim committing a major sin was an apostate. The term for labelling someone as an apostate is *takfir*, and the Khariji interpretation of this term has been revived by many modern radical groups. The Kharijis believed that in order to exterminate evil and re-establish justice the apostates must be either forced to believe or killed.

During the "great *fitna*" about who should be caliph, a battle was fought at Siffin in northern Iraq (657). After this battle Caliph 'Ali agreed to accept arbitration on the leadership dispute. Some of his followers were angered by this decision. They believed that the assassination of his predecessor, Caliph 'Uthman, had been just, given that 'Uthman had sinned. Quoting the Qur'anic motto "Judgement belongs to God alone", they held that the question of who should be caliph was not an appropriate subject for human arbitration. They withdrew from 'Ali's camp, stating that he had lost the right to the caliphate by making this concession to sinners, and that he and his followers were therefore no longer Muslims. Because they had withdrawn they were called Kharijis (meaning "seceders"). The following year 'Ali defeated the Kharijis at the Battle of Nahrawan, but was himself assassinated by a Khariji in 661.

The Kharijis held that the appointment of both 'Uthman and 'Ali to the caliphate had been valid, but that each had forfeited their right to the position by later sinning and therefore – in the eyes of the Kharijis – becoming apostates. They considered that all Muslims who supported either 'Uthman or 'Ali were likewise apostates.

The Kharijis rebelled almost constantly for two centuries against first the Ummayad and then the 'Abbasid Sunni Islamic regimes, with battles being fought in Persia, Iraq and North Africa. As has already been noted, they were brutal and ruthless in war. Despite many defeats, the Kharijis managed to establish states in the Arabian peninsula and in North Africa which survived for varying lengths of time. While the Kharijis themselves were eventually suppressed and exterminated by about 900, small remnant communities of a more moderate sub-sect of the Kharijis called the 'Ibadis survive in Oman, East Africa and North Africa. Some Berber-speaking 'Ibadis are found in Algeria, where they are called Mzabis after the desert region in which they are concentrated.

The Kharijis were extremely puritanical and legalistic. They forbade all luxuries such as music, games and ornaments. They held that Muslims who committed major sins had effectively left the faith, i.e. apostatised, and were therefore liable to be killed. Unlike the other sects, they did not accept an oral profession of faith as sufficient to assure a person's status as a Muslim but believed that a life of righteousness and good works was also necessary. Their rebellions were motivated by the belief that any caliph who sinned must be deposed by force (unless he repented). The goal of the Kharijis was to create an Islamic community in which no one could deviate from the duties of Islam. Jihad by the sword was a vital part of their faith, a duty so binding that it was considered a "pillar of Islam" on a par with fasting, praying etc.

They stressed that all Muslims were equal and that the position of caliph should be held by the most pious Muslim in every generation, whether Arab, non-Arab, slave or even a woman. They rejected the Shi'a argument that the imam must be a descendant of 'Ali, and also rejected the Sunni practice of appointing to the caliphate (and all the main government posts) only those from Muhammad's tribe, the city-dwelling Quraish. This egalitarianism appealed particularly to non-Arab Muslims and also to the desert-dwelling Bedouin Arabs, whose warriors had done much of the fighting but felt they had not received a fair share of the spoils of war.

Apart from the equating of sin with apostasy, Khariji doctrines were based firmly on the Qur'an and on the words and example of Muhammad. They cannot therefore be regarded as heretical, but should be seen as a valid mainstream sect alongside Sunnis and Shi'as. In many ways they were simply taking literally what other Muslims found more convenient to interpret non-literally. Furthermore, the Khariji attacks were on other Muslim sects and regimes; they did not attack people who called themselves non-Muslims. Because they considered other Muslims to be apostates from Islam (and therefore to be killed on sight) these other Muslims were far worse in Khariji eyes than, for example, Jews and Christians, the People of the Book. In this way they differ very importantly from modern radical Islamist groups.

The Khariji doctrine of *takfir* – labelling other Muslims as infidels worthy of the death sentence for any perceived violation of the Shari'ah – has been revived in various modern groups of Islamist radicals including the Wahhabis, the Salafiyya movement, and many violent groups in Egypt, Jordan, Yemen, Algeria and Pakistan. These groups include the Muslim Brotherhood and al-Jama'at al-Islamiyya in Egypt, the Armed Islamic Group (GIA) in Algeria and Al-Qa'eda. It is thus that they justify their jihad against Muslim regimes which they consider insufficiently Islamic. Unlike the Kharijis, these modern groups attack not only Muslims but also non-Muslims. The Khariji model and their concept of *takfir* are irrelevant to the modern radicals' jihad against non-Muslims.

Isma'ilis

The Isma'ili sect began to be differentiated from the main body of Shi'as at the time of Imam Ja'far as-Sadiq (d. 765). They trace their imamate through one of his sons, Isma'il, and await the return of Isma'il's son Muhammad ibn Isma'il as the Mahdi. Also known as

"Seveners", they focus on the seventh imam, (whom some Isma'ilis consider to be Ism'ail, although other Ismaili sub-sects identify other individuals as the seventh imam). The Isma'ilis carried the Shi'a concept of secret [batini] teaching to great extremes, believing that only 'Ali and his descendants knew the real meaning of religious truth.

They developed what could be termed an intelligence service (i.e. the secret infiltration of normal society and the regime establishment as a way to prepare for the final onslaught on the corrupt state power) and practised taqiyya to a high degree. The emissaries they sent out across the Muslim world tried to nurture any anti-government feeling and social unrest whether based on racial antipathies, economic discontent or whatever the cause. They would create doubt, stress the need for an authoritative leader and impose an oath of secrecy and obedience. They would represent their own beliefs as Khariji to the Kharijis, as Shi'a to the Shi'as, as anti-Arab to the Persian nationalists etc. What they actually believed – apparently revealed only to the higher echelons of the movement – seems to have been a kind of mystic philosophy far removed from orthodox Islam.[2]

In the tenth century the Isma'ili message culminated in the appearance in North Africa of a certain 'Ubaydullah, who claimed to be the Mahdi and the legitimate ruler of all Muslims by virtue of his descent from Muhammad's daughter Fatima through Muhammad ibn Isma'il. He established the Fatimid Caliphate in Egypt.

Today Isma'ilis are found mainly in India and Pakistan, with smaller numbers in Yemen, Syria, Central Asia and Iran. Many have emigrated from the Indian sub-continent to East Africa and some to Europe and America.

Assassins

Amongst the many divisions and sub-sects of the Isma'ilis were the Assassins, based at Alamut in Persia, who were active for nearly two centuries starting around 1090.

The Assassins developed political killings (i.e. assassinations) by suicide devotees [fida'iyun] as the most effective tool to spread terror in the general populace and deter enemies from attacking them. They attacked only the great and powerful, and never harmed ordinary people. They always killed with a dagger since this was more likely to lead to capture and execution i.e. martyrdom, which would take the believer directly to paradise. More discreet methods, such as poison or killing from a safer distance with a bow and arrow, ran the "risk" of the Assassin getting away with it.[3]

The Assassins terrorized Syria and Iraq from their fortresses in the time of the Crusades. They were also a constant challenge to the Sunni rulers of Persia. Their power continued until 1256 when the Mongols attacked their fortress at Alamut in such overwhelming numbers that the Grand Master surrendered and was executed. The present Aga Khan traces his descent from this last Grand Master of Alamut.

Thus contemporary Muslims wishing to re-enact the methodology of the early Muslims find encouragement to use force as well as espionage against opponents and presumed enemies in the very model which they revere.

Later reform movements

Islam has seen a cycle of puritanical reform movements in the pre-modern era, which were a reaction to cultural, religious, political and economic decline at a time when Muslim states were under pressure from western imperialism. Typically their leaders would seek to purge Islam of the various accretions it had accumulated over the centuries and to return to the fundamentals of the Qur'an and *hadith* and the first Islamic state established in Medina.

Many of these movements had a messianic element in that their leaders claimed to be the long-awaited Mahdi come to bring deliverance to Muslims and restore their glory. General Gordon was killed in a Mahdi-led Islamic uprising in Sudan in 1885 which was eventually put down by Kitchener in 1898, thirteen years after the Mahdi's own death.

Wahhabism

One of the most enduring of these movements was that founded in the Arabian peninsula by 'Abd al-Wahhab (1703-1792) who linked his movement to the House of Saud. Al-Wahhab considered Muslim society at the time to be little better than paganism, and he revived the Khariji practice of *takfir*, i.e. condemning all Muslims he disagreed with as apostates in order to justify jihad against them. The strictly puritanical Wahhabism remains today the predominant Islamic movement within Saudi Arabia.

In 1979 Juhayman al-'Utaybi (1943-1979), a strict Wahhabi who was disillusioned by the profligate lifestyle of the Saudi royal family, attempted to revolt against the Saudi regime in the name of Muhammad ibn-'Abdullah al-Qahtani, a student at the Islamic University in Riyadh, believed to be the Mahdi. Qahtani's Mahdi status had been revealed in dreams to his wife and sister. He fulfilled many of the predictions about the Mahdi which occur in the *hadith*: the Mahdi was to appear at the *ka'ba* at the turn of the Islamic century (1979 overlapped with the year 1400 in the Islamic calendar), and was to have the same name as the Prophet and similar physical characteristics. Juhayman and his followers believed that after a long period of deviation from true Islam, the Mahdi would appear and put an end to corrupt, tyrannical regimes. They seized the Grand Mosque in Mecca but were eventually dislodged by the Saudi security forces after a violent siege.[4]

Salafiyya (neo-Wahhabism)

Wahhabism was a key factor in the development of the Salafiyya movement which became widely influential across the Muslim world, shaping the activist ideology of Islamist radicals from Morocco to Indonesia. Founded by Rashid Rida (1865-1935),[5] Salafiyya sought to return to the example of the "pious ancestors" [*salaf*] i.e. Muhammad, his companions, and the "rightly guided" caliphs. Like Wahhabism it looked back for inspiration to the Khariji in the early days of Islam and followed their example in the use of *takfir*, condemning secular Muslim society as heretical and apostate. Salafiyya added to Wahhabi puritanism an element of reinterpreting the origins of Islam in order to face the modern world. Another source of inspiration were the writings of Ibn Taymiyya in the thirteenth and fourteenth centuries.

Its organizational principles are those of the Saudi Ikhwan movement – a movement of radically extremist settlers who were sent in the 1920s and 1930s by the Saudis to found settlements on the Saudi borders. (Ironically they subsequently became a real danger for the Saudi regime.)

During the 1950s the Saudi religious establishment was active in disseminating Salafiyya, also known as neo-Wahhabism. In the 1990s it was the Salafiyya trend that caused various different Islamist radical groups to strengthen their links with each other.

Deobandi

The Deobandi movement grew out of the Indian Mutiny against the British in 1857, an event of major significance to the Muslim community in India. The Dar-ul-Uloom Deoband Islamic school was founded in 1867 in Peshawar. The Deobandi school taught a complete rejection of western influence and values and a return to classical, conservative Islam. So successful was the Deobandi movement that by the time of its centenary in 1967 there were over 9,000 Deobandi schools and *madrassas* [Islamic religious schools] across South Asia. Today the Deobandi movement remains extremely influential amongst Muslims in India, Pakistan and Afghanistan and has helped to shape a distinctly South Asian, as opposed to Middle Eastern, brand of conservative Islam.

In recent years the Deobandi movement has become much more involved with Islamist militancy as a result of the jihad in Afghanistan against the Soviet Union in the 1980s, as they sought to defend their fellow-Muslims whose land had been occupied by non-Muslims.

The movement has come to the attention of the West because of its close connection with the Taliban and several key Pakistan-based Islamist militant groups. The Taliban emerged as a religious movement amongst ethnic Pathans very much growing out of Deobandi mosques and *madrassas* in Pakistan. During their rule in Afghanistan they continued to receive massive support and backing from the Deobandi school in Pakistan and even after the disintegration of their rule in 2001 the various Taliban and Al-Qa'eda cells left in Pakistan's North West Frontier Province are believed still to receive close support from the Deobandi school. In Pakistan itself the Islamist group Jamiat Ulema-e-Islam, which has links to Islamist militants fighting across Asia, is also firmly embedded within the Deobandi tradition.

Tablighi Jama'at

The Tablighi Jama'at was established in 1926 in what was then British India under the leadership of a Deobandi-associated Sufi scholar, Mawlana Muhammad Ilyas. Like the Deobandi school itself the Tablighi Jama'at is a movement which began as basically non-violent but later developed a violent element. In the case of the Tablighi Jama'at this change was a result of infiltration. The organization, which is based near Delhi, is hugely influential with branches all over the Islamic world. Gatherings of supporters near Lahore, Pakistan, constitute the second largest assembly of Muslims in the world, surpassed in numbers only by the annual pilgrimage to Mecca. Tablighi Jama'at is very popular amongst Muslims from all sections of society, but particularly amongst educated, westernised elites.

The Tablighi Jama'at considers that the most valuable kind of jihad is moral self-improvement. It stresses that Islam should be spread and promoted amongst nominal Muslims and unbelievers, not through force and compulsion, but through persuasion and peaceful means. They see physical jihad as secondary and inferior. However, during the 1980s the ISI (Pakistan's intelligence agency) and the CIA worked to infiltrate this hugely influential, and until then largely peaceful, Islamic organization in order to recruit individuals to fight in the jihad against Soviet troops in Afghanistan.

This helped to generate a violent element within the movement. The organization is extremely large and diverse, and there is little interaction between different cells, making it difficult to gauge the extent to which this hugely influential and ostensibly peaceful organization may be linked to groups involved in violent activity.

Contemporary movements

The various contemporary Islamist terrorist groups are closely enmeshed with each other, networked and interwoven, providing recruits and funds for each other, offering safe houses and serving as clearing houses for funds, arms and fighters. They have established a large array of front organisations such as legal businesses, charities, trusts, welfare, educational and other institutions to bankroll and whitewash their activities while raising large amounts of funds and many recruits for their cause. Some of the fund-raising is by drug-trafficking, hostage-taking and other criminal activities. Individuals who do not engage directly in violence nevertheless provide vital help to those who do engage in violence.

Further strands were added to the mesh in the 1990s when many extremist movements had to move from their country of origin, where radical militants were being repressed, to the West (especially western Europe and North America), where they found freedom to continue their operations. Global communication technologies meant that such re-location did not hinder their work, but rather gave them a new pool of local western Muslims from which to draw financial support and recruit new members.

Western attempts to focus exclusively on Al-Qa'eda and isolate it from the mainstream Islamic tradition fail to understand the nature of Islamist terrorist networks. A good comparison would be the multitude of western NGOs or anti-globalisation groups. These organizations have a great deal of interaction and overlap with each other; they support each other, evolve coalitions on issues of common interest, and combine their causes together. The boundaries between them are not clearly defined. In addition key individuals can be involved as trustees or directors of several different groups at once. Another feature of this comparison is the way different groups merge and split, or close themselves down only to reappear under a new name or as several different new groups. Contemporary Islamist terrorism is manifested in the same kind of fluid, complex, ever-shifting networks, closely linked to and resourced by mainstream Muslim society, not as a lone, clearly defined entity.

An eschatological worldview continues to be an important influence on today's radical groups, many of whom believe themselves to be living in the End Times. This mindset also results in abundant conspiracy theories. They view Muslim history as a prelude to the End and the various battles as End-Time battles or at least dress-rehearsals for them. They perceive a series of cycles of victory and defeat, and are therefore not dismayed by defeat as this is only to be expected periodically, while ultimately God will bring them victory. This final victory, achieved by God himself when the Muslims face overwhelming odds, will be superior to the victories which the Muslims themselves have gained in the past by their own strength.[6]

Classic Muslim eschatology includes various signs of the End Times. Sunnis expect the appearance of the Mahdi and of the Anti-Christ [Dajjal]. Osama bin Laden is in many ways a Mahdi-like figure, who has achieved an almost mythical status. His austere and devout lifestyle, zeal for Islam, reported exploits, legendary wealth, and international renown fit the classical Mahdi picture and have increased his popular appeal to Muslims around the world.[7]

Shi'as, on the other hand, await the return of the Hidden Imam who will set up a righteous rule on earth. The rise to power of Ayatollah Khomeini resonated with classical Shi'a eschatological symbols. Many Iranians believed that he was the Hidden Imam who had returned, or at least his representative sent to prepare the way for the End Times. Ali Shariati (1933-1977), the main ideologue of the Iranian Islamic Revolution, reinterpreted the Shi'a concept of *intizar*, the waiting for the return of the Hidden Imam, as an active accelerating of his coming – a struggle towards the goal of revolution.[8]

Having recognised how fluid and interlinked the various groups are, there is nevertheless some value in trying to characterise them individually and analyse their relationships with each other.

Movements in the colonial period

Out of the Salafiyya movement emerged the Muslim Brotherhood. This Egyptian group, founded by Hasan al-Banna (1906-1949) in 1928, was the first grass-roots Islamist militant movement, the first of the groups who are often termed "fundamentalist". Al-Banna, who had connections to Sufism, glorified active defensive jihad: "The supreme martyrdom is only conferred on those who slay or are slain in the way of God. As death is inevitable and can happen only once, partaking in jihad is profitable in this world and the next."[9] The movement developed branches in Syria, Palestine and Sudan.

Movements in the post-colonial period

Following independence, most Muslim-majority nations did not deliver the promised improvements in social conditions. Their political, social, and economic failures contributed to the rise of radical Islam as a mass movement demanding a return to Islam as an authentic alternative political ideology. (See appendix four on Various Brands of Radical Islam.)

Mawdudi (1903-79) and Jama'at-i Islami

On the Indian subcontinent Abu'l A'la Mawdudi (1903-1979), influenced by al-Banna, founded the Jama'at-i Islami in 1941 as an elitist vanguard organization aimed at establishing an Islamic order. His goal was the complete transformation of individual, society and politics in line with Islamic ideology, a transformation that should be attained gradually through the efforts of a highly motivated vanguard of enlightened Muslims acting as catalysts of the revolution. The Islamic state ruled by Shari'ah was seen as the panacea for all the problems Muslims faced worldwide. He defined jihad as primarily individual exertion "in the way of Allah" to alter the ideology and social order. While embracing the classic military understanding of Islam, he also considered jihad to cover non-violent means such as campaigning by speech and writing.[10]

Both the Muslim Brotherhood and the Jama'at-i Islami claim that Islam is a total ideological system that must dominate all public life (political, societal, economic), as well as personal matters and private worship. It is not enough for society to be composed of Muslims – it must also be Islamic in its basic structures.

Qutb (1907-66)

Mawdudi in turn influenced Sayyid Qutb, the main ideologue of the Muslim Brotherhood in Egypt. Qutb's writings (especially *Ma'alim fi al-Tariq*, translated as *Signposts on the Road* or *Milestones*) became the primary ideological source of contemporary radical Islamist movements, providing them with the criteria by which to judge contemporary regimes and societies. In this work he promoted the Khariji doctrine of *takfir*, the process of judging Muslims (individuals, regimes, societies and states) as infidels if they do not wholly conform to the Shari'ah.

Qutb transformed the meaning of the Islamic term *hijra* (emigration) from a simple description of Muhammad's migration from Mecca to Medina to a distinct stage in the development of all true Islamic societies. *Hijra*, in Qutb's terminology, is the response of true Muslims to the state of ignorance and immorality prevalent in their society. He called this ignorance and immorality *jahiliyya*,[11] a term normally confined to the paganism of pre-Islamic Arabia. Qutb identified the enemy as all *jahili* societies, thus supplying a specific focus for revolutionary action. *Jahiliyya* is always evil in whatever form it manifests itself, always seeking to crush true Islam, he asserted, and therefore jihad by force must be used to annihilate *jahili* regimes and replace them by true Muslim ones.[12] He put an emphasis on the *qital* aspect of jihad[13] and strongly rejected the defence-only interpretation.[14] He saw jihad as a method for actively seeking to free all peoples on earth from non-Islamic authority.[15]

Most violent extreme groups of today like al-Jamaʿat al-Islami-yya, Hamas, Hizb al-Tahrir, the GIA of Algeria, and many more, were born out of the Muslim Brotherhood as reinterpreted by Qutb. They have developed in two general trends excellently defined by Reuven Paz, academic director of the International Policy Institute for Counter-Terrorism, in his January 2000 paper on *The Heritage of the Sunni Militant Groups: An Islamic internacionale?*[16] from which the following analysis is drawn:

1. *Islamic Jihad groups:* These groups hold that the leaders of their countries are not true Muslims and therefore legiti-mate the use of violence against them, if not the wider pop-ulace. In general terms they are better integrated with soci-ety at large than are the more isolationist Takfir groups (see below), they do not consider their leaders to be sent by Allah in any exceptional way, and they accept the teaching of later Islamic scholars and leaders as authoritative alongside the earlier sources of Islam.

   Egyptian groups which fall into this category include al-Jihad, now led by Sheikh Omar Abdul Rahman, and al-Jamaʿat al-Islamiyya with its own various groups. Faraj, the founder of al-Jihad, accepted the tradition of waiting for the Mahdi, but believed this should not lead to passivity but rather that true Muslims should be active in fulfilling God's mandate to spread Islam to the whole world before the end times and the appearance of the Mahdi. He held that lack of messianic leadership was no reason to postpone the struggle, as leadership can be given in the interim by the best Muslim in the community.[17]

   Three members of the radical Egyptian group al-Jamaʿat al-Islamiyya included in their declaration of faith:

   > We have no doubt that the awaited Mahdee (or rightly-guided Imam) will come forth among the *Ummah* of the Prophet at the end of time (on earth). We believe in the Signs of the Hour. The

appearance of ad-Dajjal (false Messiah, or Antichrist). The descent from heaven of 'Isa,[18] son of Mary. The sun rising from the West. The emergence of the Beast from the earth. And other signs mentioned in the Qur'an and the authentic Hadeeth of the Prophet.[19]

In the Levant, this category includes the faction of the Palestinian Islamic Jihad led by Sheikh As'ad Bayoud al-Tamimi (as opposed to the Shqaqi faction which was primarily affiliated with the Islamic revolution in Iran), alTali'ah al-Islamiyya in Syria, and two groups in Lebanon – al-Tawhid group in Tripoli and al-Jama'ah al-Islamiyya in Saida.

Also in this category are the various Afghan Mujahidin groups (taking inspiration from the Palestinian Dr 'Abdallah 'Azzam[20]). It is from the Afghan Mujahidin that the gigantic network Al-Qa'eda emerged. There are also several other small groups in the Arab world and in Pakistan.

2. *Takfir groups*: In general terms the Takfir groups are much more isolationist than the Jihadists. They withdraw from wider Muslim society, the members of which they consider to be apostates, and by this interpretation they justify the indiscriminate murder of civilians to achieve their aims. Their leaders are sometimes seen as being exceptional, even Mahdis. They accept as authoritative the Qur'an, the teachings of Muhammad in the *hadith* and the rulings of the first four caliphs, and reject all later Islamic traditions.

One of the main Takfir groups was the Egyptian group Jama'at al-Muslimin (more often known as al-Takfir wal-Hijra, a name given to them by the Egyptian authorities, based on their ideology). This was a Mahdist movement with an eschatological worldview. They saw signs of the End Times in disbelief, oppression, immorality, famines, wars, earthquakes and hurricanes. Their charismatic leader, Shukri Mustafa (1942-1978), a disciple of Qutb, was seen as the promised Mahdi who would found a new Muslim community, conquer the world, and usher in God's final reign on earth.[21] In 1978 al-Takfir wal-Hijra gained prominence when they kidnapped and murdered the Egyptian Minister of Endowments Hasan al-Dhahbi. They had embraced the extremist ideas of the Saudi Ikhwan, including the idea of emigrating to the desert to found a pure Islamic society. However their main influence was to spread the concept of *takfir* in the sense of labelling other Muslims as apostates and hence justifying violence against them. When most of the group had been tried and jailed, they lost their ability to act as an organised entity in Egypt.

Paz describes some offshoots of the Takfir trend including:

Egyptian Salafist groups: Al-Najoun min al-Nar [Survivors of the Fire/Hell], comprised of remaining Egyptian members of al-Takfir wal-Hijra, was active in Bosnia and later Albania. They have a small number of Palestinian followers in the Gaza Strip. This group considers their main enemy to be the secular Arab regimes (not Israel). They therefore took no part in the Palestinian *intifada* and have no links with Hamas or Palestinian Islamic Jihad. They are considered by the latter two groups to be deviant.

The Jordanian Takfir: Other Salafiyya groups have spread, by means of Saudi guidance and finance, to Jordan and what is now the Palestinian National Authority Area. They were present in the Gaza Strip until 1986 when they lost their identity by merging into the developing groups of the Islamic Jihad. In Jordan they have faced strong opposition from the authorities which has obliged them to keep on the move. During periods of imprisonment they were involved with members of Hizb al-Tahrir al-Islami (The Islamic Liberation Party), another illegal Palestinian/Jordanian militant group which has a different ideology but has carried out a substantial amount of terrorism in Jordan, Egypt, Turkey, Lebanon and Uzbekistan. Hizb al-Tahrir also has strong bases in the West

Bank, UK and Central Asia. In recent years the Jordanian Takfir, another development of the Salafiyya in Jordan, has acquired a large following of various nationalities but including many Egyptians. In April 1996 the Egyptian authorities demanded the extradition of 57 members of the Egyptian Takfir group who had fled to Jordan.

Others: The Pakistani militant group Harakat ul-Mujahidin (HUM) is also part of the Takfir movement, as is the London-based Committee for the Defence of Legal Rights (CDLR) which is the political wing of the Islamist opponents of the Saudi royal regime. The Algerian GIA (Groupe Islamique Armée, i.e. Armed Islamic Group) also shares the *takfir* ideology. Nine GIA members, who were specialists in the smuggling of weapons and false identity documents, were arrested in northern Italy in May 1998 in connection with the Soccer World Cup in France that summer. According to the Italian police, they belonged to a Takfir group active in Europe, especially France and Germany. Another apparent Takfir group are the Islah, based in Yemen. They also have a base in London under the name of Ansar al-Shari'ah [Supporters of Shari'ah] led by the Egyptian Abu Hamzah al-Masri. The group in London cooperates with Al-Muhajiroun [The Immigrants], led by Sheikh Omar Bakri Muhammad, which was founded after a split within the British Hizb al-Tahrir (usually known in the UK as Hizb ut-Tahrir).

Al-Qaʿeda [22]

It is worth looking briefly at the infrastructure of Al-Qaʿeda, surely the largest of contemporary Islamist militant movements, but by no means typical. It emerged in 1988-9, under the leadership of Osama bin Laden, from the Afghan Mujahidin organization Mekhtab al-Khidemat. However its name Al-Qaʿeda al-Sulba [The Solid Base], composition, aims and purpose were originally defined in 1987 by Dr ʿAbdallah ʿAzzam who can be considered the ideological father of

Al-Qaʿeda. With a network of its own cells as well as associated terrorist groups and other affiliated organisations, Al-Qaʿeda has links in some 55 countries. This makes it robust, flexible and quick to regenerate after suffering damage. According to the CIA Al-Qaʿeda can draw on the support of 6-7 million radical Muslims, of whom 120,000 are willing to take up arms.

Under the headship of Osama bin Laden is a pyramidical structure for strategic direction. The *majlis al-shura* [consultative council] is at the top, making major policy decisions on terrorist operations and issuing *fatwas*. Reporting to the *majlis al-shura* are four operational committees with the following responsibilities: (1) military (2) financial (3) *fatwa* and Islamic study (4) media and publicity. There is also a travel office. The global terrorist network is de-centralised into regional groupings called "families". Each nationality or ethnic group is assigned a particular geographical region as their responsibility. Some also have other responsibilities e.g. Libyans ran the documentation and passport office in Afghanistan, Algerians run the fraudulent credit card operations in Europe, and Egyptians have run most of the training facilities worldwide. Individuals may sometimes be sent on specialist missions outside their normal area.

The bulk of Al-Qaʿeda's funding comes from Osama bin Laden's personal fortune but donations are also received from around the world amounting to tens of millions of dollars. It has a global financial network with a multiplicity of bank accounts and "front" organisations. It also raises funds through investments, business, Islamic charities and financial crime.[23] It is proving difficult for western governments to curtail the cash-flow to Al-Qaʿeda.

Shiʿa Movements

Space precludes analysis of Shiʿa movements such as Hizbullah in Lebanon, but they are included in the *summary* diagrams in Appendix 2 and Appendix 3.

The Motivation of Terrorists and Suicide Bombers

The primary motivation of terrorists and suicide bombers is theological, compounded mainly of duty and reward. But there are also other reasons which serve to inspire them. Martyrdom has a very special position in Shi'a Islam because Hassan and Hussain, the martyrs, are seen as models to be emulated, and suffering is sought after.

1. Duty to God

It is important to realise that most Islamist terrorists are devout and sincere in their faith. They can speak without irony of the "holy bomb" that killed nearly 200 non-Muslims in Bali, Indonesia on 12 October 2002.[1] They are men and women of religion, who consider themselves to be following the example of the founder of their faith, no matter what the personal cost.

They look back to the original sources of Islam and interpret them as justification for violence. An example of this logic could be seen on the Chechen website www.qoqaz.com (now removed) where articles appeared which directly used verses in the Qur'an and incidents from the life of Muhammad to legitimise the execution of non-Muslim prisoners and hostages. For example:

> In an article titled 'A Guide to the Perplexed Regarding the Permissibility of Killing Prisoners' which appeared in the column 'Jihad News from the Land of the Caucasus' the author suggests that the Islamic religious scholars present five different alternatives, drawn from the various interpretations of the Qur'an:

A polytheist prisoner must be killed. No amnesty may be granted to him, nor can he be ransomed.

All infidel polytheists and the People of the Book (i.e. Jews and Christians) are to be killed. They may not be granted amnesty, nor can they be ransomed.

Amnesty and ransom are the only two ways to deal with prisoners.

Amnesty and ransom are possible only after the killing of a large number of prisoners.

The Imam, or someone acting on his behalf, can choose between killing, amnesty, ransom or enslaving the prisoner.[2]

Mention has already been made of an article in the Kuwaiti newspaper *Al-Watan* which used examples from Muhammad's life to legitimise the killing of non-combatants (including women and children) if they are citizens of countries with which Muslims are at war and if their actions are connected even in the most remote sense to any war effort. Referring to Israel the author states:

> It is common knowledge that the Zionist society is a military society, and every one of them takes part in warfare, whether as a soldier in the army, as a reservist, by paying taxes to the Jewish state and its army which kills Muslims, or by voting to put Sharon in a position to give the orders to kill Al-Dura and other Palestinian children.[3]

The same kind of argument was expressed by a failed suicide bomber interviewed on British television.[4] According to this logic American and British citizens would also be legitimate targets merely because they pay taxes or vote for a government which sends troops to fight in Islamic countries.

In another example Suleiman Abu Gheith, an Al-Qa'eda spokesman, states that,

Allah said: 'He who attacked you, attack him as he attacked you,' and also, 'The reward of evil is a similar evil,' and also, 'When you are punished, punish as you have been punished.'

He cites the *hadith* collections of Ibn Taymiyya, Ibn al-Qayim and others to argue from this for the use of weapons of mass destruction on the basis of reciprocity of punishment. By estimating the number of Muslim deaths caused by America's intervention and foreign policy in Afghanistan, Iraq, Somalia, Palestine, Sudan, the Philippines, Bosnia, Kashmir, Chechnya etc. Abu Gheith calculates how many American deaths can be legitimately sought in return:

We have not reached parity with them. We have the right to kill four million Americans – two million of them children – and to exile twice as many and wound and cripple hundreds of thousands. Furthermore, it is our right to fight them with chemical and biological weapons, so as to afflict them with the fatal maladies that have afflicted the Muslims because of the [Americans'] chemical and biological weapons."[5]

Of course many Muslims would reject Abu Gheith's method of reasoning.

Although there are abundant arguments to demonstrate that jihad in general is a duty, there is a debate within contemporary Islam as to whether suicide killings are also a duty, or even legitimate. Some extreme radicals have revived the Khariji and Assassin traditions of suicide killings as a legitimate weapon in their contemporary jihad. In order to do this, a theological distinction previously drawn in Islam between deliberately going to one's certain death at the hands of an overwhelmingly strong enemy (as the Assassins did) and dying by one's own hand (as modern suicide bombers do) had to be blurred.[6]

Another interesting comment on this issue comes from Shaybani in an imagined scenario whereby a Muslim pierced by a (long-handled) lance would have to deepen his own wound in order to reach his opponent with his own (much shorter) sword.

I asked: if a [Muslim] warrior is run through by a lance, would you dis-
approve if he advances – though the lance be piercing him – in order to
kill his adversary with the sword?

He replied: No.

I asked: Do you not think that he helped against his own life by so doing
[i.e. that he committed suicide, which is forbidden]?

He replied: No.[7]

Suicide killings are described as martyrdom (*istishad*). To fight for
Islam, and more particularly to die in jihad, is considered a testimony [*shahada*], a term more normally used of the Islamic creed as
verbally professed. Hence the use of the term *shahid* to mean a martyr.[8] The cult of martyrdom has always been strong amongst Shi'a
extremists, but the concept has now spread also to Sunni groups,
motivating their members to acts of violent martyrdom.[9] Suicide
bombings are an important component in their arsenal of weapons as demonstrated by Hamas, Islamic Jihad and other Palestinian
groups in Israel and the suicidal plane attacks on the World Trade
Center in New York by Al-Qa'eda members.

The debate within contemporary Islam about the legitimacy of
suicide attacks arises from the fact that suicide *per se* is regarded as
a serious sin.[10] However, the evidence for this from the Qur'an is
somewhat tenuous.

> And spend of your substance in the cause of God, and make not your
> own hands contribute to (your) destruction; but do good; for God
> loveth those who do good. Q 2:195

Although this is a Qur'anic verse often cited as forbidding suicide, A. Yusuf Ali's comment[11] interprets the verse as concerned
not with suicide but with the use of one's wealth. He sees it as a
command to give generously in support of a just war in the cause
of God and a warning that those who are reluctant to give freely

may be "helping in their own self-destruction". Alternatively if they spend their money on something other than "the cause of God" the enemy may gain an advantage and thus they will have contributed to their own self-destruction. The word "your" before "destruction" does not appear in the Arabic original, but Ali has inserted it in his translation.

> O ye who believe! Eat not up your property among yourselves in vanities: but let there be amongst you traffic and trade by mutual good-will: nor kill (or destroy) yourselves: for verily God hath been to you most merciful! Q 4:29

Asra Rasheed sees this as a prohibition on suicide,[12] but A. Yusuf Ali interprets it as a command not to kill fellow-believers and not to destroy oneself by squandering one's wealth.[13]

As so often, the *hadith* is less ambiguous, and some record clear-cut condemnations by Muhammad of suicide:

> The Prophet said, "A man was inflicted with wounds and he committed suicide, and so Allah said, "My slave has caused death on himself hurriedly, so I forbid Paradise for him." *Sahih Bukhari Volume 2, Book 23, Number 445: Narrated by Thabit bin Ad-Dahhak*

> ... if someone commits suicide with anything in this world, he will be tortured with that very thing on the Day of Resurrection .... *Sahih Bukhari Volume 8, Book 73, Number 72: Narrated by Thabit bin Ad-Dahhak*

Others too long to quote here in full describe those who commit suicide as "disobedient"[14] and as "dwellers of hellfire".[15]

It is important to note that Islamist radical groups involved in suicide attacks do not use the phrase "suicide bombers" but instead refer to *shahids* (martyrs or witnesses, Arabic plural *shuhada*) making it clear that they view the bombers as noble victims who have sacrificed their lives in jihad, not as suicides. In the selection and training of bombers, any suicidal individuals are weeded out so that the motives of the *shahids* are kept pure.

The concept of suicide killings has received support not only from radicals but from many mainstream Islamic leaders as well. It was noticeable that following September 11th 2001, no *fatwa* condemning suicide attacks was issued.[16] In fact, Sheikh Muhammad Sayyid Tantawi, whose significance lies in being Imam of Al-Azhar, the foremost institution of Sunni Islam, changed his previous position[17] in April 2002 to permit the killing of civilians by Palestinian suicide bombers. He stated that "every martyrdom operation against any Israeli, including children, women and teenagers, is a legitimate act according to [Islamic] religious law, and an Islamic commandment, until the people of Palestine regain their land …"[18] After US-led coalition forces entered Iraq in March 2003 Tantawi issued a *fatwa* ordering Muslims to fight against the "invaders" of Iraq and, if necessary, to carry out suicide bombings to prevent the overthrow of Saddam Hussein's regime.[19] The mufti of Egypt, Sheikh Dr Ahmad Al-Tayyeb, has expressed support for suicide attacks in the Palestinian context too.[20] A congress of 50 Islamic scholars from seven countries, meeting in Lebanon in January 2002, also affirmed the legitimacy of suicide attacks against Israel.[21] Three months later, a meeting of the Organisation of the Islamic Conference in Kuala Lumpur, representing all the Muslim nations, refused to condemn suicide bombings.[22] Likewise Sheikh Yousef al-Qaradhawi, head of the European Council for Fatwa and Research, gave a report to the Council at their meeting in Stockholm in July 2003, which approved suicide attacks in Palestine on the basis that it was a situation of extreme necessity and thus normal prohibitions became irrelevant.

> What weapon can harm their enemy, can prevent him from sleeping, and can strip him of a sense of security and stability, except for these human bombs – a young man or woman who blows himself or herself up amongst their enemy? This is a weapon the likes of which the enemy cannot obtain, even if the U.S. provides it with billions [of dollars] and the most powerful weapons, because it is a unique weapon that Allah has placed only in the hands of the men of belief. It is a type of divine justice

on the face of the earth ... it is the weapon of the wretched weak in the face of the powerful tyrant...[23]

He also argued that suicide attacks were not suicide as such but martyrdom, because of the different motives – advance and attack by self-sacrifice for a higher goal, or escape and retreat by fleeing life because of failure and weakness.[24]

Because of the debate about the validity of suicide bombings, it is essential for any particular suicide bomber that his death is declared to be a martyrdom.[25] Without the confidence that this will happen he will be reluctant to go ahead with the suicide. He also needs to be sure that any debts he may have will be promptly paid off after his death, because there is a belief that the martyr will not go to heaven if he is in debt.[26]

Another belief of Palestinian suicide bombers is that the bomber must repeat the Islamic creed just before he dies. If he fails to do that he will be questioned by two angels about his motives for suicide, and if he cannot truthfully say he died in the cause of God he will go to hell.

2. Heavenly reward

To die in jihad is to die a glorious and noble martyr and to ensure oneself an immediate place in paradise, with all sins forgiven. A martyr will not have to face examination in the grave by the two "interrogating angels" or any temporary punishment in hell. He will be given the highest of the various ranks in paradise, nearest the throne of God, a crown of glory, seventy or seventy-two virgins and other heavenly delights. Many would-be martyrs speak of their hope of being kept alive and sustained by God. Furthermore a martyr's intercession will be accepted for up to seventy of his relatives so that they too can go straight to paradise.[27] Female martyrs expect to find themselves given a prestigious place in paradise, close to Muhammad[28] or to become one of the heavenly virgins.[29] One woman caught before she could blow herself up had expected to become after martyrdom "the purest and most beautiful form of angel at the highest level possible in heaven".[30]

These various rewards and honours in the afterlife are stressed by the groups who recruit *shahids*. However, since dying in jihad is generally considered the only guaranteed way to paradise[31] it is probably this – the certainty of going straight to paradise – more than the seventy virgins, which motivates most suicide bombers. Indeed, Esposito asserts that the belief that a *shahid* goes directly to paradise is the "main motivator" for Muslims in war against non-Muslims.[32]

> Think not of those who are slain in God's way as dead. Nay, they live, finding their sustenance in the presence of their Lord. Q 3:169

The rewards for dying in jihad are promised in both the Qur'an and the *hadith*. Examples from the Qur'an include:

> Let those fight in the cause of God who sell the life of this world for the Hereafter. To him who fighteth in the cause of God, whether he is slain or gets victory – soon shall we given him a reward of great (value). Q 4:74

> But the Apostle, and those who believe with him, strive and fight with their wealth and their persons: for them are (all) good things: and it is they who will prosper. God hath prepared for them gardens (paradise) under which rivers flow, to dwell therein: that is the supreme felicity. Q 9:88-89

A relevant *hadith* runs as follows:

> The Apostle of Allah (peace_be_upon_him) said: If anyone fights in Allah's path as long as the time between two milkings of a she-camel, Paradise will be assured for him. If anyone sincerely asks Allah for being killed and then dies or is killed, there will be a reward of a martyr for him. Ibn al-Musaffa added from here: If anyone is wounded in Allah's path, or suffers a misfortune, it will come on the Day of resurrection as copious as possible, its colour saffron, and its odour musk; and if anyone suffers from ulcers while in Allah's path, he will have on him the stamp of the martyrs.
> *Sunan Abu Dawud Book 14, Number 2535: Narrated Mu'adh ibn Jabal*

We have already seen how the Assassins made sure of being captured after completing their killing, so that they too would be killed and go to paradise as a martyr. Similarly one of the Muslim troops at the Battle of Badr (624), 'Auf b. Harith, was so inspired by Muhammad's talk of martyrdom for those slain in battle that he removed his armour and fought until he was killed.[33]

According to Osama bin Laden there is an extra reward for killing Americans, or perhaps all Jews and Christians (People of the Book).

> These youths know that their rewards in fighting you, the USA, is double than their rewards (sic) in fighting some one else not from the people of the book. They have no intention except to enter paradise by killing you.[34]

Someone who dies in jihad on the battlefield is buried in a different way from other Muslims. Instead of ceremonial preparation – being washed and dressed carefully as if to go to the mosque – the martyr is left just as they are in their bloodstained clothes. Traditionally they were buried where they fell.[35] This follows the example of what Muhammad ordered for Muslims who were killed in the Battle of Uhud (625):

> .... He ordered them to be buried with their blood on their bodies and they were neither washed nor was a funeral offered for them. *Sahih Bukhari Book 23, chapter 37, nunber 676 narrated Jabir bin 'Abdullah*[36]

So great is the honour of being a martyr that often the relatives will not express grief at the death but rather gratitude for the martyrdom. (This was particularly true of the mothers of the Iranian soldiers killed in the Iran-Iraq war of 1980-88.)[37]

This emphasis on the heavenly rewards which Muslim suicide bombers can expect to receive contrasts sharply with the psychology of the suicide bombers of the Tamil Tigers. In Sri Lanka the cause of the Tamils is overwhelmingly political and the religious dimension is not emphasised in the way it is in the Palestinian context. For the Tamil Tigers the ethos of suicide bombing is one of sacrifice rather than heavenly reward. The individual sacrifices himself or herself for a political cause which is greater than the life of one man or woman.

It is the suffering of their fellow Tamils and the value of their sacrifice, rather than any reward in the afterlife, which are stressed during their training.

The Tigers carry cyanide pills around their necks, in order to ensure they are not captured alive and forced to divulge information. This indicates another key difference from Islamist suicide bombers who would view the use of a suicide pill as genuine suicide and not martyrdom. Suicide in the Tamil tradition is not viewed with the same abhorrence. Other differences from the Islamic tradition include the greater use of female suicide bombers, and the institutional taking and training of bombers from a very young age.

3. Response to humiliation

One of the characteristics of Islam is its emphasis on honour and power for the Muslim community. True faith – Islam – based on God's final revelation must be protected from insult and abuse. (Other faiths, being false or incomplete in Muslim opinion, have no right to such protection.) When Baghdad fell to the US-led coalition forces in April 2003 Muslims around the world, particularly Arabs, were in shock and denial; the defeat of a Muslim leader by non-Muslims caused enormous anguish.

Shame and humiliation cannot be borne and are considered legitimate justification for a violent response. Muslim statements of outrage concerning the imposition of non-Muslims on their territory or rights are often phrased in terms of "humiliation", with the unspoken assumption that this is the greatest grievance possible. Many Islamist terrorists and suicide bombers see their task as contributing to the vital process of redeeming Islam's honour from the humiliation imposed on it by the West.

In the words of Osama bin Laden,

> The walls of oppression and humiliation cannot be demolished except in a rain of bullets...

Death is better than life in humiliation! Some scandals and shames will never be otherwise eradicated.[38]

Saad al-Fagih, a Saudi dissident and director of the Movement for Islamic Reform in Arabia, commenting on the presence of American troops in Iraq after the ousting of President Saddam Hussein said:

> The sight of US tanks in Baghdad is the most humiliating event for Muslims and Arabs since 1967. Baghdad, the capital of the Islamic Caliphate for 600 years, occupies a central place in the Muslim memory and means more even than Riyadh or Cairo.[39]

The following quotation comes from an Indonesian manual on jihad. Gaining dignity is placed on a par with spreading Islamic power as fuel for the "spirit of jihad".

> Let the spirit of jihad burn among the Muslims at all times and situations because jihad is the fortress of defence for Islam and the way to improve the dignity of the Muslims from the scorn and contempt heaped on it. The jihad may not cease until all the world is free from the oppression/cruelty and bows to the power of Islam.[40]

Even Sheikh Tantawi of Al-Azhar University teaches that it is permissible for Muslims to fight non-Muslims in other countries for no greater injury than that the non-Muslims are "actively condemning or belittling" Muslims or the religion of Islam.[41]

4. The importance of history

Islamist terrorists have a highly developed and clear sense of history. The humiliations of the Crusades,[42] the loss of Islamic Spain to Ferdinand and Isabella in the Reconquista, western colonialism, and the end of the last Islamic caliphate with the collapse of the Ottomans following the First World War are all still keenly felt by Islamist militants. For many extremists these events, which happened decades and even hundreds of years ago, carry a sense of immediacy and urgency, a burden of humiliation at the hands of the West which has lost none of its potency with the passage of time.

This characteristic is described with proud sarcasm as a "fault" by the radical Saudi sheikh, famed for his anti-Americanism, Sheikh Safar bin Abdur-Rahman Al-Hawali. In his *Open Letter to President Bush* he appears to despise Germany and Japan for not still holding a grudge against the US for their defeat in the Second World War.

> Mr President, don't suppose that I want to recount your few faults and forget our own (in your eyes) very many faults. No, I will mention to you a serious fault of us Muslims: we don't forget our tragedies no matter how much time has passed. Imagine, Mr President, we still weep over Andalusia and remember what Ferdinand and Isabella did there to our religious, culture and honor! We dream of regaining it. Nor will we forget the destruction of Baghdad, or the fall of Jerusalem at the hands of your Crusader ancestors. That is, we are not (in your opinion) at the level of civilisation enjoyed by the Germans and Japanese who support your hostilities and forget your past treatment of them. Moreover, the African Muslims who embraced Islam after the fall of Andalusia cry along with the Arabs, just as the Indonesians do who only recently heard about Andalusia. It may be a problem for us, but who will pay the price after a while?[43]

5. Identification with heroes

Shahids are heroes. They are honoured and admired and held up as ideals to be imitated and followed. In India *shahids* of old are worshipped, and the devout seek their intercession.[44] Self-denying leaders such as bin Laden, who abandoned a wealthy lifestyle for one of austerity, are also heroes. Many who volunteer to be *shahids* are inspired by such examples.

A Palestinian suicide bomber is given a large, prestigious funeral. His family (who would have known nothing about his mission until he was dead) are fêted and honoured in public testimonials from groups like Hamas and Islamic Jihad. They are generally proud and delighted at what has happened.[45] The organisation which recruited, trained and sent the bomber provides his family with ongoing financial support. King Fahd of Saudi Arabia also sends funds to the families of martyrs, as did the former Iraqi president Saddam Hussein. Gifts may also come from Arab charities. A bomber's family can receive in the region of $25,000 in cash.

The Palestinian Authority runs summer camps for children at which talks and activities are used to present terrorists as role models and heroes for the children. Some of the camps are named after individual terrorists or suicide bombers, and others are simply called "*shahid*".[46] The first female Palestinian suicide bomber, Wafa Idris (who has had educational programmes as well as summer camps named after her), was celebrated in song on Palestinian Authority TV.[47]

6. Training

The training given to potential terrorists and suicide bombers involves a deliberate process of imbuing the students with a fanatical hatred of the West and a perception that the West is responsible for all the woes of the Muslim world. Those who have been through this process emerge highly motivated to expend their lives in jihad against the West. Furthermore, if the training process is violent, as it sometimes is, those who have been brutalised by it may lose all compunction or compassion for their future victims, and emerge absolutely single-minded and ruthless.

7. *Bay'a*

An important concept in Islam is that of *bay'a*, the swearing of an oath of allegiance and obedience to a religious or political leader. When Muhammad died the Muslim community made their *bay'a* to his successor Abu Bakr, the first caliph. In posters for the referendum on extending Saddam Hussein's presidency held in Iraq on 15 October 2002 (naturally a foregone conclusion) the word *bay'a* was used, and the day described as the "day of the oath of allegiance". As such the Iraqi people were swearing their oath of allegiance to Saddam Hussein as their caliph. For Islamist terrorist groups the concept has particular significance. Many Islamist militants have performed *bay'a* to their leaders such as Osama bin Laden, as the title *Sheikh*, often used to refer to him, indicates. Interestingly, western converts to Islam are often encouraged to perform *bay'a* as well. *Bay'a* can be passed on by a leader to his successor or can be distributed to a number of his followers, thus creating a network, as for example the network of Islamic centres created in nineteenth century India when various *pirs* passed *bay'a* to each other.[48]

Bay'a, which is a lifelong and personal commitment, indicates the intensely strong nature of the bonds of loyalty and co-operation which can exist within and between Islamist terrorist networks. Western intelligence agencies have found it correspondingly difficult to infiltrate or establish informers amongst such networks.

A distinction needs to be drawn between an oath of allegiance to a leader such as Saddam Hussein who is political, and one to a much more overtly religious leader like bin Laden. Allegiances to the former can shift very easily and quickly depending on the varying circumstances and fortunes of the political leader. However, an oath of allegiance to a religious leader is far more binding since it is a matter of faith. In seeking out potential terrorist movements, one could therefore examine where *bay'a* is made, and to whom.

8. Specific grievances

All radical Islamist movements share a common hostility to western influences and their perceived corruption of Islamic societies; such influences are viewed as a continuation of colonialism and imperialism by other means. The West is held responsible for the decline and loss of the Islamic empires such as the Mughals, the Ottomans and Safavi Iran i.e. for blasphemously spoiling the God-ordained order of the world in which Muslims rule over non-Muslims. Western civilization is blamed for the corruption of all that is good in the world and for encouraging the evils of secularism, atheism, alcohol, drugs, sexual permissiveness, family breakdown etc. Globalisation, capitalism, secularism, materialism and consumerism are other western characteristics which are condemned. It is interesting to remember that Muhammad was strongly opposed to commerce and trade in Arabia, believing them to be the cause of social ills. Islamists hold that western values must be rejected as they lead to moral chaos and threaten Muslim identity and self-esteem.

The USA is seen as the leading western power, imposing its immoral and secular values by means of its economic superiority, cultural hegemony etc. and thus humiliating Muslims and robbing them of their culture and dignity. Islamic revival has come to focus on the USA as the enemy of God, the incarnation of evil, a diabolical opponent of all that is good. Israel is seen as a "dagger in the heart of the Arab world", a western creation which is causing suffering to Palestinian Muslims. American support for Israel is perceived as one-sided.

Dependency, failure, powerlessness, humiliation and jealousy all lead to a search for scapegoats for the ills of Muslim society and thus to conspiracy theories. Christianity, the West, the USA, Jews, Freemasons etc. are thought to be conspiring against Islam in some kind of a global cultural war, whose battlefields include Palestine, Iraq, Lebanon, Tajikistan, Kashmir, the Philippines, Somalia, Eritrea, Chechnya, Bosnia and others. Sayyid Qutb thought that Marxists were participating in a conspiracy against Islam with the Christian West and with Jews.[49] Taqiuddin an-Nabhani (1909-1977), founder of Hizb ut-Tahrir, believed that Orientalists and Christian missionaries were conspiring with western states to get revenge on Islam for Christendom's defeat in the Crusades; he saw western colonialism and the military conquest of Arab lands in the First World War as part of this conspiracy.[50] Ayatollah Khomeini expressed his fears as follows:

> The hands of the missionaries, the orientalists and of the information media – all of whom are in the service of the colonialist countries – have cooperated to distort the facts of Islam in a manner that has caused many people, especially the educated among them, to steer away from Islam and to be unable to find a way to reach Islam.

Islam is the religion of the strugglers who want right and justice, the religion of those demanding freedom and independence and those who do not want to allow the infidels to dominate the believers.

But the enemies have portrayed Islam in a different light. They have drawn from the minds of the ordinary people a distorted picture of Islam and implanted this picture even in the religious academies. The enemies' aim behind this was to extinguish the flame of Islam and to cause its vital revolutionary character to be lost, so that Muslims would not think of seeking to liberate themselves …

The colonialists and their lackeys have made these statements [that Islam has nothing to do with society or government] to isolate religion from the affairs of life and society and to tacitly keep the 'ulama of Islam away from the people, and drive people away from the 'ulama because the 'ulama struggle for the liberation and independence of the Muslims. When their wish of separation and isolation is realized, the colonialists and their lackeys can take away our resources and rule us.[51]

The car accident which killed Britain's Princess Diana and her Egyptian Muslim boyfriend Dodi Al-Fayed in 1997 is believed by many Muslims to have been arranged by the British intelligence service to ensure that no Muslim could enter the senior levels of the monarchy. The suicide attacks on the World Trade Center on September 11th 2001 are considered to have been organised by Jews with the intention of throwing the blame on to Muslims. Malaysian Prime Minister Mahathir Mohamad claimed in a speech to the Organisation of the Islamic Conference in October 2003 that "the Jews rule this world by proxy. They get others to fight and die for them."[52]

Coupled with anti-westernism is a nostalgia for Islam's glorious past. Those contemporary Muslim regimes who rely on oppression and western support for their continued existence are considered illegitimate. Furthermore, nationalism and socialism are deemed to have failed to deliver, more or less wherever they have been tried. The solution is therefore seen as a return to traditional, conservative Islam.[53]

Various specific aims have been adopted by different contemporary groups over the course of time:

Fighting their own governments

The plethora of twentieth century extremist Islamist groups, differing from each other in the details of their theology and methodology, would at first each focus their violent activities on destabilising and destroying the "infidel" regimes in their own countries. This was in obedience to the Islamic injunction to fight the enemies near at hand before dealing with enemies further afield.[54] Examples include Mawdudi in the Indian subcontinent, Qutb in Egypt[55] and Khomeini in Iran.

Sheikh Omar Abdul Rahman in his book *The Present Rulers and Islam: Are they Muslims or Not?* promotes the view that the *umma* is justified in removing the country's leader by force if he or she is not ruling according to the Shari'ah. While many other Islamic authorities, working on the principle of the lesser of two evils, say this should only be done if it does not lead to *fitna* (disorder and conflict), Rahman prefers to overthrow the regime even if *fitna* results.[56]

Fighting repression of Muslims

The disparate groups were brought together in the 1980s and especially in the 1990s by common causes around the world. These causes were those where Muslims perceive their co-religionists to be under threat from non-Muslims, such as Afghanistan. Thousands of volunteers from across the Muslim world joined the jihad against the Soviet Union in Afghanistan in the 1980s. Under Afghan influence a "brotherhood of the persecuted" developed among the groups, leading them to cooperation and mutual assistance despite their differences. This cooperation was accompanied by a spread of the ideas of the Takfir groups to the Jihad groups, especially in regard to the struggle in the Arab world against rulers perceived as collaborators with the "western infidel culture".

Many Afghan veterans returning home after the Soviet withdrawal instigated a radicalisation of Islamist groups and a marked increase in violence in their home countries, especially in Algeria and Egypt. Others however found new sponsors and moved to other flashpoints where they sensed infidel attacks on Muslim communities, such as Kashmir, Bosnia, Chechnya, Daghestan, Kosovo and the Philippines. They have been instrumental in intensifying the militancy of Islamist movements in Indonesia and in sub-Saharan Africa.

Fighting the USA

The Gulf War of 1990-1 further radicalised these groups by endorsing their perception of the West as aiming to re-colonize Muslim states. Their sensibilities were especially outraged by the permanent stationing of American troops in Saudi Arabia. The polluting presence of *kafir* [infidel] soldiers near Islam's holiest places, Mecca and Medina, was perceived as an aggressive act aimed at dominating the Muslim heartland.[57] The USA thus became an "enemy near at hand" and therefore a focus of attention for groups such as al-Jama'at al-Islamiyya.

One of the consequences of the influence of *takfir* ideology on the Egyptian group al-Jihad was the anti-American extremism that led them to carry out the bombing of the World Trade Center in 1993, and several other bombing attempts in the US. Prior to the early 1990s al-Jihad had confined their terrorist operations to Egypt.

Osama bin Laden's Al-Qa'eda was in the forefront of those who encouraged interaction and networking between a wide variety of such movements around the world, preparing for assaults that would really hurt and humiliate America. Petty squabbles and enmity towards corrupt regimes in Muslim lands became secondary in the light of this jihad against the greater *kufr* [unbelief]. The results of this shift have now been seen, among others, in the bombings of the American embassies in Nairobi and Dar-es-Salaam in 1998 and in the dramatic attacks on the World Trade Center in New York and the Pentagon in Washington DC on September 11th 2001 using hijacked civilian planes.

Such apparently "senseless" attacks in fact fit perfectly the classical terrorist strategy defined by the Brazilian guerrilla Carlos Marighella as "turning political crisis into armed conflict by performing violent actions that will force those in power" into a military response "that will alienate the masses."[58] The response of the West to September 11th 2001 in Afghanistan and Iraq has indeed led to a hardening of public opinion across the Islamic world and growing support for Osama bin Laden and others like him. A similar policy can be seen in other contexts such as Kosovo and Macedonia where violence has provoked military responses which in turn have led to international intervention, ultimately producing results favourable to the terrorist groups which began the cycle. This may also be the strategy in Palestine and Kashmir.

9. Personal grudges

Some terrorists and suicide bombers have the additional motivation of seeking to avenge a personal hurt or insult they have suffered. One such was a Palestinian interviewed on a British television programme who explained that as a boy of twelve he had been slapped by an Israeli border guard for no reason. He said that, being a Muslim his principle, was, "If you slap me once, I will slap you twice,"[59] and viewed the suicide attacks he was helping to organise as the retaliatory double slapping.[60]

Basic requirements for the motivation of suicide bombers

The multiplicity of motives which go to create suicide bombers can be summarised as five main requirements:
- a political cause worth dying for
- a theology which affirms the legitimacy of suicide-martyrdom
- the assurance that after death he/she will be authoritatively declared a martyr
- economic and financial support for the martyr and his family after death
- media involvement – a martyr must also be a public hero

If one or more of these is missing there is likely to be a scarcity of recruits for suicide missions.

Further comments on the Islamic theology of martyrdom

There are two main categories of martyr[61] – those who die on the battlefield and those who do not.

1. *Martyrs both in this world and the next*

   The battlefield martyrs are called "martyrs both in this world and the next", their martyrdom in this world being recognised by the special burial rites described above (see page 155) which – according to most Islamic authorities – do not include washing the body. There are many detailed rules concerning the purpose of the battle and how long a time may pass between injury and death in order to qualify as a battlefield martyr.

   Perhaps most important is the intention of the martyr. Someone who went into battle for the wrong reason, for example to show off or in the hope of spoils, would not be a true battlefield martyr. However, since only God knows the intentions of the heart, all who die on the battlefield will be buried as if they were true battlefield martyrs. Those who did not go with the right intentions or with true belief will not receive a martyr's reward in heaven, and may even go to hell. They are therefore known as "martyrs in this world only".

2. *Martyrs in the next world only*

   This includes all those who fail to qualify as battlefield martyrs. Examples would be someone who accidentally wounds themselves fatally with their own weapon on the battlefield, someone who dies in battle against Muslims, or who dies defending their family against Muslim brigands or highway robbers. Within this category are many different types of martyrs:

(i) Those who died violently or prematurely

(A) Those murdered while in the service of God. This is sometimes taken to include Muhammad himself since his death was supposedly precipitated by tasting a piece of poisoned mutton he was offered by Zaynab bt. al-Harith.

(B) Those killed for their beliefs, i.e. Muslims killed by non-Muslims because they adhered to Islam. John the Baptist and various other pre-Islamic prophets are also included here.

(C) Those who die from disease or accident. Early *hadith* collections mention victims of plague and pleurisy as well as those who drowned or burned to death, and women who died in childbirth. The logic is that elevation to the rank of martyr is divine compensation for the painful deaths they suffered.

(D) The "martyrs of love". These are people who fell in love, remained chaste, concealed their secret and died.

(E) The "martyrs who died far from home". These are Muslims who fled their homeland in time of persecution in order to preserve their faith, and died in a foreign country.

(ii) Those who died a natural death

(A) while engaged in a meritorious act such as pilgrimage or prayer or a journey in search of knowledge.[62]

(B) after leading a virtuous life – i.e. who had waged successfully the "greater jihad" against their soul. This is particularly strong amongst Shi'as.

(iii) Living martyrs Those who are engaged in successful war against their own souls i.e. are living according to Islamic teaching. This concept was promoted by the Sufi scholar Abu 'Abd al-Rahman al-Sulami (d. 1021) who held that a battlefield martyr is only a *shahid* externally, whereas someone who kills his own soul while living in accordance with Sufi teaching is a true martyr.

The Making of an Islamist Terrorist

Of the many Muslims who would acknowledge the continuing validity of the classic teachings of Islam on war and expansion of Islamic territory, only a small number put their beliefs into practice in the most literal way and become active terrorists. This chapter seeks to examine the psychology, selection and training of Islamist militants, with special reference to suicide bombers.

Psychology

Most terrorists are extremely devout Muslims, who regularly say prayers and attend mosques. A good proportion have come to Islam from another faith; they have the zeal of the convert and may feel the need to prove themselves worthy Muslims.[1] All are motivated with a sense of intense rage, hatred and revenge towards those they see as their oppressors who have humiliated their religion and their people. They feel they are breaking out of a state of impotency and striking back from their position of humiliation.

Suicide bombers within the Islamic tradition are almost all young and single.[2] In most contexts they are commonly men, except in Chechnya where there are many women (including widows) amongst the suicide bombers (see page 179). A few months before his assasination Sheikh Ahmed Yassin, the leader of Hamas, reversed the former policy of his organisation by issuing a *fatwa* permitting women to carry out suicide attacks. Soon after his *fatwa*, a Palestinian mother of two from Gaza blew herself up at the Israeli military checkpoint at the Erez crossing on 15 January 2004.[3]

Many terrorists are well educated. However, some failed Palestinian suicide bombers interviewed for television described themselves as young and ignorant, and indicated that, because of this, they were content simply to do what they were told by those who recruited and trained them, without questioning.[4]

Studies show that most tend to be introverts. However, there is no indication that they are mentally ill in any medical sense. Far from being lone individuals, Islamist suicide bombers are recruited, trained, supported and backed up by Islamist militant groups at every level. In addition, in Palestine, suicide bombers come from a background where they are venerated and treated as heroes after their death on television, on the radio, in the newspapers, in the mosques, in public murals and at every conceivable level.

Recruits may be involved with such organizations for some time before they become suicide bombers themselves, sometimes forming close, intense friendships with their comrades. Those who volunteer to be suicide bombers – and are accepted – undergo a period of rigorous training from which there is no turning back.

Rather than being spontaneous acts of pure emotion and frustration, almost all suicide bombings are the result of deliberate, reasoned planning over some time; in the case of the September 11th 2001 attacks years had been spent in planning and preparation. Palestinian suicide bombers settle their debts if they can,[5] write farewell letters and record videos for their families before leaving home for the last time. A typical video will consist of a prayer, a speech asserting the Palestinians' resolve never to be crushed by Israel, and then family messages.

It seems highly unlikely that the phenomenon of Islamist suicide bombing could exist on anything like the same scale, if at all, without this overwhelming institutionalisation of the idea in the prevailing culture. Likewise lone Islamists striking at international targets are likely to be amateurish and ineffective without groups like Al-Qaʿeda to train them and back them up.

Socio-economic deprivation

It is generally held that communities struggling to survive in grinding poverty, with few educational opportunities, widespread unemployment and little prospect of change are good breeding grounds for terrorism. The logic is that frustrated young men, who have no other way to change their situation and no other purpose to motivate them, are likely to find terrorism an attractive option. They have nothing to lose and potentially could gain personal glory and play a part in ushering in the true Islamic state which they see as the solution to all their ills. Lack of education, it is argued, makes them more susceptible to the rhetoric and persuasion of terrorist organisations.

While there is surely truth in this, it must be remembered that many Islamist terrorists are both affluent and well educated. Indeed many have been educated up to tertiary level in the West. So poverty and deprivation can be a contributory factor to the making of an Islamist terrorist, but would rarely be the only factor.

Selection and recruitment

Individuals with the right predisposition to become terrorists or suicide bombers are usually spotted and recruited at mosques, schools and religious institutions.

There has been an explosive growth in the number of *madrassas* all around the world and particularly, since the Soviet-Afghan War of 1979-89, in the Pakistan-Afghanistan region. Many of these schools are less concerned with education than with military training for young Muslims to wage jihad. Funding comes mainly from Saudi Arabia, either direct or through a network of charities. Ironically Saudi Arabia was originally encouraged in this endeavour by the USA, in the hope that it would provide a bulwark against extremist Shi'a Islam.

Pakistan's Ministry for Religious Affairs estimates that more than 1.5 million Pakistani children attend *madrassas*, while the Brussels-based think tank, International Crisis Group, believes that nearly one-third of school-going children in Pakistan are getting their education at a *madrassa*.[6] They are often from the poorest families, who cannot afford to give their children any other kind of education. The *madrassas* provide not only a free education, but also free board and lodging. In addition there are students at the *madrassas* from all across the Muslim world, for example, Malaysia, Thailand, Nigeria, Philippines, Indonesia and the Gulf.

The students, who may be as young as nine or ten, are taught the Qur'an interpreted according to Wahhabi Islam. Very little if any other education is provided. Treatment can be brutal. Some students go on to become a new generation of imams and Muslim clerics all around the world, while others become jihad fighters in various different countries. The Taliban (a term which means "students") trained in these *madrassas*. In 1997 the Haqqania School near Peshawar closed down and sent all its pupils (who numbered more than 2,800) to Afghanistan to fight for the Taliban against the Northern Alliance.[7]

In Turkey the *madrassas* were abolished by Atatürk after his proclamation of the republic. In the 1950s and 1960s the state established schools for imams and preachers. However in the later decades of the twentieth century they formed a base for newly emergent Islamist political parties, which in turn produced the first non-secular Turkish prime minister, Necmettin Erbakan, who came to power in 1996.[8]

Malaysia's privately run religious schools, known as Sekolah Agama Rakyat (SAR), are a breeding ground for future Muslim terrorists, according to the independent Malaysian think-tank, the Malaysian Strategic Research Centre. Its director, Abdul Razak Baginda, warned in January 2003, "The government must now watch these SARs more closely to ensure their students are not recruited by terrorist groups.... We have to take strong action or else we are finished." The SARs are run by individuals and groups aligned to the opposition political party the Parti Islam SeMalaysia.[9]

An appallingly brutal Islamist school in Kenya, the Khadija Islamic Institute for Discipline and Education in Eastleigh, Nairobi, was attended by teenage boys from Kenya, Ethiopia, Sweden and the UK. They were taught the Qur'an, English, Arabic and Maths.

According to one former pupil, the killing of Christians was glorified. "They told us it's called jihad. They said if you enter a church with bombs and kill yourself you will go to heaven."[10]

Singaporean Muslims are recruited to the Jemaah Islamiyah terrorist group at religious classes offered for a general mass audience. From amongst those recommended for consideration, the Jemaah Islamiyah leaders seek to identify those who are interested to know more about the plight of oppressed Muslims around the world. The recruitment process usually takes about eighteen months.[11]

In the UK young Muslims are recruited from the mosques by recruiting agents who stand outside giving away leaflets, get chatting and invite potential recruits for a meal. Recruits are often social misfits, perhaps fresh from prison and without money or friends. They may be given pocket money and somewhere to live. Gradually the meetings they attend become more political and they are taught to despise moderation and tolerance. Many are converts to Islam, and their ignorance of Arabic can be exploited by giving them the most extreme possible interpretations. Without Muslim relatives to give them a different interpretation of Islam, they may hear no other form of Islamic teaching but what their recruiters give them. Promising individuals are sent on training camps where they are taught horse-riding and how to handle guns.[12]

While British recruits often have a criminal record, it appears that a different strategy was employed by Assirat al-Moustaqim [The Straight Path], the Moroccan Islamist group responsible for the bombing in Casablanca on 16 May 2003. Assirat al-Moustaqim recruited operatives who lived in Casablanca and had no police records or previous involvement with radical Islam.[13]

An Indonesian jihad manual describes how to select individuals to serve in the "martyr brigades", defined as elite troops whose role is to engage in terrorism, sabotage, propaganda and psychological warfare. This is a somewhat different job description from that of the suicide bomber, but the willingness to die is emphasised throughout. The chosen men must have a strong faith and a true love of martyrdom. They must be courageous, skilled and always ready to sacrifice themselves if the conditions require it. They are chosen from among the strong and brave Muslims who no longer think of this earthly life and are supported with weaponry suitable to their tasks.[14]

In Chechnya those recruited as suicide bombers are often women, particularly women who have lost husbands and brothers to the Russians, who tend to target young men for arrest, torture and disappearance. The bereaved women are encouraged to offer themselves for suicide missions in order to get their revenge. Shamil Beno, who was the Chechen foreign minister during the republic's brief self-proclaimed independence in the 1990s, estimates that there are 30,000 families "that could produce *shahids*, families that have suffered terribly and see no alternative". Interestingly he sees the suicide response as not so much religiously motivated but the only practical way in which women can retaliate.[15]

Al-Qa'eda has fourteen mandatory qualifications for membership: knowledge of Islam, ideological commitment, maturity, self-sacrifice, discipline, secrecy and concealment of information, good health, patience, imperturbability, intelligence and insight, caution and prudence, truthfulness and wisdom, the ability to observe and analyse, and the ability to act.[16]

Recently recruitment of Islamist terrorists by means of Internet message boards has become popular. For example a Malaysian posted a message on an Arabic-language message board as follows: "Dear Brothers, I have already succeeded with the grace of Allah and his help, to go to Kurdistan for jihad through one of the brothers in this forum. Praise be to Allah, I have fought there, by the grace of God and his bounty. But martyrdom was not granted to me, and therefore I ask Allah to give me more lifetime and to make my deeds good. I ask anyone who has capacity to organize for me to go to another jihad front to correspond with me." There are reported to be hundreds of such message boards.[17]

Training

Once they become involved with Islamist militant groups the recruits enter a world where their rage is directed, channelled, and given a sense of purpose and an outlet. They are shown videos of Muslims suffering and are taught to demonise their future targets, who become utterly dehumanised in their thinking - they are to be sacrificed for Allah without a hint of pity. An example of this kind of thinking comes from a columnist identified as Seif Al-Din Al-Ansari, writing in the online magazine Al-Ansar, which is affiliated with Al-Qa'eda:

> Regardless of the norms of "humanist" belief, which see destroying the infidel countries as a tragedy requiring us to show some conscientious empathy and ... an atmosphere of sadness for the loss that is to be caused to human civilisation – an approach that does not distinguish between believer and infidel ... - I would like to stress that annihilating the infidels is an inarguable fact, as this is the [divine] decree of fate...[18]

According to Iraqi police, not only "brainwashing" but also drugs are used on young Iraqis being recruited for suicide missions. The main drug involved is said to be Artane, an antipsychotic drug which can give a sense of invulnerability.[19]

Palestinian suicide bombers are trained within a small cell of activists who between them cover the following functions: recruiter, bomb-maker, trainer, transport of the suicide bomber to the target area, and the bomber himself or herself. The cell chooses the target and carefully guides the bomber in the making of the farewell video.[20] Suicide bombers are not taken to reconnoitre their target areas beforehand lest they should begin to feel compassion for their future victims.[21]

The Jemaah Islamiyah in Singapore give their new recruits a strong sense of exclusivity and self-esteem. They are told they will be martyrs if they die for the cause, and also that any who leave the organisation are infidels.[22]

An Indonesian jihad manual lists thirty "military doctrines of Islam". These are a mixture of spiritual exhortation and practical advice, tactics and rules of engagement, each one backed up with a selection of quotations from the Qur'an and *hadith*. Some examples are:

> Plant the goal of jihad in the way of Allah as to die a martyr, fall in the way of Allah, or gain victory by establishing Islam on the face of the earth.

> Love jihad more than anything else other than Allah and His apostle.

> In planning to attack the enemy or during an attack, do not argue a lot, something that will cause you to lose strength and boldness as a result of division.

> Know clearly and in detail where the enemy is that must be attacked so that you don't make any mistakes and attack your own side.

> Do not feel proud and boastful when you see that the enemy forces are smaller than yours. Large numbers do not necessarily defeat small numbers, if there is pride.

> In making an attack the first priority must be to kill all the leaders/commanders of the enemy because that will cause chaos among their followers.

> Have faith to the fullest extent; life and death are in the hands of Allah. There is no one who can be killed except with His permission. From all of this, do not retreat because of fear of death in the face of a strong and powerful enemy.

> If you hear rumours, news of peace etc. do not be caught up and spread them, but examine them first, then tell them to the leader/commander.

> Be just towards your enemies who surrender. Do not kill them. So too with women and children unless they fight against you.

> Give shelter (amnesty) to the heathen and idolater who are reluctant to fight against the Muslims.[23]

Another section describes how "martyr brigades" should operate.

> They must be organised according to a tight system with a secret network that the enemy will have difficulty in analyzing. The commando structure must be complex with small teams which consist of a few members according to the need. Each of them must be expert in the field of arms. It would be excellent if every team had their own experts, in weapons, explosives etc. They will use special codes and will be very secretive in their operations, and will have all the supplies necessary to support the success of the martyr brigades.

> Control of the field: it is necessary to evaluate the targets that will be destroyed. The first choice is the facilities vital to the enemy so that they will be weakened. The principle, "strike once, destroy the enemy" must be implanted in these troops.

> Control of guerrilla tactics, both jungle, mountain and especially city guerrilla tactics vital to enemies in the city.

> These troops will not disclose the secrets of their troops even though they have to die, for the sake of the security and the continuation of the struggle.[24]

Al-Qa'eda's terrorists are amongst the best trained and most disciplined. It has several training manuals, the main one being a multi-volume work, running to 7,000 pages, called *Encyclopaedia of the Afghan Jihad*. Much of the material was culled from American and British military manuals and it was put together by Egyptians and Saudis who had been educated in the US and UK. It is written simply and clearly so the instructions on weapons, tanks, explosives, intelligence, first aid etc. could be followed easily by someone who was not highly educated. First published in book form in Arabic in 1996, a CD version appeared in 1999.[25]

Another of Al-Qa'eda's military training manuals is called *Declaration of Jihad Against the Country's Tyrants*. It presents an interpretation of Islamic teaching that justifies kidnapping for ransom, torture, killing and the exchange of hostages, especially if the victim is non-Muslim.

> We find permission to interrogate the hostage for the purpose of obtaining information. It is permitted to strike the non-believer who has no covenant until he reveals the news, information and secrets of his people ... The religious scholars have also permitted the killing of a hostage if he insists on withholding information from Muslims. They permitted his killing so that he would not inform his people of what he learnt about the Muslim condition, number, and secrets .... The scholars have also permitted the exchange of hostages for money, services, expertise and secrets of the enemy's army, plans and numbers.[26]

Al-Qa'eda runs training camps at which three standard courses are taught. Basic training involves guerrilla warfare and Shari'ah. Advanced training covers explosives, assassination techniques and heavy weapons. Specialised training includes surveillance and counter-surveillance, forging identity documents and conducting suicide attacks by vehicle or at sea.[27]

Al-Qa'eda have also launched an online magazine called *Al-Battar Training Camp*,[28] whose aim is to "spread military culture among the [Muslim] youth" by means of basic lessons in "sports training, through types of light weapons and guerrilla group actions in the cities and mountains, and [including] important points in security and intelligence". The introduction of the first issue (December 2003 or January 2004?) bemoans the fact that "many of Islam's young people" do not yet know how to bear arms, not to mention use them" and urges that preparing for jihad is a personal commandment that applies to every Muslim. The magazine finishes by saying "O Mujahid brother, in order to join the great training camps you don't have to travel to other lands. Alone, in your home, or with a group of your brothers, you too can begin to execute the training programme."[29]

However Al-Qa'eda considers that the most important form of training is psychological preparation, chiefly by religious indoctrination. The subjects covered include Islamic law, Islamic history, contemporary Islamic politics, how to preserve one's faith when interacting with non-Muslims, how to wage jihad, the life of Muhammad.[30] The hijackers of the September 11th 2001 planes had had little military training but were chosen because of their psychological state and their willingness to be martyrs.[31]

While hardly classified as "training", Hizbullah's computer game *Special Forces* shows the kind of attitudes imbued by real training procedures. It begins with target practice at a boot camp, shooting at the faces of Israeli leaders. This is followed by replications of actual Hizbullah operations. Finally there is a gallery of fallen Hizbullah heroes. Hizbullah claimed to have sold more than 7,000 copies in the first two months of the game's launch and say that it allows a form of participation for the "thousands" of would-be volunteers that they have to turn away.[32] A helper at Champions computer arcade in Beirut, where *Special Forces* can be played, makes clear that he understands the intention of the game to be training: "It serves a certain goal. It's not just for fun. It's a way to teach youngsters to know their enemy better and be patriotic."[33]

Recognising a suicide bomber

Although a suicide bomber does not normally inform his family of his intentions, there is a pattern of behaviour which might be spotted by those who know him. He will develop a new circle of friends, and drop old friends. He will probably stop going to the local mosque and start attending another one. He will be quiet and polite, yet outspoken about issues of faith with an uncompromising attitude. He will avoid places and situations where women are likely to be present, so as not to meet women whose heads are uncovered or non-Muslim women. He will refuse to associate with women (apart from close relatives), even if he has known them for a long time.

In Muslim contexts he will grow a beard and begin to dress very conservatively, with long sleeves and high necklines. He will be devout and reluctant to socialise or take part in any non-religious gatherings. However, in western contexts he may deliberately adopt the opposite behaviour, in an attempt to conceal how he is thinking. In this case, he would dress in casual western clothing, take care to be seen at nightclubs, leave tell-tale beer cans around etc. Shortly before the date of the attack, the suicide bomber may indulge in unusual extravagances, such as taking family and friends out to meals, which in retrospect are recognised to have been farewells.

The next generation of suicide bombers is expected to prove well nigh impossible to detect. Practising *taqiyya* to a high degree, they will effectively blend into the society in which they are living. In a western context they would be clean-shaven, will avoid visiting radical mosques or meeting in person with anyone publicly known as an extremist. Communication with their radical colleagues will be conducted by a variety of secure means. They will avoid travelling to places such as Afghanistan or any other theatre of armed conflict but rather will go on holiday to expensive resorts. They will consort with non-Muslims of the opposite sex, drink alcohol and eat pork, and generally participate in popular culture e.g. sport, music etc. Many would be likely to have good jobs in industry and commerce, probably involving IT and communication skills. They will not use traditional "handlers" or follow the classic cell patterns. This will make detection and monitoring by the security forces extremely difficult.

Contemporary Muslim Debate

Currently Islamic teaching on war is in a state of flux. The Muslim press, in particular Muslim cyberspace, is filled with debate and discussion about the Islamic doctrine of war. Although the traditional doctrine is no longer all-pervasive and unquestioned, it is nevertheless still very influential – as President Sadat of Egypt found to his cost[1] Before making a peace treaty with Israel, he took the precaution of obtaining a ruling from the respected Al-Azhar University to say that the treaty did not violate the Shari'ah. Many Muslims however remained unconvinced, including those who assassinated him for neglecting what they asserted was the Islamic duty to fight non-Muslims.[2]

Parts of the traditional Islamic doctrine of war clearly run counter to modern international agreements such as the Geneva conventions and protocols and UN General Assembly resolutions. Even Sobhi Mahmassani, a renowned Lebanese legal expert whose general stance is that Islamic and international principles are compatible, admitted that rules about war are an exception to this.[3]

Much of the contemporary debate centres on the justification for war, in contrast to the pre-modern debate in which jurists focused mainly on devising rules for the conduct of war, the treatment of prisoners etc. Some argue for a stricter interpretation than classical Islam, others for a more lenient interpretation. Space permits only a few examples.

Is jihad defensive only?

A prominent Arab Muslim, Dr Muhammad Maʿruf al-Dawalibi, a counsellor to the King of Saudi Arabia and formerly a professor in the Faculty of Law at Damascus University, wrote an article in the Arab press[4] outlining (amongst other things) many of the usual arguments of modern liberal Muslims against a militaristic and aggressive inter- pretation of jihad (see pages 12-18). Four weeks later the same Arab daily newspaper printed an article by Ahmad Naser al-Rajihi contain- ing a pointby-point rebuttal of each of al-Dawalibi's arguments, and asserting that jihad does indeed mean literal fighting of non-Muslims and that this is by no means limited to self-defence.[5]

Must Muslims engage in warfare?

Another area of discussion centres on whether Muslims must engage in jihad (the classical Islamic understanding) or whether they can refrain on the basis that God has already promised to annihilate the infidels so that Muslims themselves need not take responsibility for ensuring this annihilation. The Qur'anic verse which presents this possible get-out clause runs:

> ... we can expect for you either that God will send His punishment
> from Himself, or by our hands. Q 9:52

Seif al-Din al-Ansari[6] argues strongly for the classical position i.e. that Muslims must engage in warfare. He agrees that "the elements of the collapse of western civilisation are proliferating" anyway, but disagrees that this absolves Muslims from working for the annihila- tion of the infidels. He argues that unless Muslims get involved in the annihilation of an "infidel country", it might simply be replaced by another infidel regime, rather than by the Islamic state.

Does the end justify the means?

The respected Saudi Sheikh Ibn ʿUthaymeen has condemned the activities of Palestinian suicide bombers, declaring that they "have wrongfully committed suicide", they are not martyrs and they will go to hell. Unusually, his reasoning is wholly pragmatic: such suicide killings do not benefit Islam because (1) they do not result in conversions to Islam but tend rather to make the enemy more strongly anti-Muslim (2) the Israeli response to a suicide bombing usually kills more Muslims than the number of Jews killed by the bomber.[7] Presumably he would feel suicide bombers were justified if the results were more positive.

Jihad is to preserve pluralism and variety?

Sheikh 'Abd al-Hamid al-Ansari, dean of the faculty of Shari'ah at Qatar University, is renowned for his liberal views. Writing in the London-based Arabic daily, Al-Hayat,[8] he puts forward a very unusual understanding of jihad.

> Jihad, in its real meaning, is a means of preserving the right of pluralism and variety and guaranteeing freedom of choice for all, because diversity is considered a natural and universal truth...

This is of course the exact opposite of the classic Islamic doctrine of jihad which is intended to spread Islamic power, not to preserve pluralism and diversity.

Sheikh al-Ansari is also unusual in that he calls for dialogue with non-Muslims, urging Muslims to forget past wrongs done to them by the West, to put aside conspiracy theories, and to engage in some self-criticism. The opposite position was taken by a prestigious group of Islamic scholars in Saudi Arabia, headed by the Grand Mufti, Sheikh Ibn Baz, who issued a *fatwa* condemning "debates, meetings and dialogue" with non-Muslims as "invalid" and "rejected by Allah". Their reasoning was apparently that such dialogue might enable the non-Muslims "in achieving their desires, fulfilling their aims, breaking the bonds of Islam, and bending the fundamentals of Islamic faith".[9]

Suicide or martyrdom?

The London-based Saudi daily *Al-Sharq Al-Awsat* abandons normal Islamic vocabulary and refers in its news reporting to "suicide attackers" instead of "martyrs". The paper defends its action on the basis of journalistic professionalism and neutrality, and points out that its editorials (as opposed to news reports) do use the term "martyrdom".[10]

Are Jews and Christians allowed to live?

The London daily newspaper *Al-Hayat* published an article on 21 October 2001[11] by Khaled Muhammad Batrafi, a regular columnist on the paper. Batrafi, a Saudi, was reporting an argument he had had with a friend, following a sermon he had heard at the mosque which called for the annihilation of Christians and Jews. As we have seen above, classical Islam teaches that Christians and Jews, as "People of the Book", are not to be killed or forced to become Muslims, but may live in an Islamic state albeit with an inferior status to the Muslim citizens. Batrafi therefore said the preacher's words were heresy and quoted to his friend some Qur'anic verses in support of humane treatment of Christians and Jews (Q 3:64; Q 60:8). His friend however, quoted other texts in support of the preacher's stance, and the two of them discussed the various possible interpretations, their historical contexts and how to apply them to Christians and Jews today.

Discerning trends

Amidst the diversity of opinion about war amongst contemporary Muslims, Ann Elizabeth Mayer detects the emergence of certain trends. One trend seeks to prove the essential compatibility of Shari'ah with international law in order to justify Muslims adhering to public international law. The most common way of approaching this is to argue that international law is actually derived from Islamic law. This is completely contrary to the findings of scholarly research, where the prevailing opinion at present is that international law derives primarily from European thought.[12] Muslim scholars argue that European thought came under the influence of Islam during the Crusades and in Islamic Spain.[13] However, as Mayer points out, "Regardless of the strength of its scholarly underpinnings, the theory that international law derives from Islam can function like a benign fiction that facilitates the reception of international law in the Muslim world."[14]

Another trend is to abandon the traditional division of the world into *Dar al-Harb* and *Dar al-Islam*;[15] some do this by replacing *Dar al-Harb* with various alternative categories of territory e.g. *Dar al-Sulh* (House of Truce)[16] and *Dar al-'Ahd* (House of Treaty)[17] indicating peaceful co-operation with the non-Muslim world, or *Dar ash-Shahada* (House of Testimony) meaning that Muslims can freely practise their faith there. The validity of these alternatives has always been a subject of debate amongst Muslim jurists, and the distinctions between them are difficult to define.[18] A further position is that a country which was once *Dar al-Islam* and is now ruled by non-Muslims remains *Dar al-Islam* and only lapses into *Dar al-Harb* when most or all of the requirements of Islam are no longer possible.[19] Sir Syed Ahmed Khan believed that India under the British Raj could be considered *Dar al-Islam* because the Muslims were free to pursue their religious and social duties.[20]

The issue of whether or not a truce or treaty is believed to be in place is of great practical significance. Anjem Choudhary, the head of the British Islamist organisation Al-Muhajiroun, has said that his organisation does not encourage its followers in Britain to carry out attacks in Britain because they were living under a "covenant of security" that required them not to strike at the host country where they lived. Yet his organisation heaped praise on the suicide attackers who killed over 3,000 people on September 11th 2001 and said that any Muslims who condemned the attack were apostates whose opinion should carry no weight.[21]

A further trend is to consider certain features of traditional teaching on jihad in the light of international law and concepts of a just war. Since armed aggression (as in classical Islamic law) is forbidden in Article 2(4) of the UN Charter, jihad must therefore be redefined as for defence only. For example, Hasan Moinuddin argues that Muslims must not begin hostilities.[22] Others however may have definitions of "self-defence" which are not quite the same as those of international law. Sobhi Mahmassani's definition includes "to protect freedom of religion, to repel aggression, to prevent injustice and to protect social order"[23] – a much broader definition than in international law, which permits anticipatory self-defence only when the need to attack is immediate, overwhelming and leaves no other option.[24] To some Muslims, "self-defence" can even include ridding a society of polytheism and destroying anything that obstructs the propagation of Islam.[25]

Similarly, Ala'Eddin Kharofa, an Iraqi professor of Islamic law, seems to extend the definition of "self-defence" to include fighting all non-Muslims so that they cannot plot against Muslims: "The Qur'an also carries the command to the Muslims to fight all disbelievers so as they would not be able to plot against them. See al-Baqara [i.e. *sura* 2 of the Qur'an]: 190-193 and al-Tauba [i.e. *sura* 9 of the Qur'an]:36)"[26]

Imam Mohammed al-Asi, writing in the UK-based *Crescent International*, likewise looks at Q 2:193, and argues that Muslims cannot at present "enjoy freedom of conscience and will, and a truly independent state" so therefore:

> Our understanding of the Qur'an and Sunnah obliges us to carry the burden of jihad to deter all forms of persecution, discrimination, and hurt and injury premeditated by inimical forces. Muslims, like all other people, are entitled to security: security for their lives, their possessions and their faith.[27]

He condemns all, whether Muslims or non-Muslims, who try to argue that jihad is no longer an obligation for Muslims. He also condemns "those who try to deceive the Muslim public into believing that self-determination (Islamic self-determination) is obtainable through international forums, American patronage or zionist channels. [i.e. those who say] Anything will do provided that it is not *jihad* and *qital* for the cause of Allah." Al-Asi appears to consider that anything less than Islamic self-determination amounts to persecution of Muslims, and thus jihad is necessary. His inclusion of the word *qital* emphasises his belief in the need for physical warfare. (He does not, however, permit the forcible conversion of non-Muslims to Islam.)

Another modern variation on traditional Islamic teaching on jihad is to redefine it so as to legitimise the use of force on behalf of liberation struggles against oppressors in the developing world. One of these struggles is the Palestinian cause. Numerous calls have been made for a jihad to liberate Palestine and Jerusalem from Israeli control, and even before Israel existed there were calls for jihad against the Jewish settlers in Palestine. In the case of Palestine jihad has been so re-defined by some Muslims as to make it an obligation even on non-Muslims![28] Mayer believes that the existence of the Palestinian issue, which is so prominent in Muslim consciousness around the globe, may have hampered progress towards bringing Islamic law on war in line with public international law.[29]

A rather complex issue which some Muslim thinkers are tackling is the question of what entity can conduct a jihad. In classical Islam it was the *umma*, the entire Muslim community, but in today's world of nation-states that is impractical. Yet the goal of every liberation struggle is a nation-state. According to Hassan Hanafi, an Egyptian intellectual, Islam supports the idea that every people deserves its own nation-state,[30] a position that seems to be gaining adherents. Further support comes from the Organisation of the Islamic Conference, implicitly by its very structure and explicitly in its 1972 Charter, which recognises the right of "all peoples" to self-determination (especially Muslims and most particularly the people of Palestine).[31]

Any attempt to determine trends in current Muslim thinking on jihad may be complicated by political rhetoric. For example in the Iran-Iraq war of the 1980s, each side justified the war as a jihad against the other, surely an impossibility under any definition of jihad.[32]

Furthermore, there is often a difference between statements addressed to the West and statements intended for a Muslim audience. A phrase used by Professor Kharofa concerning a fellow-Muslim is revealing. Kharofa writes that he finds himself "having to remind him of the linguistic and Islamic idiomatic meanings of the word [jihad], and how Muslims understand it *without any misrepresentation to gain the pleasure of Westerners.*"[33] Westerners should be aware that some comments they hear or read on jihad may well be a case of being "given what they want to hear" rather than the true opinion of the speaker or writer. Thus Ayatollah Khomeini stated on one occasion that jihad was nothing to do with defence but meant "expansion and the taking over of other countries" and that Muslims are obliged "to fight and to spread Islamic laws throughout the world", whereas another time he denied any intent to use armed force or wars of aggression to achieve his objectives which were to be accomplished by spiritual means.[34] The doctrine of *taqiyya* (see pages 89-92), particularly strong amongst Shi'as like Khomeini, should not be forgotten.

Many Muslims assert that Islamic international law is superior to modern international law. Their argument is based on the fact that Islamic international law was formulated thirteen centuries ago, whereas the present system of international law came into being only about four centuries ago. For example, they say that the Islamic requirement to warn the enemy of an impending attack pre-dates by many centuries the 1907 Hague Convention's ruling on the opening of hostilities. They also argue that Islamic international law was more humane than other systems at the time it was created.[35] They claim that it enshrined the principles of equality, reciprocity and peace long before these were recognised internationally[36] (a claim that seems impossible to justify if these terms are understood in their normal western sense). Another reason given for the superiority of Islamic law is that it is based on religion and therefore has a moral sanction.[37]

Responses to Islamist Terrorism

Military strategists recognise the importance of "knowing your enemy". Yet following September 11th 2001 it appeared that American and British political leaders went to great lengths to deny any connection between Al-Qaʿeda and mainstream Islam i.e. to consider Al-Qaʿeda as mindless extremists, motivated by a pointless blind fanatical hatred of the West. They were referred to as "enemies of civilization", "enemies of our way of life" or simply "terrorists". Seen as such, it is a struggle to comprehend what can have possibly motivated them to carry out such apparently senseless acts of violence.

However in the context of radical Islamists' understanding of Islam, with its historical teaching of jihad, *Dar al-Islam* and *Dar al-Harb*, together with the historical development of a theology of violence amongst sects and jihad groups through the ages, their actions are far from senseless but rather are guided by a clear logic. With this understanding one can begin to look seriously at how to address them.

Islamist terrorists do not function in isolation. Not only are they networked to each other but also they are linked to the Muslim community at large, from which they draw funds and new recruits to enable their continued operation. The interconnections resemble a multiplicity of spiders' webs. To remove a single individual, for example Osama bin Laden, from this scenario would have relatively little effect on the overall position. It is the networking of groups which gives them their great strength, so efforts should be made to isolate the groups from each other, and prevent the flow of funds, personnel and expertise.

In order to begin to tackle Islamist terrorism effectively, greater surveillance and penetration of these networks is vital. However, it is particularly difficult to infiltrate Muslim groups, as Muslims are very unwilling to act as agents for the non-Muslim world and non-Muslims find it difficult to pass themselves off convincingly as Muslims. Also the cellular structure makes penetration from outside difficult, in particular where such groups are ethnic-, tribal- or even family-based. As well as current terrorist activities it is important to research all matters relating to Islamic theology, history, interpretation and practices and to analyse the findings in terms of their influence on the terrorist networks and individuals. A spider weaves its web in secret in a dark corner, and cannot be tackled until a light is shone upon it. Similarly, a light must be shone on the network of Islamic groups and interconnections to reveal the true complexity of the situation.

Given these precautionary and preparatory tactics, what broad strategies are available for dealing with Islamist terrorism?

1. Elimination

At one end of the spectrum of responses is the elimination of all individuals involved in terrorist activities by killing them, as for example in the elimination of the Kharijis by mainstream Muslims. This is also how the Assassins were dealt with in the Middle Ages when their main centre at Alamut in Persia was wiped out by the Mongols under Hulagu in 1256. Those based in Syria were subjugated by the Mameluke Sultan Baybars, who had captured all their castles by 1273.[1]

In one sense the USA's determined pursuit of Islamist terrorists could unwittingly evolve into such a response. Because of the way in which terrorists are interlinked, to remove just the perceived "ringleaders" is very unlikely to have any effect on the movement as a whole. The Americans may therefore go on to extend their targeting more broadly resulting in a spiralling with unpredictable consequences. Without making a conscious or deliberate policy of mass elimination, their actions could thus develop in that direction.

Even if this method were considered acceptable, it could not be permanently effective. Sooner or later terrorism would re-emerge, as individual Muslims examined the roots of Islam, gave them a particular interpretation, and made their own decisions to return to the violence of the early days of their faith. Given the theological character of Islam, the non-violent Muslim masses are bound to give rise to violent individuals from time to time. The removal of the Assassins centuries ago has not prevented the development of Palestinian suicide bombers now. Non-violent Islam is like a cone balanced on its point; it cannot exist in that state indefinitely but is bound to fall i.e. to give rise to violent elements.

2. Military defeat

History shows that until now the advance of Islam has only ever been stopped by military defeat. We have already seen how Kaegi's analysis indicates that it was military factors that were the primary cause of the success of the Muslim invasions of the Levant. In western Europe it was only Christendom's military might which reversed the Muslim advance into France at the battle of Tours (732, also known as the battle of Poitiers) and drove Islam out of Spain in the Reconquista (1492). Similarly in eastern Europe militant Christendom turned back the Muslim advance in Austria at the siege of Vienna (1683).

Historically Europe was attacked by Muslim armies and could be defended by conventional warfare. Now it is faced with terrorist activities, and it is not clear how to defeat these militarily, as has been demonstrated recently in Afghanistan where even finding the enemy has proved virtually impossible. However, a modern example illustrating that the likelihood or otherwise of a strong physical response can still be an important motivation for Islamist terrorists is described by Bernard Lewis.

One of the most surprising revelations of those who held the American Embassy in Teheran from 1979 to 1981 was that their original intention had been to hold the building and the hostages for only a few days. They changed their minds when statements from Washington made it clear that there was no danger of serious action against them. They finally released the hostages, they explained, only because they feared that the new President, Ronald Reagan, might approach the problem "like a cowboy".[2]

3. Colonialism

It is noteworthy that Islamist terrorism was in abeyance throughout the eighteenth and nineteenth centuries when European colonial powers ruled most of the Muslim world. It was only in the mid-twentieth century, when the colonial yoke was being thrown off all around the world, that radical Islam re-appeared on the scene. It would seem that strong western colonial rule prevents the rise of active militants within Islam. For example, in 1921 the British arrested and tried for conspiracy Pir Ghulam Mujaddid Sirhindi who made inflammatory anti-British speeches and denounced the presence of Muslims in the British army.[3] This particular *pir* was willing to endure the discomforts of prison, but many others were not and also felt that the humiliation and disgrace of prison endangered their special status in society. Many therefore quickly gave in when punishment loomed.[4] One such Khilafat supporter, Maulvi Muhammad Sadiq of Nawabshah, had served only a week of his one-year sentence for refusing to furnish security for good behaviour when he changed his mind and acceded to the authorities' demands. He justified this with a verse from the Qur'an:[5]

> He who takes up a burden which he has not the power to bear commits a sin.[6]

Abdul Ghaffar Khan felt that jihads against the British were of no use, serving only to provoke them into greater violence and ruthlessness. He considered that the British presence in the North-

West Frontier was so firmly established that it was not possible to oust them by violence. "Earlier, violence had seemed to me the best way to revolution ... but experience taught me that it was futile to dig a well after the house was on fire."[7] We have already seen how Muridism in Senegal responded to French colonialism with passive resistance and eventually cooperation. (See page 96.)

However, colonial rule does not necessarily prevent the rise of the ideas, as for example in Egypt where the Muslim Brotherhood came into existence during a period of British military and political influence in the country (albeit not full colonialism).

4. Brutal repression

The majority of Muslim governments today face opposition from Islamist movements who seek to topple the existing regime by terrorism and replace it with their own, more Islamic, system. Many of these countries respond to the threat with brutal repression. Terrorists and suspected terrorists are arrested, tortured, imprisoned without trial etc. Some may be formally executed or surreptitiously murdered. Countries which fall into this category include Egypt, Syria, Tunisia, Algeria and Saudi Arabia.

It is noteworthy that in Egypt the Muslim Brotherhood have now abandoned their policy of violence and are pursuing their goals by political means. A similar thing seems to be happening in Algeria. However, if the movements seeking to reform society change only their methods and not their aims, the question remains as to what they will do once they have attained power through the political processes. Will they continue to allow some form of democracy or will they install a totalitarian regime?

5. Denial of human rights

In western democracies the method of brutal repression is not an option, hence the flourishing centres of radical Islam which now exist in the western world, directing and funding the activities of the terrorists. The most the West can do to control or limit these activities is a suspension of certain human rights to permit, for example, the detention of suspects without trial. This is difficult to sustain because of the protests of human rights activists, as has been seen with regard to both American and British actions against terrorists since September 11th 2001. For such a method to be workable it requires overwhelming public support which in turn requires a public awareness of the threat of Islamist terrorism.

6. Financial restrictions

A more acceptable way might be to stem the flow of funds to terrorist organisations. The sums involved are vast. Steven Stalinsky's well documented report[8] on Saudi donations to Palestinian jihad fighters concludes that the Saudi royal family has been their main financial supporter for decades. He calculates that in a period of five and a half years (January 1998 – June 2003), over US$4 billion has been donated. Much of this was specifically designated for the families of martyrs. King Fahd himself has pledged to support 1,000 Palestinian families of martyrs. If these funds could be prevented from reaching the terrorists it is likely that their activities would soon have to be severely curtailed.

7. Economic uplift

Many have suggested that Islamist terrorism is the expression of frustrated impoverished young Muslim men, without education or employment, who have no earthly hope. It has therefore been suggested that a massive injection of aid into the poorest Muslim regions to enable development and economic improvement would see an end to militant Islam. Unfortunately this theory is belied by the fact that many Islamist terrorists, particularly in the Gulf and Middle East, are neither poor nor uneducated. A good proportion, especially those in leadership, are from the comfortable, cultivated middle-classes. Osama bin Laden is immensely wealthy and funds much of Al-Qa'eda's activity from his own pocket. The terrorists' motivation is theological, not just psychological. Sadly the theory of paying Islamist terrorism to disappear seems to be more wishful thinking than grounded in reality.

Nevertheless economic assistance may mean that fewer individuals are interested in becoming terrorists. A comparison of Chechnya and Turkey in recent years is very illuminating. In Chechnya the Russian army has targeted not just the Chechen rebels but the also ordinary Chechen civilians, whose lives have been devastated by an indiscriminate scorched-earth policy which has destroyed the Chechen economy. It is also reported that Russian soldiers routinely rape Chechen women. There has been no let-up in the Chechen rebellion, which has become ever more desperate, with many suicide bombers including women. Turkey took a different approach to the Kurdish rebel group, the PKK. The Turkish military targeted the PKK activists only, crushing them militarily, cutting off international support, and arresting their leader. They avoided attacking the general Kurdish population, who were instead given much economic assistance in the form of social welfare programmes to improve agriculture and women's education etc. The Turkish government has invested over $32 billion in the Kurdish region, which is more per capita than any other part of Turkey. They have also yielded to various Kurdish demands on language, cultural freedom and educational reforms. It is presumably as a result of this that the PKK's suicide bombing campaign of the late 1990s has dwindled to almost nothing.[9]

8. Yield to the terrorists' requests

In theory terrorist activity should cease if the terrorists are given what they want. This is the analysis of the BBC's World Affairs Editor, John Simpson, citing the examples of the IRA in Northern Ireland and ETA in Spain:

> There is only one method of defeating political violence. It begins by mobilising the support of governments who might otherwise be quietly sympathetic to extremists, and goes on to isolate those responsible for the violence *by reducing the causes of discontent*.[10]

In the case of Islamist terrorists their immediate goal is to rule the Muslim world according to the strictest forms of Islam. Some might argue that the non-Muslim world should withdraw from any involvement in Muslim regions, should cede Palestine, Chechnya, Kashmir, south Thailand, Mindanao in the Philippines, and all the other areas where Muslims are seeking to establish Muslim or Islamic states, and put up an "Islamic curtain" between the Muslim and the non-Muslim world. It is relevant to remark that whilst Samuel Huntington's thesis of a "clash of civilisations" may at first have seemed an extreme position, there is now some recognition of the validity of his argument.

But would this permanently satisfy the terrorists? Or is it possible that, because of their ultimate global agenda i.e. to change all the remaining *Dar al-Harb* to *Dar al-Islam*, they would break through the "Islamic curtain" and continue the struggle for dominance?

9. Peace treaty

As we have seen, the traditional Islamic doctrine of war has much to say about when and how Muslims are permitted to make peace treaties with the enemy. This suggests the possibility of the non-Muslim world making some kind of formal peace with the Muslim community worldwide. However, there are a number of serious difficulties with this, not least the fact that peace treaties in classical Islam are supposed to be only temporary. Another problem is that there is no single Islamic authority accepted by all Muslims with whom to negotiate. Thirdly, there are sections of the Muslim community who believe that Muslims may freely break any agreement made with non-Muslims.

10. Theological undermining

An ingenious method is reported to have been employed on various occasions. According to the stories, dead Islamist terrorists are buried with pig body-parts. Because the pig is considered unclean in Islam, some Muslims believe that this kind of treatment will prevent the deceased from going to paradise. If the certainty of going immediately to paradise is the main motivation of terrorists and suicide bombers, then this relatively cheap and easy response might possibly prove to be an effective deterrent.

Places and times where this method is reported to have been used include Peshawar in British India in 1882,[11] the Philippines in about 1911,[12] and the Gaza Strip in 2002.[13] It was also suggested by the deputy Israeli police minister Gideon Esra in the Israeli newspaper *Yediot Aharonot*, a few weeks before September 11th 2001[14] and again by an Israeli rabbi in 2004 who proposed hanging bags of pig fat in Israeli buses as a deterrent to Palestinian suicide bombers, who frequently target buses.[15]

Even if the method has never actually been used, the logic behind it would be hard to defy, if Muslims really do believe that contact with pig parts will stop a martyr going to paradise. However, there does not appear to be any warrant for this belief in Islamic theology and Philps reports that Palestinian Muslims scorned the idea.[16] Raeed Tayeh, public affairs director of the Muslim American Society Freedom Foundation, has also denied that Muslims would be barred from heaven by such treatment.[17] Furthermore, even if the method were workable, its very offensiveness raises the question of whether it could ever really be recommended.

However, there are other ways in which the theological basis for suicide bombers could be undermined. Since no individual suicide attack is a martyrdom unless Islamic leaders say it is, there is the possibility of an Islamic leader declaring that a particular suicide attack was *not* martyrdom. This means the bomber will not go straight to heaven. The bomber will also have been relying on a financial payout for his family (that will also clear his own debts if any, a necessary pre-requisite for going to heaven) which might not be forthcoming. If militants begin to fear that they may not be "covered" by this kind of theological and financial support, they will be less willing to kill themselves in suicide attacks.

So if at least some Islamic leaders could be persuaded to publicly condemn at least some suicide bombings, not just to western audiences, but also in the relevant religious terminology for their own community, this particular method of terrorist attack, which is so hard to deal with militarily, might lose its popularity. An example of this occurred when Saudi Arabia's Crown Prince Abdullah made a rare televised statement after three suicide attacks in Riyadh in May 2003 which killed 34 people including some Saudi civilians. He warned that the terrorists who committed the atrocity "have a destiny that is very harsh in hellfire".[18] In other words, he proclaimed that the suicide bombers were not martyrs going to heaven but murderers going to hell.

Similarly Saudi Arabia's Council of Senior Clerics, headed by Grand Mufti Sheikh Abdul-Aziz al-Sheikh, issued a *fatwa* in August 2003 stating that acts of sabotage, bombing and murder in their country were not a part of "jihad for the sake of God". It stated that those who assisted or sheltered the perpetrators were guilty of "great sin".[19] It appears that this condemnation may have been limited only to terrorist attacks within the boundaries of Saudi Arabia.

Similarly if the Islamic media were to refrain from making heroes of the suicide bombers, it is possible that fewer young men would be motivated to follow in their footsteps. Perhaps a small beginning was made when the Italian branch of the Muslim World League dismissed the newly appointed imam of Rome's Grand Mosque, the largest mosque in Europe, for having praised Palestinian suicide bombers in his sermon at Friday prayers on 6 June 2003 and having called on Allah "to annihilate the enemies of Islam".[20]

However, this is complicated by the fact that the bombers usually look chiefly to their own militant group for backing, affirmation and the assurance of heaven. Statements by those outside the group, even if they are respected Islamic religious leaders, may carry little weight with the bomber in comparison with statements by the leaders of his or her own small group. The statements of more prominent leaders may, for example, be dismissed as merely designed to please western governments.

Historically there was a great difference of opinion between the Kharijis, who considered that death in battle against "unrighteous" governments was martyrdom, whilst Sunni theologians considered that rebellion against the government was not a jihad and therefore could not lead to martyrdom.[21]

11. Reform of Islam

If terrorism is going to be dealt with at its source, Islam has to change and undergo a transformation. In the long term it would appear that the only way to bring an end to Islamist terrorism is to reform the teachings of Islam with regard to war and violence. Christianity underwent its own reformation in the fifteenth and sixteenth centuries but this has not happened to Islam, at least not yet. Reform of Islam would require a new *ijtihad* to reinterpret the original sources. The current debate within Islam as to whether or not a new *ijtihad* can take place at this stage has involved a number of individual Muslims who have embraced the concept of change and are calling for the origins of their faith to be reinterpreted in the light of modern standards of human rights, freedom, democracy etc. These lone voices do not have substantial followings as yet, but they are becoming more numerous. As long as they remain few in number they are at physical risk themselves.

Ulil Abshar-Abdalla of the Liberal Islam Network, based in Jakarta, Indonesia, urges a contextualised interpretation of Islam for the modern day by means of *ijtihad* to "seek a new formula" to translate the universal values of Islam into the context of contemporary life. He considers that the type of Islam established by Muhammad at Medina "was one possible translation of the universal Islam... But there are possibilities of translating Islam in other ways, in different contexts." Amongst other recommendations, he recommends that "All those legal products of classical Islam which discriminate between Muslims and non-Muslims should be amended on the basis of the universal principle of human equality" and that religion should be separated from public life and political power. When his article on this subject was published in Kompas, an Indonesian daily newspaper, it resulted in a death sentence being passed on him by certain Islamist groups in Indonesia.[22]

Perhaps the ideal kind of reformed Islam would relegate the *hadith* to a minor source or ignore it altogether. A new Shari'ah would be formulated based on the Qur'an alone, interpreted for modern times. The theory of abrogation would be abandoned or preferably reversed giving the Meccan verses primacy over the Medinan verses in any case of contradiction.

Even calling for a new *ijtihad*, let alone opining on what conclusions it should reach, can be seen as hugely controversial in Islamic circles as the majority believe that "the door of *ijtihad*" has been closed for a thousand years. Islamic societies have a long tradition of condemning as blasphemers, heretics and apostates, those who suggest ideas which differ from orthodoxy, and in Islam the penalty for apostasy is death. Groups like the Mu'tazilites in the eighth and ninth centuries suffered massive and rapid suppression when their theology fell out of favour with Islamic orthodoxy.

So for real, permanent and widespread change, the central institutions of Islam need to be engaged so that they can bring about this reform. Following the suicide attacks in Saudi Arabia on 12 May 2003, in which Saudi civilians were killed, it has been reported that Saudi Arabia intends to set up a commission to formally re-examine the concept of jihad in Islam.[23] But the author is not aware of any other institutional efforts in this direction.

It may be possible for the West (and other non-Muslims) to assist this process by encouraging the individuals and by putting pressure on the leading Muslim institutions to bring about reform that would eliminate from Islam military jihad, suicide martyrdom, the empire-building thrust etc. This encouragement would need to be given with great care, perhaps behind the scenes, as overt western support might lead to a loss of credibility with the Muslim public in general.

Another reservation is that there is no way of guaranteeing that a new *ijtihad* will have the desired effect of producing a mainstream Islam which rejects the violent traditions of the past. When Sir Syed

Ahmed Khan returned to the original sources of Islam he concluded that jihad could only be permitted in the direst necessity of self-defence. By contrast, when those like the Takfir groups have sought to strip away later Islamic teaching and return to the very oldest sources of Islam, they have emerged more militant as a result. A new *ijtihad* could open Pandora's box.

Choosing options

Of these eleven options, a number are difficult to contemplate because the end would not justify the means. Others, less drastic, are unlikely to succeed. Still others are irrelevant because they cannot be used unless the clock is put back to the days of colonialism or of a different style of warfare.

The best hope in the long term would seem to be the route of Islamic reform, a non-violent method which, despite its drawbacks, has the potential to permanently eliminate the threat of Islamist terrorism. This method is closely linked to that of undermining the terrorists' motivation by theological pronouncements. Without a theology to fuel it, Islamist terrorism would eventually shrivel and die. The cone of nonviolent Islam would now be resting on its base, stable and very difficult to knock over. Consequently, individuals who interpreted the sources in the traditional way would have a problem trying to gain a following from the Muslim public at large. In seeking to promote a reform of Islam resulting in the removal of its violent tradition the West would be moving towards a strategy which begins to address the underlying ideology rather than merely combating the numerous individuals who will continue to emerge hydra-like from it. It is vital that the West should begin to give active support to Muslims seeking reform and to challenge the leaders of the Muslim world to take up this cause with urgency. Such a strategy could thus isolate remaining Muslim militants from their support base amongst wider Islamic society. This method however must be pursued with great care, as western intervention in Muslim affairs, especially

Muslim theology, would be seen by many Muslims as being itself a justification for violent jihad.

This could create space for more conventional tactical approaches of dealing with the current situation – structures and individuals – at an economic, political, intelligence and military level without such a widespread fear of popular backlash from the Islamic world. Of these more immediate methods the restriction of funding could well prove to be amongst the most effective.

Such a dual approach, coupled with going some way towards meeting certain Muslim grievances, could offer the possibility of a more peaceful future.

Conclusion

One vital aspect of what the Chinese general Sun Tzŭ described some two and a half thousand years ago as "the art of war" is the skill now termed "enemy recognition". It is essential for those engaged in war to be able to distinguish foe from friend. Much time in training is given, for example, to learning to recognise the silhouette of an enemy tank, and not just from one direction but from any angle.

Similarly, Sun Tzŭ endorsed the saying:

> If you know the enemy and know yourself, you need not fear the result of a hundred battles.[1]

Knowing the enemy

Lack of knowledge of their enemy has often created difficulties for non-Muslims under attack by Muslims. Even in the earliest days the Byzantine forces failed to appreciate the nature of their Muslim Arab enemies, and the significance of the fact that they were no longer pagans. In Kaegi's analysis of the early defeats of the Byzantine Christian army by the Muslim Arabs he observes:

> Part of Byzantium's difficulties was generally poor intelligence on the Muslims and failure to act rapidly, properly and decisively on what intelligence they did acquire about the Muslims. Although some Byzantines were immediately aware of the Islamic component in the motivation of Arabs, Byzantines generally underestimated the religious motivation of Arabs as Muslims and understood very little about this new religion.[2]

A variety of interpretations have been suggested with respect to contemporary Islamist violence. Huntington has spoken of Islam's "bloody borders" and has interpreted war in its contemporary expression in terms of a clash of civilizations. By contrast, Fukuyama, following his idealistic predictions of a post-Cold War period characterized by liberal democracies, argues that current Islamist violence represents the death throes of a religion unable to compete and coexist with liberal democracy.[3]

Following the attacks on September 11th 2001 and the US's subsequent overthrow of the Taliban in Afghanistan and Saddam Hussein in Iraq and its pursuit of Al-Qa'eda terrorists worldwide, the debate on the nature of the conflict has taken centre stage. Many Muslims interpret the situation in terms of the West waging war on Islam, while those in the West, particularly the American and British governments, have been at pains to assert that the West is at war only with terrorists and terrorism, not with the household of Islam.

The American government has shown a marked reluctance to define their enemy any more specifically than by such epithets as "terrorists", "evildoers", or "a bunch of cold-blooded killers". This vagueness is a serious handicap for them in pursuing their war. It prevents them from knowing either their enemy or themselves. The careful omission of the words "Islamist" and "Islamic" means that the enemy's motives remain a complete mystery as does the enemy's extent. For, as this book has sought to show, the activities of militant Muslims are nourished by a whole network of other traditionally-minded Muslims, whose interpretation of Islamic theology encourages them to become supporters of those who actively engage in this kind of violence.

As long as America's enemy remains so ill-defined, America will also find difficulty in identifying allies. The most important of these in the long term would be liberal Muslims who interpret the sources of their faith in a more peaceable manner and are willing to contemplate making adjustments appropriate for modern times and values.

A vaguely defined enemy means that war goals too can be no more than vague. The US Secretary of Defence, Donald Rumsfeld, declared that his aim was to prevent terrorists "from adversely affecting our way of life". But this is only to tackle the symptoms, not to get to the root of the matter. Unless the militant interpretation of Islamic sources is recognised as the basic cause of Islamist terrorist activities, there is little hope of a lasting solution.[4]

British Foreign Office Minister Mike O'Brien takes a similar line to official US government policy by arguing that the conflict hinges on the Kharijis, whom he describes as a radical heretical Islamist terrorist group in contrast to Islam itself which he sees as essentially peaceful and lacking in war-like intentions.[5] Likewise, as has been surveyed earlier, many Muslim descriptions of their own faith in the context of war have painted a picture of peace and tolerance, denying that war is central to their faith.

Nevertheless wars continue to be fought in which the name of Islam as a religion is invoked along with the concept of jihad; as has been seen, this reflects the mainstream interpretation of Islamic scholars in the classical period of Islam. A twenty-first century imam, who feels strongly that Islam is oppressed by the tyrannous and unjust governments of the US and Europe, comments:

> We say it proudly that Islam recognizes the near-inevitability of recourse to war.[6]

Islam in its classical interpretation finds it difficult to coexist with the modern world. Such coexistence will remain a challenge unless Islam can examine itself and make modifications. No matter how much is done to improve the socio-economic status of impoverished Muslim populations, no matter how carefully the West tries to avoid causing any kind of "humiliation" which might inflict psychological pain on Muslims, there will still remain reasons for Muslims to wage war on non-Muslims, unless Islam itself can change. How far the Islamic world is capable of coming to terms with its own history, theology and practice is hard to estimate. Typically Islam finds great difficulty in admitting fault or the need for change. However, there are contemporary Muslims who are beginning to face this reality.

Writing in the *Wall Street Journal* Hussain Haqqani, former adviser to Pakistan's prime ministers Benazir Bhutto and Nawaz Sharif, has said:

> Muslims have suffered a great deal from their tendency to shun discussion of ideas, especially those relating to history and religion and their impact on politics. Hard-liners won't tolerate questioning of their views that Islam has nothing to learn from "unbelievers" or that Muslims have a right to subdue other faiths, by force if necessary. The notion of an Islamic polity and state – supported by extremists, questioned by moderates – is also an issue which must be aired.[7]

The same idea has been expressed by other Muslims, particularly in the Saudi press immediately after the suicide attacks there in May 2003.[8] The following two examples were admittedly in the English-language press – not always an accurate reflection of Muslim opinion – but nevertheless are worth quoting.

> Crushing them [the terrorists] will not be enough. The environment that produced such terrorism has to change. The suicide bombers have been encouraged by the venom of anti-Westernism that has seeped through the Middle East's veins, and the Kingdom is no less affected. Those who gloat over September 11, those who happily support suicide bombings in Israel and Russia, those who consider non-Muslims less human than Muslims and therefore somehow disposable, all bear part of the responsibility for the Riyadh bombs.[9]

> The time of pretending that radicalism does not exist in Saudi Arabia is long past. How can we expect others to believe that a majority of us are a peace-loving people who denounce extremism and terrorism when some preachers continue to call for the destruction of Jews and Christians, blaming them for all the misery in the Islamic world?[10]

Similar sentiments appeared in the Arabic-language press as well. For example:

> What many of the official sheikhs and columnists – who do not awaken until a catastrophe occurs – say about the phenomenon does not deal with

the real causes and roots of the ideology of jihad ... Jihad groups find ideological cover in the religious message spread by the mosques and schools.[11]

If Islamic theologians continue to argue a simple two-fold division
of the world into *Dar al-Islam* and *Dar al-Harb*, if they continue to
dehumanize the enemy,[12] if a majority of Muslims continue mean-
while to deny that these things are happening, if western politicians,
media, church leaders and others continue to acquiesce with the
assertion that religion is not a factor in terrorist violence and therefore that Islam need not change, it is difficult to see how peace can
be achieved unless the whole world is under the rule of Islam.

Today's secular West perhaps struggles to take religion seriously,
and finds it difficult to believe there could be wars of religion in
our time. There is a reluctance to take at face value the statements
expressing religious commitment and the priority of religion which
are made by many Muslim leaders, as for example, the following
quote from Pakistan's former president, General Zia-ul-Haq.

> The professional soldier in a Muslim army, pursuing the goals of a
> Muslim state CANNOT become "professional" if in all his activities
> he does not take on " the colour of Allah". The non-military citizen of
> a Muslim state must, likewise, be aware of the kind of soldier that his
> country must produce and the ONLY pattern of war that his country's
> armed forces may wage.[13]

It is relevant to note that the institutional motto of the Pakistani
army is "Iman, Taqwa and Jihad Fi Sabil-Lilah" [Faith, Piety and
Jihad is the way of God].

In this there is nothing new, as Islam has always emphasized the
spiritual aspect of warfare. Ibn Khaldun asserted that military victory depended not only military preparedness but also spiritual
insight, the latter meaning "the dedication of the commander, the
morale of the army, the use of psychological warfare, and informed
and inspired decision-making".[14]

Wars of religion, for example Europe's Thirty Years War (1618-48),
have often had appalling consequences, but to pretend that a religious

war is not a religious war does nothing to ameliorate the situation. Denying reality is no more effective in dealing with danger than the ostrich's strategy of sticking its head in the sand.

Following September 11th 2001, many westerners were eager to make statements dissociating Islam from violence and terrorism, but discovered this argument could not be substantiated. They then tried to argue that although violence and terrorism do occur within Islam they are a mere aberration, not a part of true Islam. This argument likewise was revealed to be invalid. They then tried to distinguish between a moderate Islam and an extremist Islam, but it became apparent that – to echo the words of Jordan's King Abdullah II[15] – there is no such thing as extremist Islam and no such thing as moderate Islam. Islam is one. It has a classical formulation which can be regarded as "the standard" from which a range of variants has developed. Finally it has been acknowledged, at least implicitly by at least some,[16] that violence and terrorism do form an intrinsic part of classical Islam.

Although Islam is one, there is still an important distinction which must be drawn between Islam the ideology and Muslims the people who follow it. While Islam the ideology may cause great hardship and suffering to non-Muslims it also causes great hardship and suffering to many Muslims (particularly women). If an "enemy" is to be defined, then the enemy is not Muslims but the classical interpretation of Islam.

Finding solutions

Having identified the causes of Islamist terrorism, the question remains as to how best to work for peace. Given the easy accessibility of the materials necessary to create weapons of mass destruction (chemical, biological or nuclear), the current growth in radical Islam, and the calls even by moderate Muslim leaders such as Malaysia's then prime minister Mahathir Mohamed for technological advance in weaponry, it is imperative that violence in Islam be addressed.

Obviously there should be no more repetitions of western powers deliberately raising up Islamist terrorists for their own purposes, as the US did in Afghanistan in the 1980s. The American mistake seems to have been that they regarded religion as a neutral force and thought that they could channel religious conviction to serve their own agenda without realising how the Islamist agenda would itself gather momentum from the impetus they had given it. This fundamental mistake has been made by many other governments, who believed that they could use or work with Islamists, not realising the likely future effects of giving assistance to the Islamist cause. The ongoing consequences continue to be seen in events such at September 11th 2001.

In the short term, it is instructive to recall that force has in the past managed to reverse the Islamist expansion, when no other method has been effective. Sheikh Ibn Uthaymeen's reasoning that suicide bombing was not legitimate *because it did not help the Islamic cause* adds further weight to arguments for a physically strong response to Islamist terrorism. A physical response would formerly have meant simply a military response, but in today's world another way physically to limit the activities of Islamic terrorists would be by financial restrictions to prevent the flow of funds to terrorist organisations. Economic power, perhaps in the form of trade sanctions or trade agreements, could also be used to exert force indirectly by encouraging Muslim governments to curtail the activities of radicals and the promulgation of radical ideologies within their borders. Another possibility would be to make security treaties conditional on the protected government implementing certain policies, for example, promoting a more liberal kind of Islam.

However, as already argued, the most realistic way to provide a permanent solution to the problem of Islamist violence in the long term is the reform of the Islamic doctrine of jihad i.e. for one of the peaceable non-classical variations to supersede the classical interpretation and to be acknowledged as the new norm. This would not, of course, mean a complete cessation of all violence from Islamic contexts, but it would mean a cutting of the link between religion and violence. The historic churches like the Church of England are often said to be built on scripture, tradition and reason. So too is Islam, built as it is on Qur'an, *hadith* and *ijtihad*. It is the third factor, reason, which is important in ameliorating the more strident aspects of scripture and particularly of tradition, and which must be encouraged within Islam, provided always that it leads to a more liberal interpretation of the sources.

Islam takes great pride in the concept of the *umma*, the whole body of Muslims worldwide. The received wisdom is that Islam displays a unity and cohesion that gives it immense strength. This was certainly what the Byzantine armies experienced when they found to their surprise that their normal tactic of inducing some of their Arab enemies to defect no longer worked now that those Arabs had become Muslims. But the idea of Muslim unity continuing throughout the succeeding centuries is very much open to question. Modern Muslims tend to believe that any tensions within the *umma* are a result of western conspiracy despite the fact that, as this book has sought to show, there is a huge range of theological differences within Islam, not to mention ethnic and national differences.[17] Furthermore Islamic history contains many examples of distinctions drawn within the *umma* right from the beginning. Even during Muhammad's lifetime, there was a distinction made between the Muslims who had moved from Mecca to Medina with him (*muhajirun*) and the Muslims who were native-born Medinan (*ansar* [helpers]).[18] The *umma* was not so much a super-tribal loyalty but rather the domination of the other Arab tribes by the Quraish, the tribe to which Muhammad and the first Muslims belonged.[19] Islamic history has been characterised by inter-ethnic (Arabs, Turks, Persians) and inter-sectarian (Sunni-Shi'a) conflicts. Indeed, some scholars, such as van Ess, assert that the *umma* concept had little significance in early Islam and has gained its current importance only in recent times.[20]

Arab Islam is dominant in the Muslim world today and is generally considered normative. This is due to the fact that the heavenly original of the Qur'an is believed to be written in Arabic and to the fact that Muhammad and the first Muslims were Arabs. Increasingly, the issues facing the Arab world (such as the Palestinian issue) are shaping the non-Arab Muslim world as well, and arguably are reinforcing the classical doctrine of jihad. Left to its own devices, and without the constant stimulus of Arab grudges, non-Arab Islam might develop a more peaceable doctrine. Indonesian Islam did so, as manifested by the Indonesian doctrine of Pancasila which drew on China and India as well as the Middle East to provide a range of acceptable religious beliefs, both Muslim and non-Muslim. Current moves to impose Middle Eastern Islam (that is, classical Islam) as the standard in places like Indonesia are creating tensions with non-Muslim minorities in societies which had previously enjoyed inter-communal harmony. It is also creating tensions with those Muslims who reject the Arab Islamic norm.

What the West can do

If the West wants to assist in the promotion of a non-violent kind of Islam, it must do so with great care or its well-meant efforts could be counter-productive. When Mike O'Brien argued that Islamist violence is rooted in a radical heretical movement, the Kharijis, his comments were opposed by some in the Middle East who pleaded with him not to promote that interpretation. What O'Brien did not realise was that making culprits of the Kharijis has given them enormous credibility with certain sections of the Muslim community in the Muslim world. The Kharijis have become a focal point for dissent in the Middle East. The Khariji paradigm is now used to justify violent opposition to legitimate Muslim rulers who are deemed to be autocratic, corrupt or in cahoots with the West.

Another potential pitfall for western efforts to foster nonviolent forms of Islam is exemplified by Sir Syed Ahmed Khan in India. While he was happy to cooperate with and submit to British rule in the nineteenth century, other Muslims have bitterly criticised him for this. For example Jamal al-Din al-Afghani (1838-97) wrote in his *Al-Urwah Al-Wuthqa*:

The English authorities saw in Sir Sayyid Ahmad Khan a useful instrument to demoralize the Muslims so they began to praise and honour him and helped him build his college at Aligarh and called it the college of the Muslims in order that it be a trap to catch the sons of the believers and spread unbelief amongst them. Materialists like Sir Sayyid Ahmad Khan are even worse than the materialists in Europe for those in Western countries who abandon their religion still retain their patriotism and do not lack zeal to defend their fatherland while Sir Sayyid Ahmad Khan and his friends represent foreign despotism as acceptable.[21]

The French authorities would do well to ponder this reaction by Muslims to British efforts in India. In 2003 the French government created a national council of Muslims to represent the country's five million Muslims before the French state. The aim was to combat what the Interior Minister Nicolas Sarkozy described as "the Islam of cellars and garages that has fed extremism and the language of violence" and create "an official Islam for France".[22] This strategy of trying to enlist cooperative Muslims in promoting a submissive, non-violent type of Islam is in many ways similar to what Britain tried to do with Sir Syed Ahmed Khan, and which provoked such strong resentment. Perhaps the French authorities should not have been as surprised as they were when the first elections for the new council, held in April 2003, resulted in a large number of seats for Islamist extremists.[23] The mere fact of being a non-Muslim initiative can doom such a plan to failure from the start.

The part which the non-Muslim world can play in the reform of Islam can therefore never be more than indirect. Ultimately it is for the Muslim world to address the issues and consider what changes can be brought about. Reform cannot be imposed on Islam from outside. A Saudi security expert has stated clearly that it is not for the West to try to change the Muslim world; any movement for change must come from within Muslims themselves.[24] His opinion is typical. But non-Muslims can, with great care, wisdom and diplomacy, help to create an atmosphere conducive to finding a solution. Part of this would be simply to refrain from undermining the stance of liberal Muslims i.e. to refrain from making statements to the effect that Islam is already wholly peaceable and does not need to be reformed. More positively, another part would be supporting efforts towards growth in mutual understanding – non-Muslims beginning to grasp the reality of Islam and how different it is from secular materialism as well as from Judaeo-Christian traditions, and Muslims beginning to understand the basis of democracy, individual freedom of conscience and other values which are so alien to classical Islam. The importance of non-Muslims using appropriate, sensitive and tactful language cannot be overestimated; great damage can and has been done by careless and insensitive comments and vocabulary, indicative of a lack of understanding of cultural and religious factors.

Consideration of effective methodology to promote a new doctrine of jihad side-steps the most important question of all: what should that new doctrine be? At one extreme would be pacifism, but that would be to impose on Islam a restraint which mainstream Christianity has never imposed on itself in its standard teaching on just war. So where should the boundaries be drawn? Self-defence? But how would that be defined? Is there any place for the concept of *Dar al-Harb*? Can peace treaties with non-Muslims be permanent? What about the conduct of war? Civilian casualties seem to have become an intrinsic part of modern warfare, so what should Islam say about this today? It is the author's hope that the right use of force of various kinds, coupled with good diplomacy, may nudge the Islamic world forward into a debate on this subject, leading to a reformation of this area of Islamic teaching, and thus to a more peaceful and stable world.

Appendix 1: Traditional Divisions in Islam

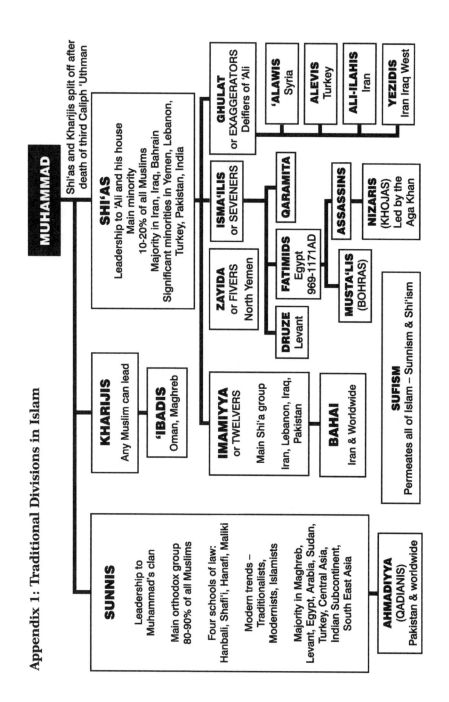

Appendix 2: Modern trends in Islam

Pre-modern revivals –
Sirihindi (India 1564-1624), 'Abd-Al-Wahhab (Arabia 1703-1792)

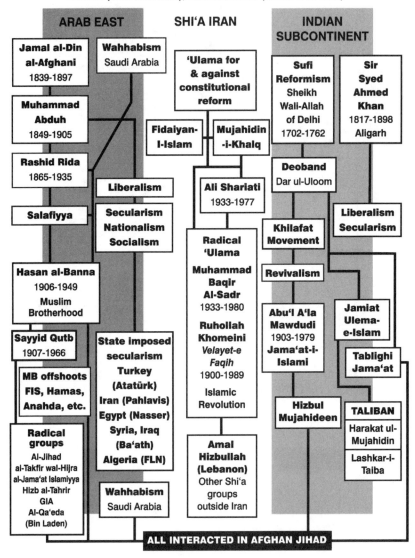

ARAB EAST

Jamal al-Din al-Afghani 1839-1897

Wahhabism Saudi Arabia

Muhammad Abduh 1849-1905

Rashid Rida 1865-1935

Salafiyya

Liberalism

Secularism Nationalism Socialism

Hasan al-Banna 1906-1949 Muslim Brotherhood

Sayyid Qutb 1907-1966

MB offshoots FIS, Hamas, Anahda, etc.

State imposed secularism Turkey (Atatürk) Iran (Pahlavis) Egypt (Nasser) Syria, Iraq (Ba'ath) Algeria (FLN)

Radical groups Al-Jihad al-Takfir wal-Hijra al-Jama'at Islamiyya Hizb al-Tahrir GIA Al-Qa'eda (Bin Laden)

Wahhabism Saudi Arabia

SHI'A IRAN

'Ulama for & against constitutional reform

Fidaiyan-I-Islam

Mujahidin-i-Khalq

Ali Shariati 1933-1977

Radical 'Ulama

Muhammad Baqir Al-Sadr 1933-1980

Ruhollah Khomeini *Velayet-e Faqih* 1900-1989 Islamic Revolution

Amal Hizbullah (Lebanon) Other Shi'a groups outside Iran

INDIAN SUBCONTINENT

Sufi Reformism Sheikh Wali-Allah of Delhi 1702-1762

Sir Syed Ahmed Khan 1817-1898 Aligarh

Deoband Dar ul-Uloom

Liberalism Secularism

Khilafat Movement

Revivalism

Abu'l A'la Mawdudi 1903-1979 Jama'at-i-Islami

Jamiat Ulema-e-Islam

Tablighi Jama'at

Hizbul Mujahideen

TALIBAN Harakat ul-Mujahidin

Lashkar-i-Taiba

ALL INTERACTED IN AFGHAN JIHAD

Appendix 3: Various networks of radical Islam (brackets link similar groups)

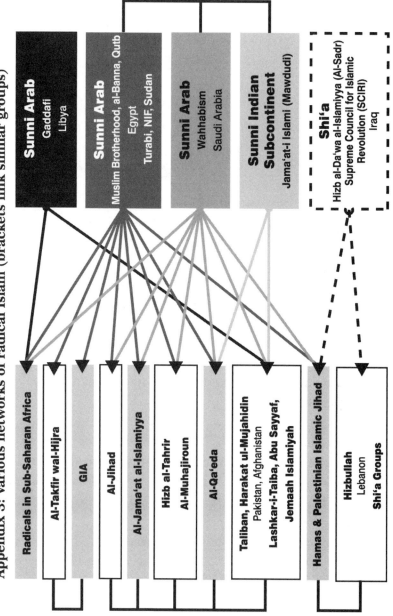

Appendix 4: "Bin Laden" Audiotape

This is a translated transcript of an audiotape said to be of Osama bin Laden, aired by al-Jazeera satellite television channel on 4 January 2004, text published by BBC news.[1]

From Osama Bin Laden to his brothers and sisters in the entire Islamic nation: May God's peace, mercy and blessings be upon you.

My message to you concerns inciting and continuing to urge for jihad to repulse the grand plots that have been hatched against our nation, especially since some of them have appeared clearly, such as the occupation of the Crusaders, with the help of the apostates, of Baghdad and the house of the Caliphate, under the trick of weapons of mass destruction.

There is also the fierce attempt to destroy the al-Aqsa Mosque and destroy the jihad and the *mujahideen* in beloved Palestine by employing the trick of the roadmap and the Geneva peace initiative.

The Americans' intentions have also become clear in statements about the need to change the beliefs, curricula and morals of the Muslims to become more tolerant, as they put it.

In clearer terms, it is a religious-economic war.

The occupation of Iraq is a link in the Zionist-Crusader chain of evil.

Gulf states 'next'

Then comes the full occupation of the rest of the Gulf states to set the stage for controlling and dominating the whole world. For the big powers believe that the Gulf and the Gulf states are the key to controlling the world due to the presence of the largest oil reserves there.

O Muslims: The situation is serious and the misfortune is momentous. By God, I am keen on safeguarding your religion and your worldly life. So, lend me your ears and open up your hearts to me so that we may examine these pitch-black misfortunes and so that we may consider how we can find a way out of these adversities and calamities.

The West's occupation of our countries is old, yet new. The struggle between us and them, the confrontation, and clashing began centuries ago, and will continue because the ground rules regarding the fight between right and falsehood will remain valid until Judgment Day.

Take note of this ground rule regarding this fight. There can be no dialogue with occupiers except through arms.

This is what we need today, and what we should seek. Islamic countries in the past century were not liberated from the Crusaders' military occupation except through jihad in the cause of God.

Under the pretext of fighting terrorism, the West today is doing its utmost to tarnish jihad and kill anyone seeking jihad. The West is supported in this endeavour by hypocrites. This is because they all know that jihad is the effective power to foil all their conspiracies.

Jihad is the path, so seek it. This is because if we seek to deter them with any means other than Islam, we would be like the one who goes round in circles. We would also be like our forefathers, the al-Ghasasinah [Arab people who lived in a state historically located in the north-west of the Persian empire]. The concern of their seniors was to be appointed officers for the Romans and to be named kings in order to safeguard the interests of the Romans by killing their brothers of the peninsula's Arabs. Such is the case of the new al-Ghasasinah; namely, Arab rulers.

Words of warning

Muslims: If you do not punish them for their sins in Jerusalem and Iraq, they shall defeat you because of your failure. They will also rob you of land of *al-Haramayn* [Mecca and Medina]. Today [they robbed you] of Baghdad and tomorrow they will rob you of Riyadh and so forth unless God deems otherwise.

Sufficient unto us is God.

What then is the means to stop this tremendous onslaught? In such hard times, some reformers maintain that all popular and official forces should unite and that all government forces should unite with all their peoples. Everyone would do what is needed from him in order to ward off this Crusader-Zionist onslaught.

The question strongly raised is: Are the governments in the Islamic world capable of pursuing this duty of defending the faith and nation and renouncing allegiance to the United States?

The calls by some reformers are strange. They say that the path to righteousness and defending the country and people passes though the doors of those rulers. I tell those reformers: If you have an excuse for not pursing jihad, it does not give you the right to depend on the unjust ones, thus becoming responsible for your sins as well as the sins of those who you misguide.

Fear God for your sake and for your nation's sake.

God does not need your flattery of dictators for the sake of God's religion.

Arabs 'succumbed to US pressure'

The Gulf states proved their total inability to resist the Iraqi forces. They sought help from the Crusaders, led by the United States, as is well known. How can these states stand up to the United States? In short, these states came to America's help and backed it in its attack against an Arab state which is bound to them with covenants of joint defence agreements. These covenants were reiterated at the Arab League just a few days before the US attack, only to violate them in full. This shows their positions on the nation's basic causes.

These regimes wavered too much before taking a stand on using force and attacking Iraq. At times they absolutely rejected participation and at other times they linked this with UN agreement. Then they went back to their first option. In fact, the lack of participation was in line with the domestic desire of these states. However, they finally submitted and succumbed to US pressure and opened their air, land and sea bases to contribute toward the US campaign, despite the immense repercussions of this move.

Most important of these repercussions is that this is a sin against one of the Islamic tenets.

Saddam arrest

Most important and dangerous in their view was that they feared that the door would be open for bringing down dictatorial regimes by armed forces from abroad, especially after they had seen the arrest of their former comrade in treason and agentry to the United States when it ordered him to ignite the first Gulf war against Iran, which rebelled against it.

The war consumed everything and plunged the area in a maze from which they have not emerged to this day. They are aware that their turn will come. They do not have the will to make the difficult decision to confront the aggression, in addition to their belief that they do not possess the material resources for that. Indeed, they were prevented from establishing a large military force when they were forced to sign secret pledges and documents long ago. In short, the ruler who believes in some of the above-mentioned deeds cannot defend the country. How can he do so if he believes in all of them and has done that time and again?

Those who believe in the principle of supporting the infidels over Muslims and leave the blood, honour and property of their brothers to be available to their enemy in order to remain safe, claiming that they love their brothers but are being forced to take such a path - of course this compulsion cannot be regarded as legitimate - are in fact qualified to take the same course against one another in the

Gulf states. Indeed, this principle is liable to be embraced within the same state itself.

Those who read and understood the history of kings throughout history know that they are capable of committing more than these concessions, except those who enjoyed the mercy of God. Indeed, the rulers have practically started to sell out the sons of the land by pursuing and imprisoning them and by unjustly and wrongly accusing them of becoming like the *Khawarij* [Kharijis] sect who held Muslims to be infidels and by committing the excesses of killing them. We hold them to be martyrs and God will judge them.

All of this happened before the Riyadh explosions in Rabi al-Awwal of this year [around May 2003].

This campaign came within a drive to implement the US orders in the hope that they will win its blessings.

'Miserable situation'

Based on the above, the extent of the real danger, which the region in general and the Arabian Peninsula in particular, is being exposed to, has appeared. It has become clear that the rulers are not qualified to apply the religion and defend the Muslims. In fact, they have provided evidence that they are implementing the schemes of the enemies of the nation and religion and that they are qualified to abandon the countries and peoples.

Now, after we have known the situation of the rulers, we should examine the policy which they have been pursuing. Anyone who examines the policy of those rulers will easily see that they follow their whims and desires and their personal interests and Crusader loyalties.

Therefore, the flaw does not involve a secondary issue, such as personal corruption that is confined to the palace of the ruler. The flaw is in the very approach.

This happened when a malicious belief and destructive principle spread in most walks of life, to the effect that absolute supremacy and obedience were due to the ruler and not to the religion of God.

In other countries, they have used the guise of parliaments and democracy.

Thus, the situation of all Arab countries suffers from great deterioration in all walks of life, in religious and worldly matters.

We have reached this miserable situation because many of us lack the correct and comprehensive understanding of the religion of Islam. Many of us understand Islam to mean performing some acts of worship, such as prayer and fasting. Despite the great importance of these rituals, the religion of Islam encompasses all the affairs of life, including religious and worldly affairs, such as economic, military and political affairs, as well as the scales by which we weigh the actions of men – rulers, *ulama* and others – and how to deal with the ruler in line with the rules set by God for him and which the ruler should not violate.

Therefore, it becomes clear to us that the solution lies in adhering to the religion of God, by which God granted us pride in the past centuries and installing a strong and faithful leadership that applies the Qur'an among us and raises the true banner of jihad.

The honest people who are concerned about this situation, such as the *ulama*, leaders who are obeyed among their people, dignitaries, notables and merchants should get together and meet in a safe place away from the shadow of these suppressive regimes and form a council for *Ahl al-Hall wa al-'aqd* [literally those who loose and bind; reference to honest, wise and righteous people who can appoint or remove a ruler in Islamic tradition] to fill the vacuum caused by the religious invalidation of these regimes and their mental deficiency.

The right to appoint an imam [leader] is for the nation.

The nation also has the right to make him correct his course if he deviates from it and to remove him if he does something that warrants this, such as apostasy and treason.

This temporary council should be made up of the minimum number of available personnel, without [word indistinct] the rest of the nation, except what the religion allows in case of necessity, until the number is increased when the situation improves, God willing.

Their policy should be based on the book of God [the Qur'an] and the *sunna* [customs] of his Prophet [Muhammad], God's peace and blessings be upon him. They should start by directing the Muslims to the important priorities at this critical stage and lead them to a safe haven, provided that their top priority should be uniting opinions under the word of monotheism and defending Islam and its people and countries and declaring a general mobilisation in the nation to prepare for repulsing the raids of the Romans, which started in Iraq and no-one knows where they will end.

God suffices us and he is the best supporter.

Appendix 5: Editorial in *Al-Masaa*

Al-Masaa is an Egyptian government daily newspaper. This editorial was published on 2 February 2004 and supports Palestinian suicide attacks, even if children are killed. The English translation is from MEMRI Special Dispatch No. 658 (6 February 2004)

We ask again, why do the various Palestinian organizations insist on publishing the name of everyone who carries out a martyrdom operation against the Zionist entity?

We have no argument regarding the question of the legitimacy of these operations, because they are considered a powerful weapon used by the Palestinians against an enemy with no morality or religion, [an enemy] who has deadly weapons prohibited by international law, that is not deterred from using them against the defenseless Palestinian people.

Even if during [a martyrdom operation] civilians or children are killed – the blame does not fall upon the Palestinians, but on those who forced them to turn to this *modus operandi.*

Ultimately, we should bless every Palestinian man or woman who goes calmly to carry out a martyrdom operation, in order to receive a reward in the Hereafter, sacrificing her life for her religion and her homeland and knowing that she will never return from this operation.

But at the same time, we wonder about the reason for publishing the names of those who carry out the [martyrdom] operations; [this publishing] is a valuable gift that the Palestinian resistance gives the

Zionist entity, since as soon as it receives this gift, the armies of the [Zionist] entity hasten to the home of the martyr's family, wounded by the loss of its son, in order to multiply its pain by destroying its home. Moreover, the home of the martyr's family is always destroyed negligently, causing serious damage to or the collapse of the neighbour's home.

We ask the leaders of these organizations: Give us one good reason for publishing the names of the martyrs whom, it can be assumed, martyred themselves for the religion, the homeland, and the people, and not for any other reason. The Lebanese resistance published [the names of] those who took this path during the years of the Zionist occupation [in Lebanon] without any logical justification. We were surprised that the Palestinian resistance is employing the same method, also without any justification.

This is even though the situation is different, as the *shahids* in the case of Lebanon, such as Sanaa Muheidali and other women, lived in territories not under the control of the Zionist occupation, while in the Palestinian case, [they live under Zionist occupation].

Appendix 6: The Zarqawi Document

This document was captured in Baghdad and released by the US authorities, who believe it to have been written by Abu Musab al-Zarqawi, a Jordanian suspected of close ties with Al-Qaʿeda and of involvement in terrorist attacks in Iraq.

The document was initially obtained by a Kurdish militia, which had captured a courier named Hassan Ghul, who confessed that he was taking the document from Ansar al-Islam, a group affiliated with Al-Qaʿeda that had been supported by Saddam Hussein, to Al-Qaʿeda operatives.

The existence of the document was first reported by Dexter Filkins of The New York Times *on 10 February 2004. The document itself is undated.*

1. The foreign *mujahidin*

Their numbers continue to be small, compared to the large nature of the expected battle. We know that there are enough good groups and jihad is continuing, despite the negative rumours. What is preventing us from making a general call to arms is the fact that the country of Iraq has no mountains in which to seek refuge, or forest in which to hide. Our presence is apparent and our movement is out in the open. Eyes are everywhere. The enemy is before us and the sea is behind us. Many Iraqis would honour you as a guest and give you refuge, for you are a Muslim brother; however, they will not allow you to make their homes a base for operations or a safe house. People who will allow you to do such things are very rare, rarer than

187

red sulphur. Therefore, it has been extremely difficult to lodge and keep safe a number of brothers, and also train new recruits. Praise be to Allah, however, with relentless effort and searching we have acquired some places and their numbers are increasing, to become base points for the brothers who will spark war and bring the people of this country into a real battle with God's will.

2. The present and future

There is no doubt that American losses were significant because they are spread thin amongst the people and because it is easy to get weapons. This is a fact that makes them easy targets, attractive for the believers. America, however, has no intention of leaving, no matter how many wounded nor how bloody it becomes. It is looking to a near future, when it will remain safe in its bases, while handing over control of Iraq to a bastard government with an army and police force that will bring back the time of [Saddam] Hussein and his cohorts. There is no doubt that our field of movement is shrinking and the grip around the throat of the *mujahidin* has begun to tighten. With the spread of the army and police, our future is becoming frightening.

3. So where are we?

Despite few supporters, lack of friends, and tough times, God has blessed us with victories against the enemy. We were involved in all the martyrdom operations – in terms of overseeing, preparing, and planning – that took place in this country except for the operations that took place in the north. Praise be to Allah, I have completed 25 of these operations, some of them against the Shi'a and their leaders, the Americans and their military, the police, the military, and the coalition forces. There will be more in the future, God willing. We did not want to publicly claim these operations until we become more powerful and were ready for the consequences. We need to show up strong and avoid getting hurt, now that we have made great strides and taken important steps forward. As we get closer to the decisive moment, we feel that our entity is spreading within the security void existing in Iraq, something that will allow us to secure bases on the ground; these bases that will be the jump start of a serious revival, God willing.

4. Plan of action

After much inquiry and discussion, we have narrowed our enemy to four groups:

A. Americans

As you know, these are the biggest cowards that God has created and the easiest target. And we ask God to allow us to kill, and detain them, so that we can exchange them with our arrested sheikhs and brothers.

B. Kurds

These are a pain and a thorn, and it is not time yet to deal with them. They are last on our list, even though we are trying to get to some of their leaders. God willing.

C. The Iraqi troops, police, and agents

These are the eyes, ears, and hand of the occupier. With God's permission, we are determined to target them with force in the near future, before their power strengthens.

D. The Shi'a

In our opinion, these are the key to change. Targeting and striking their religious, political and military symbols, will make them show their rage against the Sunnis and bare their inner vengeance. If we succeed in dragging them into a sectarian war, this will awaken the sleepy Sunnis who are fearful of destruction and death at the hands of these Sabeans, i.e., the Shi'a. Despite their weakness, the Sunnis are strong-willed and honest and different from the coward and deceitful Shi'a, who only attack the weak. Most of the Sunnis are aware of the danger of these people and they fear them. If it were not for those disappointing sheikhs, Sufis, and Muslim brothers, Sunnis would have a different attitude.

5. Way of action

As we have mentioned to you, our situation demands that we treat the issue with courage and clarity. So the solution, and God only knows, is that we need to bring the Shi'a into the battle because it is the only way to prolong the duration of the fight between the infidels and us. We need to do that because:

A. The Shi'a have declared a subtle war against Islam. They are the close, dangerous enemy of the Sunnis. Even if the Americans are also an archenemy, the Shi'a are a greater danger and their harm more destructive to the nation than that of the Americans who are anyway the original enemy by consensus.

B. They have supported the Americans, helped them, and stand with them against the *mujahidin*. They work and continue to work towards the destruction of the *mujahidin*.

C. Fighting the Shi'a is the way to take the nation to battle. The Shi'a have taken on the dress of the army, police, and the Iraqi security forces, and have raised the banner of protecting the nation and the citizens. Under this banner, they have begun to assassinate the Sunnis under the pretence that they are saboteurs, vestiges of the Ba'ath, or terrorists who spread perversion in the country. This is being done with strong media support directed by the Governing Council and the Americans, and they have succeeded in splitting the regular Sunni from the *mujahidin*. For example, in what they call the Sunni triangle, the army and police are spreading out in these regions, putting in charge Sunnis from the same region. Therefore, the problem is you end up having an army and police connected by lineage, blood, and appearance to the people of the region. This region is our base of operations from where we depart and to where we return. When the Americans withdraw, and they have already started doing that, they get replaced by these agents who are intimately linked to the people of this region. What will happen to us, if we fight them, and we have to fight them, is one of only two choices:

i) If we fight them, that will be difficult because there will be a schism between us and the people of the region. How can we kill their cousins and sons and under what pretext, after the Americans start withdrawing? The Americans will continue to control from their bases, but the sons of this land will be the authority. This is the democracy, we will have no pretext.

ii) We can pack up and leave and look for another land, just like it has happened in so many lands of jihad. Our enemy is growing stronger day after day, and its intelligence information increases. By God, this is suffocation! We will be on the roads again.

People follow their leaders, their hearts may be with you, but their swords are with their kings. So I say again, the only solution is to strike the religious, military, and other cadres of the Shi'a so that they revolt against the Sunnis. Some people will say that this will be a reckless and irresponsible action that will bring the Islamic nation to a battle for which the Islamic nation is unprepared. Souls will perish and blood will be spilled. This is, however, exactly what we want, as there is nothing to win or lose in our situation. The Shi'a destroyed the balance, and the religion of God is worth more than lives. Until the majority stands up for the truth, we have to make sacrifices for this religion, and blood has to be spilled. For those who are good, we will speed up their trip to paradise, and the others, we will get rid of them. By God, the religion of God is more precious than anything else. We have many rounds, attacks, and black nights with the Shi'a, and we cannot delay this. Their menace is looming and this is a fact that we should not fear, because they are the most cowardly people God has created. Killing their leaders will weaken them and with the death of the head, the whole group dies. They are not like the Sunnis. If you knew the fear in the souls of the Sunnis and their people, you would weep in sadness. How many of the mosques have they have turned into Shi'a mosques ("husayniyas")? How many houses they have destroyed with their owners inside? How many brothers have they killed? How many sisters have been raped at the hands of those vile infidels? If we are able to deal them blow after painful blow so that they engage in a battle, we will be able to reshuffle the cards so there will remain no value or influence for the ruling council, or even for the Americans who will enter into a second battle with the Shi'a. This is what we want. Then the Sunni will have no choice but to support us in many of the Sunni regions.

When the *mujahidin* have secured a land they can use as a base to hit the Shi'a inside their own lands, with a directed media and a strategic action, there will be a continuation between the *mujahidin* inside and outside of Iraq. We are racing against time, in order to create squads of *mujahidin* who seek refuge in secure places, spy on neighbourhoods, and work on hunting down the enemies. The enemies are the Americans, police, and army. We have been training these people and augmenting their numbers. As far as the Shi'a, we will undertake suicide operations and use car bombs to harm them. We have been working on monitoring the area and choosing the right people, looking for those who are on the straight path, so we can cooperate with them.

We hope that we have made progress, and perhaps we will soon decide to go public – even if gradually – to display ourselves in full view. We have been hiding for a long time, and now we are seriously working on preparing a media outlet to reveal the truth, enflame zeal, and become an outlet for jihad in which the sword and the pen can turn into one. Along with this, we strive to illuminate the hindering errors of Islamic law and the clarifications of

Islamic legal precepts by way of tapes, lessons, and courses which people will come to understand.

The suggested time for execution: we are hoping that we will soon start working on creating squads and brigades of individuals who have experience and expertise. We have to get to the zero-hour in order to openly begin controlling the land by night and after that by day, God willing. The zero-hour needs to be at least four months before the new government gets in place. As we see we are racing time, and if we succeed, which we are hoping, we will turn the tables on them and thwart their plan. If, God forbid, the government is successful and takes control of the country, we just have to pack up and go somewhere else again, where we can raise the flag again or die, if God chooses us.

6. What about you?

You, noble brothers, leaders of jihad, we do not consider ourselves those who would compete against you, nor would we ever aim to achieve glory for ourselves like you did. The only thing we want is to be the head of the spear, assisting and providing a bridge over which the Muslim nation can cross to promised victory and a better tomorrow.

As we have explained, this is our belief. So if you agree with it and are convinced of the idea of killing the perverse sects, we stand ready as an army for you, to work under your guidance and yield to your command. Indeed, we openly and publicly swear allegiance to you by using the media, in order to exasperate the infidels and confirm to the adherents of faith that one day, the believers will revel in God's victory. If you think otherwise, we will remain brothers, and disagreement will not destroy our cooperation and undermine our working together for what is best. We support jihad and wait for your response. May God keep for you the keys of goodness and preserve Islam and his people. Amen, amen.

Glossary

'Abbasid – the second dynasty of Sunni caliphs, based in Baghdad. c.f. Ummayad

Ahl al-Kitab – literally "the People of the Book" i.e. those who have their own revealed scriptures. The term is applied to Jews, Christians, Sabeans [followers of John the Baptist] and sometimes Zoroastrians.

Ahmadi – member of the Ahmadiyya sect

Ahmadiyya – a Muslim sect, originating in nineteenth century India, regarded as extremely heretical by other Muslims

aman – temporary safe-conduct granted to non-Muslims who want to enter *Dar al-Islam* e.g. to trade

ansar – literally "helpers". Native-born Medinan Muslims. c.f. *muhajirun*

'aqd - literally "tie". An agreement. A meeting of minds on a certain act with the object of creating legal consequences

Assassins – an Isma'ili sect (active 1090-1256) whose devotees practised suicide assassinations

al-Azhar University, Cairo – the leading scholarly institution of Sunni Islam

Banu an-Nadir – a Jewish tribe living in the Arabian peninusula in Muhammad's time

Banu Hanifa – an Arab tribe of Muhammad's time, partly pagan and partly Christian

Banu Qurayza – a Jewish tribe living in Medina who were exterminated when Muhammad had all the men killed

Banu Taghlib – a Christian Arab tribe of Muhammad's time

batini – inner, estoric

bay'a – the act of swearing allegiance and obedience to a religious or political leader

beyanname-i cihad – declaration of war [Turkish]

Byzantium – the city later known as Constantinople and now called Istanbul. The Byzantine Empire began in 330 as the Eastern Roman Empire and then evolved into a distinctive medieval Eurasian-Christian civilisation with Byzantium the centre of eastern Orthodox Christianity.

caliph – the Sunni title for the supreme ruler of the Muslim community c.f. imam

Chalcedonian – refers to the doctrine, affirmed at the Council of Chalcedon in 451, that the divine nature and the human nature are united in Christ unconfusedly but indivisibly. c.f. Monophysite and Monthelete

Dajjal – the Anti-Christ

Dar al-'Ahd – House of Treaty

Dar al-Harb – literally "house of war". Classical Islam's term for territory not under Islamic rule

Dar al-Islam – literally "house of Islam" i.e. territory under Islamic rule

Dar al-Sulh – house of truce

Dar ash-Shahada – house of testimony

Deobandi – radical movement very influential in south Asia and Afghanistan. Rejects all western influence and seeks to return to classical Islam. In recent years has become militant.

dervish – a member of one of many Sufi brotherhoods or orders. Their spirituality is characterised by seeking a state of ecstasy by dancing, whirling, repeating a name of God or other methods.

devshirme – the forced levy of Christian boys for the Janissaries

dhimma – literally "protected". The status of Jews, Christians and Sabeans in an Islamic state. They were permitted to live and keep their own faith, in return for payment of *jizya* and adherence to various demeaning regulations.

dhimmi – those with *dhimma* status

diya – financial compensation for homicide or injury

fard – obligation, duty

Fatimids – Isma'ili dynasty based in Cairo, ruling from 969 to 1171.

fatwa – an authoritative statement on a point of Islamic law

fay' – property taken from non-Muslims without fighting, which went to the state treasury

fida'iyun – literally "men of sacrifice", people who give up their life for a cause. This term was used for adherents of the Assassin sect who went on suicide missions.

fi sabil illah – in the way of God

fitna – rebellion, sedition, disorder, schism, civil strife. The "great *fitna*" was the period of conflict within the Muslim community (656-661) when it divided into three sects.

Gazâ – Turkish term for holy war on behalf of Islam

ghazi – literally "one who takes part in a ghazwa". Fighter for the faith

ghazwa – inter-tribal raid, much practised in pre-Islamic Arabia. Often called "razzia"

hadith – traditions recording what Muhammad and his early followers said and did. Some are considered more authentic and reliable than others. c.f. *sunna*

Hanafi – a Sunni school of Shari'ah, founded by Imam abu Hanifa (d.767)

Hanbali – a Sunni school of Shari'ah, founded by Imam Ahmad ibn Hanbal (d.855)

Haramayn – Mecca and Medina

harb – war

hedaya – guidance

Hidden Imam – according to Shi'a Islam, the twelfth Imam who went into hiding in 873 AD and is believed to be still alive, one day to return as the Mahdi.

hijra – emigration (of Muslims from Mecca to Medina in 622)

hudna – temporary peace treaty with a non-Muslim nation

hurub al-ridda – wars of apostasy (632-4)

'Ibadis – a modern-day sect descended from the Kharijis, found in Oman, East Africa and North Africa. Berber-speaking 'Ibadis in Algeria are called Mzabis.

idha'ah – open propagation of beliefs, the opposite of *taqiyya*

ijma' – the consensus of Muslim scholars on any given subject. Used in *ijtihad*.

ijtihad – the process of logical deduction on a legal or theological question, using the Qur'an and *hadith* as sources, which created the Shari'ah

Ikhwan – brethren (plural of *akh* "brother"). In the context of Saudi Arabia refers to a religious and military brotherhood which played an important part in the unification of the Arabian Peninsula under Ibn Sa'ud in the early decades of the twentieth century. The Ikhwan were recruited from nomadic tribesmen and then, in order to break their tribal allegiances and force them to abandon their nomadic lifestyle, were settled in pan-tribal military cantonments around oases to farm the land.

ikrahiyya – enforced *taqiyya*, to save one's life

imam – the Shi'a term for the supreme ruler of the Muslim community (equivalent to the Sunni caliph). The same term is used by Sunni Muslims to mean the prayer leader at a local mosque, similar to a Christian parish priest.

intifada – literally "a throwing off". Used of the Palestinian uprising against Israeli occupation.

intizar – waiting for the Hidden Imam

'Isa – Jesus

Islamism – the term preferred by Muslims to describe what is often called by others "Islamic fundamentalism" or "political Islam", i.e. a form of Islam characterised by zeal, activism and above all a desire to follow the Shari'ah in minute detail. Violent methods may often be used. (The adjectival form is "Islamist".)

Isma'ilis – a secretive Shi'a sect who infiltrated normal Muslim society. Also called "Seveners". Today they are found mainly in India and Pakistan.

istishad – martyrdom

jahiliyya – the time of ignorance (meaning before Islam), especially pre-Islamic Arabia

Janissaries – elite troops in the Ottoman Empire, comprised of young Christian boys who had been forcibly taken from their families, converted to Islam and trained for war

jihad – literally "striving". The term has a variety of interpretations including (1) spiritual struggle for moral purity (2) trying to correct wrong and support right by voice and actions (3) military war against non-Muslims with the aim of spreading Islam.

jihad-e-asghar – lesser jihad, often used to mean military jihad

jihad-e-akbar – greater jihad, often used to mean spiritual struggle

jizya – a tax payable by non-Muslims (Jews, Christians and Sabeans) within an Islamic state. Various practices designed to humiliate the payer were associated with this tax.

Ka'ba – literally "cube". The large cubic stone which stands in the centre of the Grand Mosque at Mecca. Muslims face the *ka'ba* when praying.

kaffara – atonement, making amends

kafir – infidel i.e. non-Muslim. This is a term of gross insult. (pl. *kafirun* or *kuffar*) c.f. *kufr*

khandaq – trench or ditch

Kharijis – literally "seceders". A puritanical sect of Islam with a highly developed doctrine of sin. Sinners were considered apostates. The sect began in 657 as a result of disputes over the succession to the caliphate, and continued to rebel against the caliphate for two centuries. They survive today in a more moderate variant, the 'Ibadis. (Arabic sing. *khariji*, Arabic pl. *khawarij*)

khawfiyya – precautionary *taqiyya* e.g. Shi'a Muslims performing Sunni acts and rituals in Sunni countries

Khilafat movement – a movement which tried to preserve the status of the Sultan of Turkey as Caliph (1919-1924)

Khudai Khidmatgaran – literally "Servants of God". A non-violent Pathan movement of the 1930s seeking a political voice in north-west British India. Nicknamed the "Red-Shirts"

kitmaniyya – arcane *taqiyya*, to conceal one's beliefs as well as the number and strength of one's co-religionists, and to carry out clandestine activities to further religious goals.

kufr – unbelief c.f. *kafir*

madrassa – Islamic religious school

Mahdi – the awaited End Time deliverer

Majalla – the Ottoman Civil Code, an 1877 compilation of rules and guidelines from the Hanafi School of Shari'ah, intended to be used as a reference text for state court judges untrained in "finding" the law in traditional Hanafi texts. Certain sections are still applicable in Palestinian courts today.

majlis al-shura – consultative council

Maliki – a Sunni school of Shari'ah, founded by Imam Malik ibn Anas (d. 795)

manakh – serious inter-tribal conflict in pre-Islamic Arabia. Compared with a *ghazwa*, a *manakh* was rare but much more violent.

mansukh – that which is abrogated or superseded c.f. *nasikh* and *naskh*

Mecca – the Arabian city where Muhammad lived until the age of 52, now the holiest city in Islam.

Medina – Muhammad and his first followers emigrated from Mecca to Medina in 622 because of persecution. At Medina Muhammad established and led the first Islamic state, where Islam developed into a more aggressive form.

Monophysite – refers to the doctrine that the incarnate Christ had only one nature (divine) c.f. Chalcedonian and Monothelete

Monothelete – The Monothelete heresy was a politically inspired compromise between the Chalcedonian and Monophysite positions, devised in the seventh century in an attempt to unite the Christians in the face of Persian and later Muslim invasions. Monotheletism asserts two natures in Christ but only one mode of activity.

mudarati – "symbiotic" *taqiyya,* the co-existence of Shi'as with Sunni for the sake of Islamic unity and power

Mughal – the Arabic and Persian form of "Mongol". Conventionally used to describe the Muslim dynasty that ruled large parts of India from the early sixteenth to the mid-eighteenth century. Also spelled "Mogul"

muhajirun – the Muslims who moved from Mecca to Medina with Muhammad c.f. *ansar*

mujahid – a person who takes part in jihad. Plural *mujahidin* or *mujahidun.*

muqaddas – holy

murid – literally "one who desires", a disciple of a Sufi *pir*

Muridism – a term used for a pacifist Sufi movement in Senegal and also for a militant Sufi movement in the Caucasus

Mu'tazilites – literally "withdrawers". A rationalist school of Islam which originated in the second Islamic century. They held that someone who sins is neither a believer nor an unbeliever, and opposed the view that the Qur'an was eternal and uncreated. They also differed from orthodox Muslims in denying predestination and in believing that God must always act justly.

Mzabis – a name given to Berber-speaking 'Ibadis living in Algeria

Naqshbandiyya – a prominent Sufi order founded in the fourteenth century in Bukhara. It is widespread in the Caucasus and Central Asia, and is characterised by its use of silence and concentration.

nasikh – a Qur'anic verse that abrogates another verse c.f. *mansukh* and *naskh*

naskh – abrogation – the rule whereby an earlier-dated verse of the Qur'an is considered subordinate to a later-dated verse c.f. *mansukh* and *nasikh*

Ottomans – a Turkish clan who established a principality in Anatolia around 1300. By military conquest their territory expanded into the Ottoman empire, which was the dominant Muslim power for some six centuries. The Ottoman Sultanate was abolished in 1922 and the Caliphate in 1924.

pir – Sufi "saint" or spiritual guide

Pukhtunwali – the Pathan code of honour, which governs all aspects of life. Its main features are hospitality, truce, vengeance and *nanawatey* (a kind of asylum by which feuds can be ended).

qibla – direction faced during prayer (originally towards Jerusalem, later towards the *ka'ba* at Mecca).

qital – fighting

qiyas - analogical reasoning, used in *ijtihad*

Qur'an – a series of "revelations" which Muhammad believed God gave him over the period 610 to 632

Quraish - the Arab tribe to which Muhammad and the first Muslims belonged

razzia – a European pronunciation of *ghazwa*

Red-Shirts – see *Khudai Khidmatgaran* and *Surkhposhan*

ribat – strengthening the frontiers of *Dar al-Islam*, a type of defensive jihad

ridda – apostasy

rightly-guided caliphs – the first four caliphs who succeeded in turn to the leadership of the Muslim community following Muhammad's death. Their rule covered the period 632 to 661.

Sabeans (Sabians) – followers of John the Baptist. Considered in the Qur'an to have a revealed religion and thus to be in the same category as Jews and Christians, i.e. not pagans. There are still some Sabeans in modern Iraq. c.f. *ahl al-kitab*

sadaqa – voluntary alms-giving. Distinguished from *zakat* (compulsory alms-giving)

sahih – true. Used before the name of a compiler of a collection of *hadiths*, to indicate reliability

salaf – pious ancestors

Salafiyya – widespread radical movement, also called neo-Wahabbism

Sanussiya – a Sufi-led rebel movement in Libya (1837-1931)

SAR – Sekolah Agama Rakyat, private Islamic schools in Malaysia

Sassanian – a Persian dynasty founded in 224. It was destroyed by the Arab Muslims in 637-651.

Shafi'i – a Sunni school of Shari'ah, founded by Imam Muhammad bin Idris ash Shafi'i (d. 820)

shahada – testimony, particularly reciting the Islamic creed. Also legal testimony in a court of law. Also martyrdom.

shahid – martyr or witness

Shari'ah – Islamic law

Shi'a – a minority sect of Islam, which broke away from the main body in 657. It is a majority in Iran and Iraq.

siyar – literally "motion". This word came to mean the types of conduct of the Islamic state in its relationships with non-Muslim communities. It was the title of a famous work by Shaybani on international relations.

Sufism – Islamic mysticism

sunna – literally "a trodden path". The customs of Muhammad and his early followers who knew him personally as recorded in the *hadith*

Sunni – the largest sect of Islam, comprising 80-90% of the Muslims today

sura – a chapter of the Qur'an

Surkhposhan – literally "Red-Shirts". A nickname for the *Khudai Khidmatgaran*

takfir – the process of declaring someone to be an apostate from Islam. This process began with the Kharijis, who applied it very broadly, as do some modern-day groups.

Taliban - literally "students" or "seekers". The ultraconservative Islamic movement which gained political power in Afghanistan 1996 – 2001

taqiyya – literally "shield" or "guard". To conceal one's real beliefs in order to save one's life. A doctrine which is very strong in Shi'a Islam, but also present in Sunni Islam. c.f. *idha'ah*

'ulama – scholars, those learned in the study of Islam

umma – the whole body of Muslims worldwide

Ummayad – the first dynasty of Sunni caliphs, based in Damascus. They followed the rightly guided caliphs and were succeeded in 750 by the 'Abbasid dynasty.

velayat-e faqih – vice-regency of the Islamic jurists i.e. government by the Islamic jurists, a doctrine devised by Ayatollah Khomeini (1900-89) the architect of the 1979 Islamic Revolution in Iran

Wahhabism – strictly puritanical form of Sunni Islam, predominant in Saudi Arabia

Yenicheri – Janissaries

Zoroastrianism – the pre-Islamic religion of Persia, strongly ethical and with both monotheistic and dualistic aspects.

References & Notes

Chapter 1

1   In his preface to his translation of *The Islamic Law of Nations: Shabyani's Siyar* (Baltimore, Maryland: The Johns Hopkins Press, 1966) p.xi

2   Akbar, M.J. *The Shade of Swords: Jihad and Conflict between Islam and Christianity* (London: Routledge, 2002) p. xvi

3   Some Muslims consider jihad to be primarily the preaching of Islam in order to persuade non-Muslims to convert. One such is Dr Mar'uf Al-Dawalibi writing in Kharofa, Ala'Eddin *Nationalism Secularism Apostasy and Usury in Islam* (Kuala Lumpur: A.S. Nordeen, 1994) p.12

4   Lewis, Bernard *The Political Language of Islam* (Chicago and London: The University of Chicago Press, 1988) pp.71-2

5   Tibi, Bassam *Conflict and War in the Middle East: From Interstate War to New Security* 2nd edition (Basingstoke and London: Macmillan Press Ltd, 1998) p.216

6   Haleem, Harifyah Abdel, Oliver Ramsbotham, Saba Risaluddin and Brian Wicker (eds.) *The Crescent and the Cross: Muslim and Christian Approaches to War and Peace* (Basingstoke: Macmillan Press Ltd, 1998; New York: St Martin's Press, Inc., 1998) pp.60-103

7   The founder of one of the four mainstream schools of Sunni Islamic law

8   Haleem et al. *The Crescent and the Cross* pp.76-7

9   The wide range of modern Muslim definitions of the term "self-defence" will be considered in chapter 8.

10   See al-Aqqad, Abbas Mahmoud *Haqa'iq al-Islam wa Abatil Khusumih* (Cairo: Dar al-Hilal, 1957) pp.187-91, quoting a survey by Ahmad Zaki Pasha of all the battles which took place in Muhammad's lifetime.

11   Qur'anic references are given as the *sura* (chapter) number followed by the number of the verse within the *sura*. All are from A. Yusuf Ali's *The Holy Qur'an: Text, Translation and Commentary* (Leicester: The Islamic Foundation, 1975) unless otherwise stated. Verse numbers vary slightly between different translations of the Qur'an so if using another version it may be necessary to search in the verses just preceding or just following the number given here to find the verse cited.

12   Shaltut, Mahmud *Al-Qur'an wa al-Qital* [The Qur'an and Fighting] (Matba'at al-Nasr and Maktab Ittihad al-Sharq, 1948). This book was written in 1940 and published in 1948, ten years before Shaltut became the Sheikh of Al-Azhar. English translation in Peters, Rudolph *Jihad in Classical and Modern Islam: a Reader* (Princeton: Markus Wiener Publishers, 1996) pp.60-101

13   Khan, Ahmed in *The Pioneer* (23 November 1871) quoted in Peters *Jihad in Classical and Modern Islam* p.123; Brown, Judith M. *Modern India: The Origins of an Asian Democracy* 2nd edition, in The Short Oxford History of the Modern World series (Oxford: Oxford University Press, 1995) p.153. Sir Syed Ahmed Khan has been vilified by many Muslims for his cooperative attitude towards the British Raj. See for example Jameelah, Maryam *Islam and Modernism* (Sant Nagar, Lahore: Mohammad Yusuf Khan, 1968) pp.49-55.

14   Bayoumi, Dr Abdel-Mo'ti "Wrong Zionist Perceptions of Jihad in Islam via the Internet" in *Al-Musawwar* (23 August 2002). English translation in *Religious News Service from the Arab World* (2 September 2002)

15   Fatoohi, Dr Louay *Jihad in the Qur'an: The Truth from the Source* (Kuala Lumpur: A.S. Noordeen, 2002) pp.3, 24, 34-5, 50, 52, 60

16   Haleem et al. *The Crescent and the Cross* p.66

17   The very same verse (quoted on page 25) was used by Ibn Taymiyya (1263-1328) to justify Muslims fighting any groups of unbelievers who refuse to convert to Islam. See Ibn Taymiyya, Taqi al-Din Ahmad *al-Siyasa al-Shar'iyya fi Islah al-Ra'i wa-al-Ra'iyya [Governance according to God's Law in Reforming both the Ruler and his Flock]* in Peters *Jihad in Classical and Modern Islam* p.45

18   Abd es-Salam, Dr Kamal Boraiq'a "Responding to Dr Bat Ye'or" (23 August 2002) in *Religious News Service from the Arab World* (2 September 2002)

19 Q 4:75 appears to encourage Muslims to fight on behalf of anyone who is oppressed, but the traditional Muslim interpretation applies it specifically to oppressed Muslims. See A. Yusuf Ali's footnote 593 to this verse.

20 Engineer, Ali Asghar "Islam and Non-violence" in Kumar, R. (ed.) *Khan Abdul Gaffar Khan: A Centennial Tribute* (New Delhi: Nehru Memorial Museum and Library, Har-Anand Publications, 1995) p.122

21 Shaltut *Al-Qur'an wa al-Qital* in English translation in Peters *Jihad in Classical and Modern Islam* pp.76-8

22 Haleem et al. *The Crescent and the Cross* p.77

23 Shaltut *Al-Qur'an wa al-Qital* in English translation in Peters *Jihad in Classical and Modern Islam* p.78

24 Bayoumi "Wrong Zionist Perceptions"

25 See pages 16-7

26 See page 37

27 Haleem et al. *The Crescent and the Cross* p.71

28 Ibid. p.60

29 For more on this vital theory of *naskh* see pages 18, 24-5

30 Shaltut, Mahmud *The Muslim Conception of International Law and the Western Approach* (The Hague: Martinus Nijhof, 1968

31 Fatoohi *Jihad in the Qur'an* (pp.27-8, 72) argues that *qital* is one aspect of armed jihad which in turn is a specialised kind of jihad.

32 Haleem et al. *The Crescent and the Cross* pp.75-6

33 Ibid. p.79

34 This is deduced by certain commentators from the words "But do not transgress limits" in Q 2:190 following a command to fight (quoted on page 25)

35 Haleem et al. *The Crescent and the Cross* p.67

36 Arabic singular *khariji*, Arabic plural *khawarij*

37 Haleem et al. *The Crescent and the Cross* p.98

38 Ibid. pp.61,109

39 Hughes, Thomas Patrick *A Dictionary of Islam* (Lahore: Premier Book House, 1885) p.199

40 Shi'a Muslims acknowledge the possibility of continuing to practise *ijtihad* (but they constitute only 10%-20% of the world's Muslim population).

41 These are explored by Fred M. Donner in "The Sources of Islamic Conceptions of War" in Kelsay, John and James Turner Johnson (eds.) *Just War and Jihad: Historical and Theoretical Perspectives on War and Peace in Western and Islamic Traditions* (Westport, Connecticut: Greenwood Press, 1991) pp.31-69. Useful analyses on the sources of Islam in general are found in Blair, John C. *The Sources of Islam: An Inquiry into the Sources of the Faith and the Practice of the Muhammadan Religion* (Madras: The Christian Literature Society for India, 1925) and St Clair-Tisdall, W. *The Sources of Islam: A Persian Treatise* transl. and abridged by Sir William Muir (Birmingham: Birmingham Bible Institute, 197?). See also S.M. Zwemer's "Analysis of the Borrowed Elements of Islam" in *Arabia: The Cradle of Islam* (Edinburgh and London: Oliphant Anderson and Ferrier, 1900) p. 178.

42 Noth, Albrecht "Heiliger Kampf (Gihad) gegen die 'Franken': Zur Position der Kreuzzüge im Rahmen der Islamgeschichte" in *Saeculum* Vol. 37 (1986) pp.240-59

Chapter 2

1 This is recorded in the Qur'an "To those against whom war is made, permission is given (to fight), because they are wronged" Q22:39

2 Kenneth Cragg discusses the difference between Meccan and Medinan Islam in "A Tale of Two Cities: Helping the Heirs of Mecca to Transform Medina" in *Mission Frontiers* (December 2001)

3 Ibn Abidin, Muhammad Amin *Radd al-Muhtar 'ala al-durr al-Mukhtar* (Cairo, 1856 or 1857) Vol. 3 pp.237-8

4 Taha, Mahmoud Mohamed *The Second Message of Islam* transl. Abdullah Ahmed An-Na'im (Syracuse, New York: Syracuse University Press, 1987) p.134

5 The Qur'an often refers to Jews, Christians and Sabeans (followers of John the Baptist) as "the People of the Book", i.e. those who had their own revealed scriptures. They were generally looked on more favourably than were other non-Muslims. Sometimes Zoroastrians were included.

6 By confining himself to Qur'anic verses which actually contain the word "jihad" and its variants, Fatoohi has managed to write a book called *Jihad in the Qur'an* without mentioning the Sword Verse. He has also been able

to assert that the purpose of armed jihad is neither to force non-Muslims to embrace Islam (p.46) nor to forcibly extend the Islamic state (p.72).

7   al-Syowty, JaLal al-Deen *Al-Atkon Fee Alom Al-Qur'an* [The Perfection of Qur'anic Theology] Vol. 2, p. 37. See also al-Kalbbi, *Al-Hafz Al-Tasshel Fi Aleolom Al Tanzel [The Easiest Revelation of Theology]*.

8   For example 3:156; 3:167-8; 4:74-6; 4:77; 4:95; 9:38-9; 9:42-52; 9:73; 9:869; 9:123; 47:4; 61:11; 66:9

9   For example 5:54; 5:85

10   For example 2:193; 8:39

11   Firestone's analysis of war verses is: nonmilitant, giving restrictions on fighting, expressing conflict between God's command and the reaction of Muhammad's followers, and strongly advocating war on behalf of Islam. Firestone, Reuven *Jihad: The Origin of Holy War in Islam* (New York: Oxford University Press, 1999) pp.67-91

12   Significantly, Louay Fatoohi, writing with the aim of conveying that jihad is primarily spiritual, has deliberately limited his sources to the Qur'an and omitted the *hadith* altogether. Rather misleadingly he writes (*Jihad in the Qur'an* pp.1-2) "The Qur'an is the undisputed source of and authority on all aspects of the religion of Islam" and goes on to say of his own work, "With its exclusive emphasis on the Qur'an this book sets itself apart from the other studies of jihad ..." In other words, he has had to omit all the usual other sources in order not to ruin his argument.

13   The reference to a *hadith* gives first the name of the person who put together the particular collection, then a reference to where that *hadith* is within the collection, then the name of the "narrator" i.e. the first person chronologically in the chain of people who passed the story on. In the original collections the names of everyone in the chain are listed. The word *sahih* before the collector's name means "true" i.e. a particularly reliable and authentic collection. The word *sunan*, which may also appear before a collector's name, is simply indicative of the fact that *hadiths* describe Muhammad's own actions, on which Muslims must model their lives.

14   An excellent text on this subject is Khaled Abou El Fadl's *Rebellion and Violence in Islamic Law* (Cambridge: Cambridge University Press, 2001)

15   A helpful discussion of what various schools of law teach can be found in Majid Khadduri's *War and Peace in the Law of Islam* (Baltimore: The Johns Hopkins Press, 1955) pp.83-137

16 I.e. the school founded by Abu Hanifa

17 *The Hedaya: Commentary on the Islamic laws* transl. Charles Hamilton (New Delhi: Kitab Bhavan, 1985) Vol. II, Book IX, chapter IV. pp.174-180

18 Ibid. Vol. II, Book IX, Chapter II p. 147

19 Kaegi, Walter E. *Byzantium and the Early Islamic Conquests* (Cambridge: Cambridge University Press, 1992) p.127

20 *The Islamic Law of Nations: Shaybani's Siyar* translated with an introduction, notes and appendices by Majid Khadduri (Baltimore: The Johns Hopkins Press, 1966)

21 Shaybani's Siyar chapter II:118-123 transl. in Khadduri *The Islamic Law of Nations* p.102

22 Khadduri reviews the stances of various Islamic jurists on this issue in *War and Peace in the Law of Islam* pp.106-7.

23 al-Mawardi, Abu'l Hasan *The Ordinances of Government: al-Ahkam al-Sultaniyya w'al-Wilayat al-Diniyya* transl. Wafaa H. Wahba, The Centre for Muslim Contribution to Civilization (Reading: Garnet Publishing Ltd, 1996) p.40. Elsewhere al-Mawardi defines other kinds of enemies who must be fought, such as apostates, insurgents, brigands and highwaymen, but distinguishes this from holy war (see pp.60-71).

24 Ibn Naqib al-Misri, Ahmad *Reliance of the Traveller: A Classic Manual of Sacred Islamic Law 'Umdat al-Salik* ed. and transl. Nuh Ha Mim Keller revised edition (Beltsville, Maryland: Amana Publications, 1997) pp.603-4

25 The meaning of his title is "The beginning for him who interprets the sources independently and the end for him who wishes to limit himself". An English translation is available in Peters *Jihad in Classical and Modern Islam* pp.27-42

26 Ibn Taymiyya translated in Peters *Jihad in Classical and Modern Islam* pp.43-54

27 Ibid. pp.47-8

28 Ibid. p.48

29 Ibn Khaldun *The Muqaddimah: An Introduction To History* transl. Franz Rosenthal (London: Routledge & Kegan Paul, 1958) Vol. 1 p.473

30 Kohlberg, Etan "The Development of the Imami Shi'i Doctrine of Jihad" in *Zeitschrift der Deutschen Morgenlaendischen Gesellschaft* Vol. 126 (1976) pp.64, 68

31 Sachedina, Abdulaziz "The Development of Jihad in Islamic Revelation
    and History" in Johnson, James Turner and John Kelsay (eds.) *Cross,
    Crescent and Sword: The Justification and Limitation of War in Western and
    Islamic Tradition* (Westport, Connecticut: Greenwood Press, 1990)

Chapter 3

1   Khadduri *War and Peace in the Law of Islam* pp.52-3. In the words of the
    respected Islamic scholar F.A. Klein: "It is the duty of the Imam to send
    an expedition, at least once or twice a year, to the land of warfare to fight
    the unbelievers. If he neglects to do so, he commits a sin, except when he
    knows that they are not strong enough to subdue the enemy." *The Religion
    of Islam* (London: Curzon Press Ltd and New York: Humanities Press Inc,
    1906, reprinted 1971, 1979) p.175

2   The doctrine of *Dar al-Harb* and *Dar al-Islam* is frequently rejected by
    modern liberal scholars. e.g. Haleem et al. *The Crescent and the Cross* p.71;
    Dr Abdel Mo'ti Bayoumi interviewed by Cornelis Hulsman "Commenting
    on Bat Ye'or's article" in *Religious News Service from the Arab World* (28
    August 2002)

3   See for example Baghdadi, Abu Mansur 'Abd al-Qahir ibn Tahir *Kitab
    Usul al-Din* (Istanbul, 1928) Vol. I p.270; Shawkani, Abu al-Fath
    Muhammad ibn 'Abd al-Karim *Nayl al-Awtar* 2nd edition (Cairo,
    1952) Vol. VIII pp.28-9; Rahim, Abdur *The Principles of Muhammadan
    Jurisprudence* (London: Luzac, printed Madras 1911) pp.396-7

4   Muslim jurists differ over some details but the consensus about the three sub-
    divisions of *Dar al-Islam* is as follows: (1) The *Haramayn*, meaning Mecca
    and Medina – non-Muslims are completely banned (2) The Hijaz – this is
    generally considered to be an area in the north-west of the Arabian penin-
    sula, about 250 miles long by 150 miles wide, containing Mecca, Medina
    and many other sites sacred in Islam. Non-Muslims may travel through it but
    not settle there permanently. Non-Muslims are also not allowed to be buried
    there, as this is considered permanent residence. (3) The rest of *Dar al-Islam*,
    where non-Muslims may live as *dhimmis*. See Khadduri *War and Peace in the
    Law of Islam* pp.158-60; Hughes *A Dictionary of Islam* on "Haramu 'l-Madi-
    nah" and "Hijaz"; B. Lewis on "al-Haramayn" and G. Rentz on "al-Hidjaz" in
    The Encyclopaedia of Islam (Leiden: Brill, 1986)

5   Cragg, Kenneth *The House of Islam* 2nd edition (California: Dickenson
    Publishing Co., 1978)

6   (New York: Simon and Schuster, 1996)

7   Overy, Richard (ed.) *The Times History of the World* new edition (London: Times Books, Harper Collins Publishers, 1999) p.303

8   Speaking at Holy Trinity, Brompton, London. Quoted in Carey, Andrew "Islam's Confused Identity" in *The Church of England Newspaper* (28 August 2003) p.8

9   Badawi, Zaki *Islam in Britain* (London: Taha Publishers, 1981) pp.26-7

10   The sermon was broadcast live on Palestinian Authority Television. Extracts in English translation in MEMRI Special Dispatch No. 370 (17 April 2002)

11   Quoted in Waddy, Charis *The Muslim Mind* 2nd edition (Longmans, 1976) p.100

12   Khadduri *War and Peace in the Law of Islam* p.68

13   Speech posted in three parts on the following web addresses: www.jahra. org/free/131313/Hamza3.wma; www.jahra.org/free/131313/Hamza5.wma; www.jahra.org/free/131313/Hamza6.wma; English translation in MEMRI Special Dispatch No. 539 (18 July 2003)

14   According to the Grand Mufti of Saudi Arabia, Sheikh Abdul Aziz Ibn Baz, the collective obligation may also become an individual obligation if the imam calls people out to fight, if Muslim territory is attacked, and for soldiers in the Muslim ranks preparing to fight (Ibn Baz, Shaykh and Uthaymeen, Shaykh *Muslim Minorities: Fatawa Regarding Muslims Living as Minorities* (Hounslow: Message of Islam, 1998) p.24). Kharofa (*Nationalism Secularism Apostasy and Usury in Islam* p.101) indicates the same. It is probably the same logic which is behind the fatwa issued by Sheikh Faysal Mawlawi, Deputy Chairman of the European Council for Fatwa and Research, on 23 March 2003 concerning American military bases in Arab and Muslim countries. This fatwa ruled that the bases were "aggressive troops" and launching jihad against them is an individual obligation incumbent on every Muslim who is able to do so (provided that such attacks do not result in internal strife between the rulers and the people of the country concerned). Mawlawi added that "in individual obligation, a Muslim does not need to seek the permission of the imam or the Muslim ruler".

15   Ibn Abi Zayd al-Qayrawani, Abu Muhammad 'Abdullah *La Risâla* (*Epître sur les éléments du dogme et de la loi de l'Islam selon le rite mâlakite*) transl. Leon Bercher, 4th edition (Algiers, 1951) pp.162-3

16   Khadduri *War and Peace in the Law of Islam* p.60. However, Mawlawi in his fatwa of 23 March 2003 (see footnote 14) stressed that "in individual obligation, a Muslim does not need to seek the permission of the imam or the Muslim ruler".

17   Khadduri *War and Peace in the Law of Islam* p.141

18   Ibid. pp.65-6

19   Ibn Khaldun *The Muqaddimah* Vol. 1 pp.257-60, 282-3

20   Ferguson, John *War and Peace in the World's Religions* (London: Sheldon Press, 1977) p.135

21   Kramer, Martin *Islam Assembled: The Advent of the Muslim Congresses* (New York: Columbia University Press, 1986) p. 55; Mango, Andrew *Atatürk* (London: John Murray, 1999) p.136. An English translation of the *fatwas* is found in Peters *Jihad in Classical and Modern Islam* pp.56-7. The *beyanname-i cihad* read: "Gather about the lofty throne of the sultanate, as if of one heart, and cleave to the feet of the exalted throne of the caliphate. Know that the state is today at war with governments of Russia, France and England, which are its mortal enemies. Remember that he who summons you to this great holy war is the caliph of your noble Prophet." The *fatwas* and *beyanname*, all in Turkish, Arabic, Persian, Tatar and Urdu, can be found in *Ceride-i ilmiyye* (Istanbul, Muharram 1333 i.e. November/December 1914) 1(7) pp.437-53 (*fatwas*) and pp. 454-80 (*beyanname*).

22   Ferguson *War and Peace in the World's Religions* p.135 Kepel, Gilles "The Origins and Devleopment of the Jihadist Movement: From Anti-Communism to Terrorism" transl. Peter Clark in *Asian Affairs* Vol. 34 No. 2 (July 2003)

23   For a full treatment of the development of the jihadist movement in modern times see Kepel, Gilles "The Origins and Devleopment of the Jihadist Movement: From Anti-Communism to Terrorism" transl. Peter Clark in *Asian Affairs* Vol. 34 No. 2 (July 2003)

24   Ancient Israel – see Deuteronomy 20:10-12. Classical antiquity – see Phillipson, Coleman *The International Law and Custom of Ancient Greece and Rome* (London: Macmillan & Co. Ltd, 1911) Vol. I pp.96-7

25   Ibn Abi Zayd al-Qayrawani *La Risâla* pp.162-3

26   In the sense of initiating a campaign against any particular enemy. Jihad per se is permanent.

27 Khadduri *War and Peace in the Law of Islam* pp.94-101, 152-154

28 Ibn Rushd, Abu al-Walid Muhammad Ibn Muhammad (Averroes) *Bidyat al-Mujtahid wa-Nihayat al-Muqtasid [The Beginning for him who Interprets the Sources Independently and the End for him who Wishes to Limit Himself]* English translation in Peters *Jihad in Classical and Modern Islam* p.37

29 These and other examples are quoted in Istanbuli, *Yasin Diplomacy and Diplomatic Practice in the Early Islamic Era* (Oxford: Oxford University Press, 2001) pp.46-7

30 al-Bukhari, Al-Imam Abu Abdillah Muhammed, *Sahih Al-Bukhari*, ed. Shaikh Qasem al-Rifaie (Beirut: Dar Al-Qalam, 1987) Vol. I, p.65; Hamidullah, Muhammad *Documents sur la Diplomatie Musulmane à l'époque du Prophete et des Khalifes Orthodoxes* (Paris: Librarie Oriental et Americane, Thesis, University of Paris, 1935) p.33

31 Hamidullah *Documents sur la Diplomatie Musulmane* p.32 "We who have surrendered" indicates "Muslims", which literally means "those who have submitted" i.e. submitted to God.

32 The letter is displayed in the Topcal Palace, Istanbul.

33 See also Osama bin Laden's declaration of war against America, quoted on page 45. It is noteworthy that the first issue of Al-Qa'eda's online training magazine *Al-Battar Training Camp* berates the Muslims of today because they "love this world, hate death, and abandon jihad". Mansour, Mu'aadh "The Importance of Military Preparedness in Shari'ah" in *Al-Battar Training Camp* issue 1 (December 2003 or January 2004?) www.hostinganime.com /battar/b1word.zip. Excerpts in English translation in MEMRI Special Dispatch Series No. 637 (6 January 2004)

34 Khadduri *War and Peace in the Law of Islam* p.67; Anderson, Professor Sir Norman *Islam in the Modern World: A Christian Perspective* (Leicester: Apollos, 1990) p.31

35 Government by the Islamic jurists, who are, according to a *hadith*, "the heirs of the prophets". The significance of the term "heirs of the prophets" is that Shi'as believe the imam must be a descendant of 'Ali, the fourth caliph, whose wife was Muhammad's daughter Fatima.

36 Johnson, Nels *Islam and the Politics of Meaning in Palestinian Nationalism* (London: Kegan Paul, 1982) pp.74-5

37 Saudi Arabia, where Mecca and Medina are located

38 The full text can be found in Alexander, Yonah and Michael S. Swetnam *Usama bin Laden's al-Qaida: Profile of a Terrorist Network* (Ardsley, USA: Transnational Publishers, Inc., 2001) (their appendix 1A) and also used to be on the website of Azzam Publications www.azzam.com/html/articles-declaration.htm (now removed).

39 I.e. William Perry, the US Secretary of Defence

40 Alexander and Swetnam *Usama bin Laden's al-Qaida* Appendix 1A, p.15

41 Full text in Alexander and Swetnam *Usama bin Laden's al-Qaida* Appendix 1B p.1-3

42 Alexander and Swetnam *Usama bin Laden's al-Qaida* Appendix 1B p.2

43 Ahlus Sunnah wal Jama'ah Ustadzjaf ar Umar Thalib, commander of the Laskar Jihad in an address broadcast on Radio SPMM [The voice of struggle of the Maluku Muslims] (1-3 May 2002). This and further excerpts can be found at www.persecution.org/news/report2002-05-15.html (viewed 20 May 2002)

44 Almascaty, Dr Hilmy Bakar *Panduan Jihad Untuk Aktivis Gerakan Islam [A Manual for Jihad for Islamic Movement Activists]* (Jakarta: Gema Insani Press, May 2001) p. 101

45 Khadduri *War and Peace in the Law of Islam* pp.74-82

46 Non-Muslims were either People of the Book or polytheists.

47 "Against them make ready your strength to the utmost of your power ..." The verse is quoted in full on page 60.

48 For example "'Abd-Allah ibn 'Umar stated that the jihad is for combating the unbelievers and the *ribat* for safeguarding the believers."

49 Fighel, Jonathan "Sheikh Abdullah Azzam: Bin Laden's Spiritual Mentor" (27 September 2001) http://www.ict.org.il/articles/articledet.cfm? articleid=388 (viewed 28 September 2003)

50 al-Tabari, Abu Ja'far Muhammad ibn Jarir *Ta'rikh al-Rusul wa'l-Muluk (Annales)* ed. M.J. De Goeje et al. (Leiden: Brill, 1879-1901) Vol. 1 p.1850

51 Including mutilation of the dead. See Khadduri *War and Peace in the Law of Islam* p.108

52 al-Tabari *Ta'rikh* Vol. III p.160; Waqidi, Abu 'Abd-Allah Muhammad ibn 'Umar *Kitab al-Maghazi* ed. Alfred von Kremer (Calcutta, 1856) p.284

53 These were the Kharijis who followed Nafi' ibn al-Azraq. See al-Bagh-dadi, 'Abd al-Qahir *Mukhtasar Kitab al-Farq Bayn al-Firaq* ed. Philip Hitti (Cairo, 1924) pp.73, 97

54 Shaybani, Muhammad ibn al-Hasan *Sharh Kitab al-Siyar al-Kabir* with commentary by Shams al-Din Muhammad b.Ahmad b. Sahl Sarakhsi, (Hyderabad, 1916-17) Vol. IV p.79

55 Ibid. Vol. I p.33

56 He repeats the same guidelines earlier in his *Siyar* as well. See chapter 2:112-3, in Shaybani's *Siyar* transl. in Khadduri *The Islamic Law of Nations* p.101

57 Shaybani Sharh *Kitab al-Siyar al-Kabir* with commentary by Sarakhsi pp.212-3

58 Khadduri *War and Peace in the Law of Islam* p.104

59 al-Tabari, Abu Ja'far Muhammad ibn Jarir *Kitab al-Jihad wa Kitab al-Jizya wa Ahkam al-Muharibin min Kitab Ikhtilaf al-Fuqaha*, ed. J. Schacht (Leiden: Brill, 1933) pp.103-4; Abu Yusuf, Ya'qub b. Ibrahim al-Ansari *Kitab al-Radd 'ala Siyar al-Awza'i* ed. Abu al-Wafa al-Afghani (Cairo, 1938) pp.837; Schacht, Joseph *The Origins of Muhammadan Jurisprudence* (Oxford: Oxford University Press, 1950) pp.34-5

60 al-Tabari *Kitab al-Jihad* pp.106-7

61 Shaybani's *Siyar* chapter II:82-89 transl. in Khadduri *The Islamic Law of Nations* pp.98-9

62 Note 1234, p.432

63 Ibn Naqib al-Misri *Reliance of the Traveller* p.604. Text in brackets comprises the comments of 'Umar Barakat (d.1890) who wrote a commentary on Ibn Naqib's work entitled *Fayd al-Ilah al-Malik fi hall alfaz 'Umdat al-salik wa 'uddat al-nasik [The Outpouring of Sovereign Divinity: an interpretation of the words of "Reliance of the Traveller and Tools of the Worshipper"]*

64 Abu Yusuf, Ya'qub b. Ibrahim al-Ansari *Kitab al-Kharaj* (Cairo, 1933) pp.195-6

65 Shaybani's *Siyar* chapter II:94-109, transl. in Khadduri *The Islamic Law of Nations* p.100-1

66 Shaybani's *Siyar* chapter II:110-111, transl. in Khadduri *The Islamic Law of Nations* p.101

67   Shaybani's *Siyar* chapter II:80-81, transl. in Khadduri *The Islamic Law of Nations* p.98

68   Shahrastani, Abu al-Fath Muhammad ibn 'Abd al-Karim *Kitab al-Milal wa al-Nihal* ed. Cureton (London, 1846) pp.90-3

69   Shaybani *Sharh Kitab al-Siyar al-Kabir* with commentary by Sarakhsi Vol. IV pp.223-5

70   al-Tabari *Kitab al-Jihad* pp.194-8

71   For example, this verse is quoted in the context of espionage in Almascaty's 2001 jihad manual *Panduan Jihad Untuk Aktivis Gerakan Islam* p.99

72   Hamidullah, Muhammad *The Battle Fields of the Prophet* (Lahore: Idra-e-Islamiat, 1993) p.117

73   Ibid. pp.120-31

74   Ibid. p.123, citing Ibn Kathir's *History* IV:6. A *hadith* describing the assassination is quoted on page 28.

75   Kandhalvi, Muhammad Zakariyya "Stories of Sahabah" in *Tablighi Nisab* (Dewsbury: Anjuman-e-Islahul Muslemeen of U.K., no date but probably soon after 1938) pp.172-3

76   Hamidullah *The Battle Fields* pp.126-7

77   Hamidullah states that in peace time there should be no difference in the treatment of male and female adult spies (*The Battle Fields* p.131)

78   Shaybani *Sharh Kitab al-Siyar al-Kabir* with commentary by Sarakhsi Vol. IV pp.226-7

79   Ibid. Vol. IV p.226; al-Tabari *Kitab al-Jihad* pp.172-3

80   Barghuthy, Omar Saleh, "A Ministry of Propaganda under the Fatimids" in *Journal of the Middle East Society* (Spring 1947) pp. 57-9

81   Ibn Asakir *History of Damascus* (1951 edition) Vol. I p.394, cited in Hamidullah *The Battle Fields* p.132

82   Ibn Sa'd II/i pp.117-8 and *Maqriziy Imta'* I:443, cited in Hamidullah *The Battle Fields* p.133

83   An expedition authorised with reluctance by Caliph 'Uthman, after Caliph 'Umar I had forbidden it. Caliph 'Umar advised all Muslims not to travel by sea, let alone fight on it. See Khadduri *War and Peace in the Law of Islam* p.112

84   Ibn Qudama, Abu Muhammad 'Abd-Allah ibn Ahmad ibn Muhammad *Kitab al-Mughni* ed. M. Rashid Rida (Cairo, 1947 or 1948) Vol. VIII pp.349-50 quoted in Khadduri *War and Peace in the Law of Islam* p.113. See also Kohlberg, E. "Shahid" in *The Encyclopaedia of Islam*. Another interesting *hadith* runs "He who becomes sick on a stormy sea will have the reward of a martyr, and he who is drowned will have the reward of two martyrs." *Mishkat al-Masabih 18:2 Narrated by Umm Haram* English translation with explanatory notes by James Robson (Lahore: Sh. Muhammad Ashraf, 1990) Vol.1 p. 815

85   Sahih Al Bukhari Vol. 4, Book 52 Number 175: Narrated by Khalid bin Madan

86   Shaybani *Sharh Kitab al-Siyar al-Kabir* with commentary by Sarakhsi Vol. I pp.25-6

87   Ibn 'Abd-Allah, Hasan *Athar al-Uwal fi Tartib al-Duwal* (Cairo, 1878 or 1879) pp. 195-8. The original work dates from 1308 or1309

88   Shaybani *Sharh Kitab al-Siyar al-Kabir* with commentary by Sarakhsi Vol. III p.265. Al-Awza'i, who opposed attacking an enemy castle with a Muslim human shield, likewise opposed trying to sink or set fire to an enemy ship with a Muslim human shield. See al-Tabari *Kitab al-Jihad* pp.4-5

89   al-Tabari *Kitab al-Jihad* p.86

90   Shaybani *Sharh Kitab al-Siyar al-Kabir* with commentary by Sarakhsi Vol. III p.269; Ardabili *al-Anwar li-'Amal al-Abrar* (Cairo, no date) Vol. II p.289

91   Shaybani *Sharh Kitab al-Siyar al-Kabir* with commentary by Sarakhsi Vol. III pp.269-70, 272

92   Ibid. Vol. III p.270

93   Kaegi *Byzantium and the Early Islamic Conquests* p.277

94   Probably from the tribe of Iyad

95   al-Tabari *Ta'rikh* Vol.1 p.2508. This English transl. in Juynboll, G.H.A. *The History of Al-Tabari* 13: *The Conquest of Iraq, Southwestern Persia, and Egypt* (Albany: State University of New York Press, 1989) p.89

96   Shemesh, A. Ben *Taxation in Islam* Vol. 2 (Leiden: Brill, London: Luzac & Co. Ltd, 1965) p.42; Kennedy, Hugh *The Prophet and the Age of the Caliphates: the Islamic Near East from the Sixth to the Eleventh Century* (Harlow: Pearson Education Limited (Longman), 1986) p.63

97 Delehaye, Hipployte "Passio sanctorum sexaginta martyrum" in *Analecta Bollandiana: A Journal of Critical Hagiography* Vol. 28 (1904) pp.289-307; Pargoire, J. "Les LX Soldats Martyrs de Gaza" in *Echos d'Orient: Revue de Théologie, de Droit Canonique, de Liturgie, d'Archaelogie, d'Histoire et de Géographie Orientales* Vol. 8 (1905) pp.40-3

98 Kaegi *Byzantium and the Early Islamic Conquests* pp.95-6

99 Ibid. p.89. A similar punishment was given to Muhammad b. Abu Bakr in 658 for his role in the murder of Caliph 'Uthman. He was not only put in an ass's stomach but then he and the stomach together were burnt – a method of execution intended to bring shame and disgrace because of his terrible crime.

100 Sophronius, Sermones. PG 87.3: 3201-364 in "Weihnachspredigt des Sophronios" ed. H. Usener *Rheinisches Museum für Philologie* n.s. 41 (1886) pp.506-7

101 *Doctrina Iacobi nuper baptizati* c.17. See Bonwetsch, N, (ed.) *Abhandlungen der Königlichen. Gesellschaft der Wissenschaften zu Göttingen.* Philologisch-Historische Klasse. Neue Folge Vol.12, No. 3 (Berlin: Weidmannsche Buchh., 1910) p.88

102 Kaegi *Byzantium and the Early Islamic Conquests* p.128

103 Rogerson, Barnaby *The Prophet Muhammad* (London: Little, Brown, 2003) pp.164-6

104 Bostom, Andrew G. "Muhammad, the Qurayza Massacre, and PBS" in *FrontPageMagazine.com* (20 December 2002)

105 Muhammad took one of the Qurayza women, Rayhanah, as his wife. She converted to Islam but begged to be kept as a concubine rather than become his wife, as she preferred to be a captive of the man who had destroyed her clan rather than enter his house as a free woman.

106 al-Mawardi *A'lam al-nubuwwa* (Cairo, 1901 or 1902?) pp.146-7 quoted in Kister, M.J. "The Massacre of the Banu Qurayza: A Re-examination of a Tradition" in *Jerusalem Studies in Arabic and Islam* Vol. 8 (1986) p.69

107 Hamidullah *The Battle Fields* p.3 footnote

108 Muir, Sir William *Mahomet and Islam* (London: The Religious Tract Society, 1895) p.151

109 al-Tabari *Kitab al-Jihad* p.145

110 Shaybani's *Siyar* chapter I:44 transl. in Khadduri *The Islamic Law of Nations* p.91

111   al-Tabari *Ta'rikh* Vol. 5 pp.2557-9

112   Khadduri *War and Peace in the Law of Islam* p.128

113   Peters *Jihad in Classical and Modern Islam* pp.143, 145, 148

114   al-Ali, Hamid Abdullah "The Legality of Killing Jewish Women and Children in Palestine" in *Al-Watan* (31 August 2001), English translation by Shira Gutgold published in the *Jerusalem Post* (5 September 2001)

115   "Mahathir urges arms as deterrent" in *Straits Times* (17 September 2003)

116   Haleem et al. *The Crescent and the Cross* p.95. Fatoohi *Jihad in the Qur'an* (p.44) writes in praise of the sword because it is much more selective than nuclear, chemical and biological weapons or even conventional bombs.

117   al-Saidi, 'Abd al-Muta'ali *Fi Maydan al-Ijtihad* (Helwan: Jam'iyyat althaqafa al-Islamiyya, no date) pp.133-9

118   Dr Hashim was speaking at a conference on "Invading Iraq and the Future of the Arab Regime" on 17 April 2003. Reported in Suleiman, Mustafa "The Rector of the Azhar University asks Arabs to Obtain Mass Destruction Weapons" in *Al-Usboa* (21 April 2003). English translation in *Arab-West Report* (17-23 April 2003)

119   Bilal, Abdul Rahman *Islamic Military Resurgence* (Lahore: Ferozsons (Pvt.) Ltd, 1991) p.204

120   "We Need Atomic Weapons and Mujahideen, says Daawa" in *Daily Times* (6 February 2004) www.dailytimes.com.pk/default.asp?page=story_6-22004_pg7_15 (viewed 6 February 2004)

121   MacAskill, Ewen and Ian Traynor "Saudis Consider Nuclear Bomb" in *The Guardian* (18 September 2003)

122   Islamic Republic News Agency (16 September 2003) reported in MEMRI News Tickers (17 September 2003)

123   Reeve, Simon *The New Jackals: Ramzi Yousef, Osama bin Laden and the Future of Terrorism* (London: André Deutsch, 1999) p.261

124   "Afghanistan invasion halted early stages of al-Qaida WMD programs, security officials say" (Associated Press, 27 January 2004) http://www.billingsgazette.com/index.php?display=rednews/2004/01/27/build/world/65-alquaidachemicalweapons.inc (viewed 30 January 2004)

125   "Bind a bond firmly (on them): thereafter (is the time for) either generosity or ransom"

126 Zuhayli, Wahba *Athar al-Harb fi al-Fiqh al-Islami. Dirasa muqarina.* (Beirut: Dar al-Fikr, 1965) pp.403-474; al-Daqs, Kamil Salama *Ayat al-Jihad fi l-Qur'an al-Karim* (Kuwait: Dar al-Bayan, 1972) pp.550-569

127 Article 13 states that prisoners of war shall not be exposed to "public curiosity".

128 "Iraq: Muslim law trumps Geneva Convention" WorldNetDaily.com (24 March 2003), quoting a BBC radio interview and Agence France-Presse.

129 al Ghunaimi, Mohammad Talaat *The Muslim Conception of International Law and the Western Approach* (The Hague: Martinus Nijhoff, 1968) pp.1845, 211; Abu Zahra, Muhammad *Al-'Alaqat al-Dawliyya fi l-Islam* (Cairo: al-Dar al-Qawmiyya li-l-Tiba'a wa-l-Nashr, 1964) pp.74-83; Zuhayli *Athar al-Harb fi al-Fiqh al-Islami* pp.362-7

130 Zuhayli *Athar al-Harb fi al-Fiqh al-Islami* pp.356-7; Mahmassani, Sobhi "International Law in the Light of Islamic Doctrine" in *Academie de Droit International, Recueil des Cours* Vol. 117 (1966) pp.53-8

131 Abu Zahra *Al-'Alaqat al-Dawliyya fi l-Islam* pp.78-9; al Ghunaimi *The Muslim Conception of International Law and the Western Approach* pp.1845; Mansur, 'Ali *'Ali Al-Shari'a al-Islamiyya wa-l-Qanun al-Dawli al-'Amm* (Cairo: al-Majlis al-A'la li-l-Shu'un al-Islamiyya, 1971) pp.281-6

132 *Hudna* was the term used by Hamas in June 2003 when expressing its willingness for a ceasefire with Israel. While *hudna* is the ordinary Arabic term for a truce or ceasefire, the Islamic religious implications of a merely temporary peace were no doubt clearly understood by Hamas followers.

133 Muhammad began this practice when he made a 10-year truce with the Meccans. See Kennedy *The Prophet and the Age of the Caliphates* pp.41-2

134 Theophanes *Theophanis Chronographia* ed. C. De Boor (Leipzig, 1883-5) AM 6126

135 Kaegi *Byzantium and the Early Islamic Conquests* pp.276-7

136 The *Hedaya* Vol. II, Book IX, chapter III, p.150

137 The *Hedaya* Vol. II, Book IX, chapter III, pp.150-1; Shaybani's *Siyar* Chapter V:602-27 transl. in Khadduri *The Islamic Law of Nations* pp.154-7

138 Other Qur'anic commands to keep promises are found in Q 5:1; 8:55-6; 16:92

139 'Abdul Khaliq, Sheikh 'Abdul Rahman *Verdict on the Treaties of Compromise and Peace with the Jews* reproduced at http://www.islaam.com/articles/treaty.htm (viewed 18 September 2001)

140 Quoted in Gold, Dore *Hatred's Kingdom: How Saudi Arabia Supports the New Global Terrorism* (Washington DC: Regnery Publishing Inc., 2003) pp.195-6

141 Shaybani *Al-Siyar al-Kabir* with Sarakhsi's Commentary Vol. IV, p.60; Rahim *The Principles of Muhammadan Jurisprudence* p.282; al-Mahmasani, Subhi *al-Nazariyya al 'Amma Li'l-Mujibat wa'l-'Uqud* (Beirut, 1948) Vol. II pp.68 ff.; *Al-Majalla* Article 103 transl. in Hooper, Charles *Civil Law of Palestine and Transjordan* (Jerusalem: Azriel, 1933-6) Vol. I p.31

142 The texts of three of his treaties in English translation may be found in Khadduri's *War and Peace in the Law of Islam* pp.205-215.

143 Shaybani's Siyar Chapter VI:628-984a transl. in Khadduri *The Islamic Law of Nations* pp.158-194

144 Price, Randall *Unholy War* (Eugene, Oregon: Harvest House Publishers, 2001) p.191

145 Enayat, Hamid *Modern Islamic Political Thought* (Austin: University of Texas Press, 1982) p.177

146 Nasif, Sheikh Mansur Ali *Al-Tajj al Jami lil-usul fi Ahadith al-Rasul* (Istanbul: Dar Ihya al-Kutub al-'Arabiyyah, 1961). Also published in Cairo by Matba'ah 'Isa al Babl al Halabi (no date). Vol. 5, p.43

147 Enayat *Modern Islamic Political Thought* p.176

148 Ibid. p.176; Corbin, Henri *En Islam Iranien* (Paris: Gallimard, 1971) Vol. I, pp.6, 30ff, 117

149 Enayat *Modern Islamic Political Thought* pp.177-8

150 al-Tabari *Ta'rikh* vol I p.2349

151 al-Baladhuri, Ahmad b. Yahya *Futuh al-Buldan [Conquests of the Countries]* ed. M.J. De Goeje (Leiden: Brill, 1866) p.130

152 Kaegi *Byzantium and the Early Islamic Conquests* p.165

153 Eutychius *Das Annalenwerk des Eutychios von Alexandrien* 282. See Breydy, Michael *Corpus Scriptorum Christianorum Orientalium* Vol. 471-2 Scriptores Arabici T.44-5 (Louvain: E. Peeters, 1985) pp.141-2 for text, pp.120-1 for translation.

154 Theophanes *Theophanis Chronographia* AM 6128 (De Boor p.340); Michael the Syrian *Chronique* ed. and trans. J.-B. Chabot (Paris: E. Leroux, 1899-1910) Vol.2 p.426

155 Kaegi *Byzantium and the Early Islamic Conquests* pp.175-6

156 Ibid. p.163

157 al-Baladhuri *Futuh al-Buldan* pp.150,156-7 whose source is Abu Ubayd al-Qasim Ibn Sallam (770-838) *Kitab al-Amwal* ed. Muhammad Khalil Haras (Cairo, 1968) pp.248, 253

158 Sachedina, Abdulaziz "Justification for Violence in Islam" in *Journal of Lutheran Ethics* (19 February 2003); Rapoport, David C. "Comparing Militant Fundamentalist Movements and Groups" in Marty, Martin E. and Appleby, R. Scott (eds) *Fundamentalisms and the State: Remaking Polities, Economies and Militance* The Fundamentalism Project Vol. 3 (Chicago and London: University of Chicago Press, 1993) p.447

159 A *murid* (literally "one who desires") is a disciple of a Sufi *pir*

160 Article by J.L. Triaud on "Muridiyya" in *The Encyclopaedia of Islam*

161 Sirriyeh, Elizabeth *Sufis and Anti-Sufis: The Defence, Rethinking and Rejection of Sufism in the Modern World* (Richmond: Curzon Press, 1999) pp.38-9

162 Shaikh Khalid's words are quoted in Abu-Manneh, Butrus "The Naqshabandiyya-Mujaddidiyya in the Ottoman Lands in the Early 19th Century" in *Die Welt des Islams* Vol. 12 (1986) p.15

163 Sirriyeh *Sufis and Anti-Sufis* p.39

164 Johnson, Paul *The Birth of the Modern: World Society 1815-1830* (New York: Harper Collins, 1991) p.275

165 Holt, P.M. *A Modern History of the Sudan* 3rd edition (London: Weidenfeld and Nicolson, 1967) pp.28-32, 78-80 & ff.

166 A radical and now violent Islamist group in South Asia. See pages 95-6.

167 Ansari, Sarah F.D. *Sufi Saints and State Power: The Pirs of Sind, 1843-1947* (Lahore: Vanguard Books, 1992) pp.78-80

168 Ibid. pp.81-3

169 Later known as Badshah Khan meaning "khan of khans"

170 Caroe, Olaf *The Pathans* 550 B.C. – A.D. 1957 (London: Macmillan & Co. Ltd, 1965) pp.272, 431-5

171 Ferguson *War and Peace in the World's Religions* p.137

172 Banerjee, Mukulika *The Pathan Unarmed: Opposition and Memory in the North West Frontier* (Karachi: Oxford University Press, 2000) p.145

173 Ahmad, Mirza Ghulam *Tohfah Golrviyah* (1902) p.82. Republished in vol. 17 of *Ruhani Khaza'in*, the collected works of Ghulam Mirza Ahmad (Rabwa, 1965)

174 Ahmad, Hazrat Mirza Ghulam *Jesus in India: Jesus' Escape from Death on the Cross and Journey to India* (London: The London Mosque, 1978) p.18

175 www.real-islam.org (4 October 2001) an Ahmadiyya website. Can now be viewed at http://www.geocities.com/Athens/Delphi/1340/reply/truth/jehad.htm (viewed 4 December 2003)

Chapter 4

1 Watt, W. Montgomery *Muhammad Prophet and Statesman* (Oxford: Oxford University Press, 1961) pp.102-9

2 Firestone *Jihad* p.134

3 Watt *Muhammad Prophet and Statesman* p.109

4 Vasiliev, A.A. *A History of the Byzantine Empire* (Madison: University of Wisconsin Press, 1958) estimates that not more than a third of the peninsula was actually dominated by Muhammad, Vol. 1 p.207.

5 Kennedy *The Prophet and the Age of the Caliphates* p.53

6 Izutsu, Toshihiko *The Structure of the Ethical Terms in the Koran* (Tokyo: Keio Institute of Philological Studies, 1959) p.49

7 Dozy, R. *Histoire des Musulmans d'Espagne* (Leiden: Brill, 1861) Vol. I, p.7

8 Obermann, Julian "Early Islam" in Dentan, Robert C. (ed.) *Lectures of the Department of Near Eastern Languages and Literatures at Yale University* American Oriental Series No. 38 (Yale University Press, 1954?) pp.253-4

9 Ibid. pp.254-5

10 Firestone *Jihad* p.31

11 Bat Ye'or *The Decline of Eastern Christianity under Islam: From Islam to Dhimmitude* (Cranbury, New Jersey / London: Farleigh Dickinson University Press and Associated University Presses, 1996) p.41

12 Khadduri *War and Peace in the Law of Islam* pp.70-1; Ibn Khaldun *The Muqaddimah* Vol. 2, p.74; Kraemer, Joel "Apostates, Rebels and Brigands" in *Israel Oriental Studies* Vol. 10 (1980) p.34. Kraemer suggests that Ibn Khaldun most likely intended to associate the attribute "just" mainly with warfare against seceders and the disobedient.

13   For a discussion of the relative reliability of many of these sources see Walter Kaegi's *Byzantium and the early Islamic Conquests* especially pp.2-18.

14   al-Tabari *Ta'rikh* Vol. 1 p.3453

15   Esposito, John (ed.) *The Oxford History of Islam* (Oxford: Oxford University Press, 1999) p.11

16   Kennedy *The Prophet and the Age of the Caliphates* p.54

17   For example Khan, Majid Ali *The Pious Caliphs* (New Delhi: Millat Book Centre, 1976) pp.35-6

18   Khadduri *War and Peace in the Law of Islam* p.77. Interestingly, execution of an apostate by burning is specifically forbidden in Islam, and there were those who objected to this method being used.

19   Holt, Lambton and Lewis *The Cambridge History of Islam* Vol. 1A p.58

20   Kennedy *The Prophet and the Age of the Caliphates* p.54; Khan, Majid Ali *The Pious Caliphs* p.35

21   Esposito *The Oxford History of Islam* p.11

22   Kennedy *The Prophet and the Age of the Caliphates* pp.54-7

23   Donner "The Sources of Islamic Conceptions of War" p.50

24   Kennedy *The Prophet and the Age of the Caliphates* p.53

25   Sicker, Martin *The Islamic World in Ascendancy: From the Arab Conquests to the Siege of Vienna* (Westport, Connecticut: Praeger Publishers, 2000) pp.10-11; Salibi, Kamal S. *Syria Under Islam: Empire on Trial 634-1097* (Delmar, New York: Caravan Books, 1977) p.19

26   Fredegarius *Chronicles* 4:66 ed. Bruno Krusch (Hanover: MGH Scriptores Rerum Merovingicarum T.2, 1888, repr. 1984) p.154; John, Bishop of Nikiu *Chronicle* 120.33, 121.2, 121,11, 123 transl. R. Charles (London, Oxford, 1916); Sebeos *History* c.32 transl. Macler, F. *Histoire d'Héraclius* (Paris: E. Laroux, 1904) pp.104-5, see also trans by Bedrosian, Robert (New York: Sources of the Armenian Tradition, 1985) p.135; John Bar Penkaye *Ris Melle* in Brock, S.P. "North Mesopotamia in the Late Seventh Century. Book XV of John Bar Penkaye's *Ris Melle*" in *Jerusalem Studies in Arabic and Islam* Vol. 9 (1987) pp.57-61; Michael the Syrian *Chronique* 11.5, 11.6 (Chabot Vol. 2 pp.418,422-3)

27   Kaegi *Byzantium and the Early Islamic Conquests* pp.26, 87

28   Ibid. pp.274, 269-70, 286

29   Ibid. p.265

30   Ibid. pp.88, 100, 270

31   Sophronius *Sermones* PG 87:3 197D

32   Kaegi *Byzantium and the Early Islamic Conquests* p.79, 104

33   Exceptions were Gaza and Ba'labakk where the local inhabitants paid for the repair of their city walls.

34   Kaegi *Byzantium and the Early Islamic Conquests* p.260

35   Ibid. pp.112-146

36. Ibid. p.144

37   Ibid. pp.173-4, 267; Jandora, John W. "Developments in Islamic Warfare: The Early Conquests" in *Studia Islamica* Vol. 64 (1986) pp.101-13

38   For example, the contemporary or near-contemporary Armenian historian Sebeos in his *History* c.32 (Bedrosian pp.134-6, Macler pp.104-5)

39   Kaegi *Byzantium and the Early Islamic Conquests* pp.189, 198-200, 203

40   Ibid. pp.198-200

41   Ibid. p.142; al-Tabari *Ta'rikh* Vol. 1 p.2089; Shahid, Irfan "Asrar al-nasr al'arabi fi futuh al-Sham" in Bildad al Sham Proceedings (1985) pp.137-147

42   Ibn Hisham, 'Abd al-Malik *al-Sira al-Nabawiyya* ed. Heinrich Ferdinand Wüstenfeld *Sirat Rasul Allah [Das Leben Muhammeds]* (Göttingen: Dieterischen Buchhandlung, 1858-60) p.958; Ibn Ibn Sa'd, Muhammad *Kitab al-Tabaqat al-Kabir* ed. Eduard Sachau et al. (Leiden: Brill, 1904-40) Vol. I pp.2, 18, 31, 83

43   Kaegi *Byzantium and the Early Islamic Conquests* pp.68-71

44   Ferguson *War and Peace in the World's Religions* pp.127-8

45   Blankinship, Khalid Yahya *The End of the Jihad State: The Reign of Hisham Ibn 'Abd al-Malik and the Collapse of the Umayyads* (Albany: State University of New York Press, 1994) pp.145-6. Blankinship's book is one of very few works to document and analyse the defeats and disasters suffered by the Muslims at this period.

46   Ibid. pp.199-236

47   Inalcik, Halil *The Ottoman Empire: the Classical Age 1300-1600* (London: Phoenix Press, 2000) p.3, see also pp.6-7

48 Palmer, J.A.B. "The Origin of the Janissaries" in *Bulletin of the John Rylands Library*, Manchester, Vol. 35, No. 1 (September 1952) passim

49 Mayer, Ann Elizabeth "War and Peace in the Islamic Tradition and International Law" in Kelsay, John and James Turner Johnson (eds.) *Just War and Jihad: Historical and Theoretical Perspectives on War and Peace in Western and Islamic Traditions* (Westport, Connecticut: Greenwood Press, 1991) p.196

50 Ibid. pp.196-7

51 As well as numerous less well known ones, such as many of the groups to be considered in the next chapter

52 Rajaee, Farhang *Islamic Values and World View: Khomeyni on Man, the State and International Politics* (Lanham, Maryland: University Press of America, 1983) p.81

53 Shaltut *Al-Qur'an wa al-Qital* in Peters *Jihad in Classical and Modern Islam* p.93

54 Haleem et al. *The Crescent and the Cross* p.96

Chapter 5

1 Watt, William Montgomery *The Formative Period of Islamic Thought* (Oxford: Oneworld Publication, 1998) pp.9-37; Anderson, Sir Norman "Islam" in Anderson, Sir Norman (ed.) *The World's Religions* 4th edition (Grand Rapids, Michigan: Eerdmans, 1975) pp.103-4; Kennedy *The Prophet and the Age of the Caliphates* pp.79-80

2 Anderson "Islam" in Anderson *The World's Religions* pp.105-6

3 Lewis, Bernard "The Revolt of Islam" in *The New Yorker* (19 November 2001). Further details in Lewis, Bernard *The Assassins: A Radical Sect in Islam* (London: Phoenix, 2003).

4 al-Yassini, Ayman *Religion and State in the Kingdom of Saudi Arabia* (Boulder, Colorado: Westview Press, 1985) pp.124-9

5 Rida was building on the ideas of Sir Syed Ahmed Khan (1817-1898) in India, Muhammad Abduh (1849-1905) in Egypt and Jamal al-Din al-Afghani (1838-1897) all of whom sought to reform a decadent and stagnant Islam by looking afresh at the original sources, but without Rida's anti-western emphasis.

6 Cook, David *Studies in Muslim Apocalyptic* Studies in Late Antiquity and Early Islam 21 (Princeton, New Jersey: The Darwin Press, 2002) pp.39, 73; Rapoport "Comparing Militant Fundamentalist Movements and Groups" pp.447, 450

7   Dawoud, Khaled "America's Most Wanted" in *Al-Ahram Weekly Online*,
    Issue No. 552 (20-26 September 2001); Pipes, Daniel "Muslims Love Bin
    Laden" in *New York Post* (22 October 2001)

8   Shariati, Ali "Intizar: The Religion of Protest and the Return to Self"
    in Donohue, J.J. and Esposito, J.L. (eds.) *Islam in Transition: Muslim
    Perspectives* (New York: Oxford University Press, 1982) pp.298-304;
    Shariati, Ali *On the Sociology of Islam* transl. Hamid Algar (Berkeley:
    Mizan Press, 1979) p.124

9   al-Banna, Hasan *Five Tracts of Hasan al-Banna (1906-1949): A Selection
    from the Majmu'at Rasa'il al-Imam al-Shahid* (Berkeley, California:
    University of California Press, 1978) pp.155-6

10 Mawdudi, Sayyid Abu'l A'la *Jihad fi Sabilillah [Jihad in Islam]*, transl. K.
    Ahmad (Birmingham: Islamic Mission Dawah Centre, 1997) pp.13-15

11 Haddad, Y.Y. "Sayyid Qutb: Ideologue of Islamic Revival" in Esposito,
    John (ed.) *Voices of Resurgent Islam* (New York: Oxford University Press,
    1983) pp.85-7; Nettler, Ronald "A Modern Islamic Confession of Faith and
    Conception of Religion: Sayyid Qutb's Introduction to *tafsir, Fi Zilal al-Quran*"
    in *British Journal of Middle Eastern Studies* Vol. 21 No. 1 (1994) pp.102-14

12 Qutb, Sayyid *The Islamic Concept and its Characteristic* (Indianapolis:
    American Trust Publication, 1991) p.12

13 Haddad, Y.Y. "The Quranic Justification for an Islamic Revolution: The
    View of Sayyid Qutb" in *Middle East Journal* Vol. 37 No. 1 (Winter 1983)
    pp.17-18

14 Nettler "A Modern Islamic Confession of Faith" pp.98-102; Solihin, S.M.
    Studies on Sayyid Qutb's Fi Zilal al-Quran (unpublished thesis, Department
    of Theology, University of Birmingham, 1993) p.284

15 Qutb, Sayyid *Islam and Peace* (Cairo: Dar al-Shuruq, 1988) pp.80-5;
    Qutb, Sayyid *Fi Zilal al-Quran* (Beirut: Dar al-Shuruq, 1987) Vol. 3
    pp.1433-5; Qutb, Sayyid *Milestones* (Lahore: Qazi Publications, no date)
    pp.88-9. Also *Milestones [Ma'alem Fil Tariq]* (Indianapolis: American Trust
    Publications, 1990)

16 Paz, Reuven *The Heritage of the Sunni Militant Groups: An Islamic interna-
    cionale?* (4 January 2000) http://www.ict.org.il/articles/articledet.cfm ?arti-
    cleid=415 (viewed 5 December 2003)

17 Faraj, Muhammad 'Abd al-Salam *Al-Faridah al-Gha'ibah [The Neglected
    Duty]*, English translation in Jansen, Johannes J. G. *The Neglected Duty: The*

Creed of Sadat's Assassins and Islamic Resurgence in the Middle East (New York: Macmillan, 1986) pp.163-4; Abdelnasser, Walid M. *The Islamic Movement in Egypt* (London: Keegan Paul International, 1994) pp.234-5

18   The Islamic name for Jesus

19   Ibrahim, Naajeh, Majid, Asim Abdul and Darbaalah, Esaam-ud-Deen *In Pursuit of Allah's Pleasure* (London: Al-Firdous Ltd, 1997) p.30

20   For more information on this influential man, see Bin Omar, Abdullah "The Striving Sheik: Abdullah Azzam" translated by Mohammed Saeed in *Nida'ul Islam*, Issue 14 (July-September 1996) http://www.islam.org.au/ articles/14 /AZZAM.HTM (viewed 28 September 2003)

21   Abdelnasser *The Islamic Movement in Egypt* p.216; Hopwood, Derek *Egypt: Politics and Society 1945-1990* (London: Harper Collins Academic, 1991) p.118

22   Two useful sources are Rohan Gunaratna's *Inside Al Qaeda: Global Network of Terror* (London: Hurst & Company, 2002) and Alexander and Swetnam's *Usama bin Laden's al-Qaida: Profile of a Terrorist Network*

23   Alexander and Swetnam *Usama bin Laden's al-Qaida* pp.3, 29, 31; Gunaratna *Inside Al Qaeda* pp.54-69, 95-8

Chapter 6

1   This phrase is reported to have been used in his confession by Imam Samudra, the Indonesian Islamist accused of masterminding the Bali bombing. Reported in Friedman, Thomas L. "Defusing the Holy Bomb" *The New York Times* (27 November 2002)

2   Summarised in MEMRI Special Dispatch Series No. 434 (27 October 2002), taken from www.qoqaz.com. This precisely follows al-Mawardi.

3   al-Ali, Hamid Abdullah "The Legality of Killing Jewish Women and Children in Palestine" in *Al-Watan* (31 August 2001), English translation by Shira Gutgold published in the *Jerusalem Post* (5 September 2001)

4   Roberts, Tom (writer and director) *Witness: Inside the Mind of the Suicide Bomber* (Channel 4, 10 November 2003

5   Abu Gheith, Suleiman, "In the Shadow of the Lances" from the Center for Islamic Research and Studies website (originally www.alneda.com then changed to http://66.34.191.223) reported by MEMRI Special Dispatch Series No. 388 (12 June 2002)

6   Lewis "The Revolt of Islam"

7   Shaybani's *Siyar* chapter II:142-145 transl. in Khadduri *The Islamic Law of Nations* p.105

8   de Vaux, Carra "Shahada" in *E.J. Brill's First Encyclopaedia of Islam 1913-1936* (Leiden: E.J. Brill, 1993) Vol. VII p.259

9   John Esposito asserts that a new understanding of martyrdom was born out of the "severe dislocations experienced by much of the Muslim world from the eighteenth century to the present". See Esposito, John L. *Unholy War: Terror in the Name of Islam* (Oxford: Oxford University Press, 2002) p.69

10 Rasheed, Asra *Death* (Birmingham: Al-Hidaayah Publishing and Distribution, 2001) pp.24,28

11 His footnote 211 p.77

12 Rasheed *Death* p.24

13 His footnote 51 p.188

14 Sahih Bukhari Volume 4, Book 52, Number 297

15 Sahih Bukhari Volume 5, Book 59, Number 514; Sahih Bukhari Volume 8, Book 76, Number 500

16 A *fatwa* carries far more weight with a Muslim than any other kind of statement, command or ban.

17 Tantawi had condemned suicide bombings against Israeli citizens at a press conference in Cairo on 3 December 2001. Reported in Gardner, Frank "Grand Sheikh Condemns Suicide Bombings" (BBC News, 4 December 2001). The fact that this was a statement made to journalists, including westerners, rather than a *fatwa* addressed to the Muslim faithful, is highly significant.

18 Spoken at a reception given for Israeli Arab Democratic Party leader, Abd Al-Wahhab Al-Darawsheh. Posted on www.lailatalqadr.com (a website associated with Al-Azhar) and also reported in MEMRI Special Dispatch Series No. 363 (7 April 2002) It is important to note that this statement was made in an Arab context and reported in the Arabic-language media; it is therefore more likely to reflect Tantawi's real opinion.

19 Taheri, Amir "Tantawi's Tantrum" in *National Review Online* (16 May 2003)

20 Quoted at www.lailatalqadr.com (a website associated with Al-Azhar) and also reported in MEMRI Special Dispatch Series No. 363 (7 April 2002)

21 "Islamic Scholars say Suicide Attacks 'Legitimate'" AFP report dated 10 January 2002, in *Middle East Times* issue 2002-2 (11 January 2002)

22 Parry, Richard Lloyd "Muslim nations defend use of suicide bombers" in *The Independent* (11 April 2002)

23 *Al-Sharq Al-Awsat* (19 July 2003), extracts in English translation in MEMRI Special Dispatch Series No. 542 (24 July 2003)

24 Ibid.

25 Muslim leaders are often heard making such announcements. Sometimes some very unexpected kinds of deaths are declared to be martyrdoms. For example a Palestinian student who was killed in a road accident was declared to have died "the martyrdom of learning". See pages 126-7.

26 A *hadith* states "The Messenger of Allah said: All the sins of a Shahid [martyr] are forgiven except debt." *Sahih Muslim Book 20, Number 4649: Narrated Amr ibn al-'As*

27 These detailed promises are derived from various hadiths. The Qur'an itself affirms in several places a special reward for those who die in the way of God, but does not go into specifics. See Kohlberg, E. "Shahid" in *The Encyclopaedia of Islam.*

28 Ashburn, Kristen "The Suicide Bombers" in *Telegraph Magazine* (15 November 2003) pp.24-7

29 Jaber, Hala and Uzi Mahnaimi, "Suicide Bombing was a Family Affair" in *The Sunday Times* (18 January 2004)

30 Hamur, Thauria interviewed by Joanna Chen "A Martyr or a Murderer" in *Newsweek* (23 February 2004) p.68

31 There are various other reputed ways of getting straight to paradise, which are believed by some Muslims though probably not with any scriptural basis. For example, some believe that if you memorise the whole Qur'an you and your family will all go to heaven (reported in the *Daily Mail*, 2 May 2003). Others hold that if you kill 40 Christians you will to go to paradise. This was the opinion of a Turkish Muslim during the Armenian massacre in Turkey in the early part of the twentieth century. He first killed 39 Christians, and then found an elderly man whom he also killed to make it up to the figure 40. Reported by Isa Dogdu in Bos, Stefan J. "Christians Near Northern Iraq Persecuted" in *Assist News Service* (5 April 2003)

32 Esposito *Unholy War* p.69

33 Muhammad said that when God's servant "plunges into the midst of the enemy without mail" it makes God laugh with joy. Ibn Ishaq *Sirat Rasul Allah* III:445 English translation in Guillaume, Alfred *The Life of Muhammad: A Translation of Ibn Ishaq's Sirat Rasul Allah* (Karachi: Oxford University Press, 1955) p.300

34 In his "Declaration of war against the Americans occupying the land of the two holy places" (23 August 1996) quoted in Alexander and Swetnam *Usama bin Laden's al-Qaida* appendix 1A p.16

35 Ferguson *War and Peace in the World's Religions* pp.132; Khadduri *War and Peace in the Law of Islam* p.62; Smith, Jane Idleman and Haddad, Yvonne Yazbeck *The Islamic Understanding of Death and Resurrection* (Albany: State University of New York Press, 1981) pp.37, 51, 54, 59

36 az-Zubaidi, Al-Imam Zain-ud-Din Ahmad bin Abdul-Lateef (compiler) *The Translation of the Meanings of summarized Sahih Al-Bukhari Arabic-English*, transl. Dr Muhammad Muhsin Khan (Riyadh: Maktaba Dar-us-Salam Publishers, 1994) p.335

37 Kohlberg, E. "Shahid" in *The Encyclopaedia of Islam*

38 In his "Declaration of war against the Americans occupying the land of the two holy places" (23 August 1996) quoted in Alexander and Swetnam *Usama bin Laden's al-Qaida* appendix 1A pp.19, 21

39 al-Fagih, Saad "The War that Bin Laden is Winning" in *The Guardian* (13 May 2003)

40 Almascaty *Panduan Jihad Untuk Aktivis Gerakan Islam* p.112

41 Summary of Tantawi's teachings at http://www.sunnah.org/history/ Scholars /mashaykh_azhar.htm (viewed 25 January 2002)

42 Ironically, Europeans consider that the Muslims won the Crusades, despite the initial successes of the Franks.

43 Al-Hawali, Sheikh Safar bin Abdur-Rahman *Open Letter to President Bush* (15 October 2001) http://202.95.140.21/¬acom/fatwas/print_view. php?id=2 (viewed 4 June 2002)

44 Björkman,W. "Shahid" in *E.J. Brill's First Encyclopaedia of Islam* 1913-1936 Vol. VII pp.260-1

45 Many quotes from the proud relatives are given in Ashburn "The Suicide Bombers"

46 Marcus, Itamar "UN is Funding Summer Camps Honoring Terrorists" in *Palestinian Media Watch Bulletin* (25 July 2003)

47 Marcus, Itamar "PA TV Glorifies First Woman Suicide Terrorist – Wafa Idris" in *Palestinian Media Watch Bulletin* (24 July 2003) . The song was broadcast on 24 July 2003, almost eighteen months after her suicide (27 January 2002), and began:

> "My sister, Wafa, my sister, Wafa,
> O, the heartbeat of pride,
> O blossom, who was on the earth and is now in heaven...."

48 Ansari *Sufi Saints and State Power* pp.78-9

49 Qutb *Milestones* pp.94-6

50 an-Nabhani, Taqiuddin *The Islamic State* (London: Al-Khilafah Publications, no date) pp.188-192

51 Khomeini, Ayatollah Ruhollah "Islamic Government" in Donohue, J.J. and Esposito, J.L. (eds.) *Islam in Transition: Muslim Perspectives* (New York: Oxford University Press, 1982) pp.315-6

52 Ellis, Eric "Mahathir Tirade at 'Jews Ruling World'" *Times Online* (17 October 2003) http://www.timesonline.co.uk/printFriendly/ 0,,1-3857059,00.html (viewed 5 December 2003)

53 For example, Amr Khaled, who appears on many of the most widely viewed Arab satellite TV channels, calls people to return to traditional Islamic beliefs and lifestyle in order to be able to restore the power associated with Islam's glorious past. One of his arguments is that if women cover their heads and behave modestly, men will not be tempted and fall into sin. The upright behaviour of the men will eventually result in the return of the great conqueror Saladdin. See www.amrkhaled.net

54 Based on Q 9:123 "Fight the unbelievers who gird you about". See page 15.

55 Just how un-Islamic the Egyptian government was is open to question. President Gemal Abdul Nasser, famed for his Arab nationalist ideology, was himself a sincere practising Muslim and convinced that Islam was essential to the Arab identity. He emphasised the revolutionary aspect of Islam and established an Islamic Congress. Armstrong, Karen *Holy War* (London and Basingstoke: Macmillan London Limited, 1988) p.81

56 Rahman, Shaykh Omar Abdul *The Present Rulers and Islam. Are they Muslims or Not?* (London: Al-Firdous, 1990) p.23

57   Osama bin Laden's "Declaration of war against the Americans occupying the land of the two holy places" has already been quoted (see note 38).

58   Quoted by Woolacott, Martin "The Bali bomb may deal a fatal blow to the Islamists" in *The Guardian* (18 October 2002)

59   Interestingly he was well aware of the Christian teaching of "turning the other cheek" towards the one who slapped you. But he said that being a Muslim he did not follow this precept.

60   Roberts *Witness: Inside the Mind of the Suicide Bomber*

61   These are well summarised in Kohlberg, E. "Shahid" in *The Encyclopaedia of Islam*

62   Hence, presumably, the "martyrdom of learning" referred to in footnote 25 for a Palestinian student killed in a road accident.

Chapter 7

1   One apparent example from Britain was Richard Reid, who hit the headlines when he allegedly tried to blow up an American plane with explosives in his shoes (22 December 2001). But there are many others, particularly in the Philippines. For further examples see Hookway, James "How a Terrorist Proves his Faith" in *Far Eastern Economic Review* (14 November 2002).

2   The British Muslim, Omar Khan Sharif, who tried to blow himself up in Israel on 30 April 2003, was very unusual in being a married man with two children.

3   Jaber, Hala and Uzi Mahnaimi, "Suicide Bombing was a Family Affair"

4   Roberts *Witness: Inside the Mind of the Suicide Bomber*

5   They believe they cannot enter paradise while in debt. See page 113.

6   Iqbal, Anwar "Islamic schools create Pakistani dilemma" United Press International (17 August 2002)

7   Wood, Rick "Wahhabism: Out of Control?" in *Mission Frontiers* (December 2001)

8   Kepel, Gilles *Jihad: The Trail of Political Islam* transl. Anthony F. Roberts (London: I.B. Tauris, 2002) p.56

9   "Religious Schools 'breeding ground for future terrorists'" *Straits Times* (Singapore, 17 January 2003)

10 Walsh, Duncan "Boys Rescued from Kenya's Islamic School of Torture" in *The Times* (30 January 2003)

11 John, Elizabeth and K.T. Chelvi, "The Chilling Jemaah Islamiyah Goal" in *New Sunday Times* (19 January 2003)

12 McGrory, Daniel and Lister, Sam "Prophets of Hate Prey on Rootless Misfits" in *The Times* (31 January 2003)

13 Crumley, Bruce "Jihad's Hidden Victim" in *Time* (2 June 2003) p.48

14 Almascaty *Panduan Jihad Untuk Aktivis Gerakan* Islam p.92

15 "The Black Widows' Revenge" in *The Economist* (12-18 July 2003) p.32

16 Gunaratna *Inside Al Qaeda* p.73

17 "Holy Warriors Enlisting Online" in *WorldNetDaily* (7 August 2003) http://wnd.com/news/printer-friendly.asp?ARTICLE_ID=33960 (viewed 7 August 2003)

18 Al-Ansar, No. 16 (24 August 2002), extracts in English in MEMRI Special Dispatch Series No. 418 (4 September 2002)

19 Colonel Karim Sultan, police chief in Karbala, quoted in Hider, James "Iraqis Drugged, Brainwashed and sent to die for Bin Laden" in *Times Online* (22 March 2004)

20 Roberts *Witness: Inside the Mind of the Suicide Bomber*

21 Reported in the *Daily Mail* (2 May 2003)

22 John and Chelvi "The chilling Jemaah Islamiyah goal"

23 Almascaty *Panduan Jihad Untuk Aktivis Gerakan Islam* pp.96-112

24 Ibid. p.95

25 Gunaratna *Inside Al Qaeda* pp.70-1,75-6

26 *Declaration of Jihad Against the Country's Tyrants, Military Series* recovered by police in Manchester UK form the home of Nazihal Wadih Raghie, 10 May 2000

27 Gunaratna *Inside Al Qaeda* pp.71-2

28 www.hostinganime.com/battar/b1word.zip

29 English summaries and excerpts in MEMRI Special Dispatch Series No. 637 (6 January 2004)

30 *Declaration of Jihad Against the Country's Tyrants*, Military Series

31 Gunaratna *Inside Al Qaeda* p.73

32 "Jihad in Cyberspace" in *The Economist* (15 March 2003)

33 Hassan Jomass, quoted in Harnden, Toby "Video Games Attract Young to Hizbollah" in *The Daily Telegraph* (21 February 2004) p.18

Chapter 8

1 Mayer "War and Peace in the Islamic Tradition and International Law" pp.197, 209

2 Jansen *The Neglected Duty* p.193

3 Mahmassani "International Law in the Light of Islamic Doctrine" pp.307-8

4 al-Dawalibi, Ma'ruf "Islam and Nationalistic and Secularistic Trends" in *Ash-Sharq al-Awsat* (31 December 1989) reprinted in Kharofa *Nationalism Secularism Apostasy and Usury in Islam* pp.11-13

5 al-Rajihi, Ahmad Naser "Heavenly Religions Encourage Legitimate War" in *Ash-Sharq al-Awsat* (28 January 1990) reprinted in Kharofa *Nationalism Secularism Apostasy and Usury in Islam* pp.25-27

6 *Al-Ansar*, No. 16 (24 August 2002), extracts in English translation in MEMRI Special Dispatch Series No. 418 (4 September 2002)

7 Ibn 'Uthaymeen, Sheikh *Riyaadhus-Saaliheen* Vol.1 pp.165-6. Available at www.fatwa-online.com/fataawa/worship/jihaad/jih004/0010915_1.htm (viewed 12 August 2003)

8 Al-Ansari, 'Abd Al-Hamid "Landmarks in Rational and Constructive Dialogue with the 'Other'" in *Al-Hayat* (London) 31 May 2002. Extracts in English translation in MEMRI Special Dispatch Series No. 386 (5 June 2002)

9 Ibn Baz, Abdul-Aziz, Abdul-Aziz Ibn Abdullah Al-Shaykh Abdullah, Salih Ibn Fawzan Al-Fawzan and Bakr Ibn Abdullah Abu Zaid (The Permanent Committee for Academic Research and Ifta) *Unification of Religions* Fatwa no. 19402 (2 June 1997) available at www.troid.org/ articles/islaamicinfo/ Islaamingeneral/whatisislaam/unificationofreligion (viewed 7 August 2003)

10 *Al-Sharq Al-Awsat* (London, 20 April 2002 and 10 May 2002). Extracts in English translation in MEMRI Special Dispatch Series No. 378 (16 May 2002)

11 Batrafi, Khaled Muhammad "Why do we hate the People of the Book?" in *Al-Hayat* (21 October 2001) extracts in English translation quoted in MEMRI Special Dispatch Series No. 295 (1 November 2001)

12 With regard to law on war, James Turner Johnson identifies five main sources of the western just war tradition from which international law on war is derived: Hebraic, Roman, Christian, classical and Germanic. See his chapter "Historical Roots and Sources of the Just War Tradition in Western Culture" in Kelsay, John and James Turner Johnson (eds.) *Just War and Jihad: Historical and Theoretical Perspectives on War and Peace in Western and Islamic Traditions* (Westport, Connecticut: Greenwood Press, 1991).

13 Armanazi, Najib *L'Islam et le Droit International* (thesis) (Paris: Librairie Picart, 1929) pp.50-2; Hamidullah, Muhammad *Muslim Conduct of State* 3rd edition (Lahore: Sh. Muhammad Ashraf, 1953) pp.66-8; Mansur *Al-Shari'a al-Islamiyya* pp.28-30; Al Ghunaimi *The Muslim Conception of International Law and the Western Approach* pp.82-6, al-Daqs *Ayat al-Jihad fi l-Qur'an al-Karim* p.88

14 Mayer "War and Peace in the Islamic Tradition and International Law" p.199

15 Ibid. p.198

16 Traditionally this involved the payment of tribute in return for a truce or armistice. Historic examples were Muhammad's treaty with the Christians of Nadjran and a treaty in 652 with the Nubians who had to pay a tribute of slaves rather than money. See the article by D. B. Macdonald's on "Dar al-Sulh" in *The Encyclopaedia of Islam*

17 *Dar al-'Ahd* is acceptable in the Shafi'i school of Shari'ah. The non-Muslims are permitted to continue to have control of their lands on condition that they pay tribute to the Muslims. Examples include Armenia in the early days of Islam, and later various Christian rulers under the Ottoman empire. See the article by Halil Inalcik on "Dar al-Ahd" in *The Encyclopaedia of Islam*.

18 If the non-Muslims must make payments to the Muslims in return for peace or possession of their property there is not much difference between these and the classic *dhimmi* status of non-Muslims living in *Dar al-Islam*, although *dhimmis* were also humiliated in various ways.

19 Anderson *Islam in the Modern World* pp.30-1; article on "Daru 'l-Harb" in Hughes *A Dictionary of Islam* pp.69-70

20 Brown *Modern India* p.153

21 Reynalds, Jeremy "Radical Islamic Group Threatens Britain After Police Raid" *Assist News Service* (30 July 2003); "Insult to the Dead" *Daily Mail* (9 September 2003)

22 Moinuddin, Hasan *The Charter of the Islamic Conference and Legal Framework of Economic Co-operation among Its Member States* (Oxford: Clarendon Press, 1987) p.28

23 Mahmassani "International Law in the Light of Islamic Doctrine" pp.320-1

24 Higgins, Rosalyn "The Attitude of Western States towards Legal Aspects of the Use of Force" in Cassese, A. (ed.) *The Current Legal Regulation of the Use of Force* (Dordrecht: Martinus Nijhoff, 1986) p.442

25 Ayatollah Mutahhari in a lecture entitled "Defence – the Essence of Jihad". See Abedi, Mehdi and Gary Legenhausen (eds.) *Jihad and Shahadat: Struggle and Martyrdom in Islam* (Houston: Institute for Research and Islamic Studies, 1986) pp.109-13

26 Kharofa, Ala'Eddin "Muhammad the Messenger of God (PBUH) and Westerners" in Kharofa *Nationalism Secularism Apostasy and Usury in Islam* p.99

27 al-Asi, Imam Mohammed "Qur'anic Teaching on the Justification for Jihad and Qital" in *Crescent International* (1-15 June 2003) p.7

28 In 1973 the Sheikh of Al-Azhar declared that jihad against Israel was incumbent on Egyptians, whether they were Christian or Muslim. See Peters, Rudolph *Islam and Colonialism: The Doctrine of Jihad in Modern History* (The Hague: Mouton, 1979) p.134

29 Mayer "War and Peace in the Islamic Tradition and International Law" p.215

30 Piscatori, James *Islam in a World of Nation States* (Cambridge: Cambridge University Press,1986) pp.86-7

31 Moinuddin *The Charter of the Islamic Conference* p. 90 and also pp.186-7 where he reproduces the relevant sections of the Charter.

32 Mayer "War and Peace in the Islamic Tradition and International Law" p.206

33 Kharofa "Muhammad the Messenger of God (PBUH) and Westerners" p.97 [emphasis added]

34 Rajaee *Islamic Values and World View pp.82-3*

35   Peters *Jihad in Classical and Modern Islam* p.137

36   Hamidullah *Muslim Conduct of State* pp.43-4; Daraz, Muhammad 'Abd
     Allah "Mabadi' al-Qanun al-Dawli al-'Amm li-l-Islam" in *Risalat al-Islam*
     2 (1950) p.149; Abu Zahra *Al-'Alaqat al-Dawliyya fi'l-Islam* pp.20-5;
     Mahmassani "International Law in the Light of Islamic Doctrine" pp. 242-4

37   Armanazi *L'Islam et le Droit International* pp.73-5; Hamidullah *Muslim
     Conduct of State* pp.190-4; Abu Zahra *Al-'Alaqat al-Dawliyya fi'l-
     Islam* pp.94-5; Zuhayli *Athar al-Harb fi al-Fiqh al-Islami* pp.150-61;
     Mahmassani "International Law in the Light of Islamic Doctrine" p.289;
     Mansur *Al-Shari'a al-Islamiyya* pp.296-303; al-Daqs *Ayat al-Jihad fi'
     l-Qur'an al-Karim* p.91

Chapter 9

1   It is interesting to note that at Banyas in 1140 it took the combined
     efforts of the Crusaders and Saracen Muslims to defeat the Assassins who
     were attacking both parties. This event gave rise to a new era in Christian-
     Muslim relations in which Crusader and Saracen nobles gathered together
     for conversation and sport.

2   Lewis "The Revolt of Islam"

3   Ansari *Sufi Saints and State Power* p.96

4   Ibid. p.95

5   *Daily Gazette* (4 November 1920) p.5

6   This author has not been able to track down the quoted text within the
     Qur'an, although two verses state that God will not place a burden on a
     soul greater than it can bear (Q 2:286 and 23:62). One wonders where the
     Maulvi found his convenient quotation.

7   Quoted in Banerjee *The Pathan Unarmed* p.49

8   Stalinsky's report "Saudi Policy Statements on Support to the Palestinians"
     is based entirely on official Saudi government sources. Stalinksy, Steven
     "Saudi Policy Statements on Support to the Palestinians" MEMRI Special
     Report No. 17 (3 July 2003)

9   Zakaria, Fareed "Suicide Bombers Can be Stopped" in *Newsweek* (25
     August – 1 September 2003) p.15

10   Simpson, John "Why Tourists are Now the Ideal Targets" in *The Sunday
     Telegraph* (1 December 2002) p.21 [emphasis added]

11 Jukes, Worthington *Frontier Heroes: Reminiscences of Missionary Work in Amritsar 1872-1873 and on the Afghan Frontier in Peshawar 1873-1890* (manuscript dated Exmouth, 1925, re-typed Peshawar, 2000) p.47

12 Drogin, Bob and Greg Miller "Spy Agencies Facing Questions of Tactics" in *Los Angeles Times* (29 October 2001); Hurley, Victor *Jungle Patrol: The Story of the Philippine Constabulary* (New York: E.P. Dutton, 1938). Also, the threat of being sprinkled with pig's blood was used in the Philippines in 1902 by Pershing to "persuade" some Muslim leaders to sign a treaty to make peace amongst themselves. See O'Connor, Richard *Black Jack Pershing* (New York: Doubleday & Co., inc, 1961) pp.62-3

13 Philps "Settlers Use Pigskin to Foil the Martyrs" www.telegraph.co.uk (26 February 2002) (viewed 5 December 2003)

14 Mikkelson, Barbara and David "Pershing the Thought" in Urban Legends Reference Pages at www.snopes.com/rumors/pershing.htm (26 February 2002) (viewed 11 December 2002)

15 "Israeli Rabbi urges Pig Fat use to Stop Bombers" Reuters (12 February 2004) http://news.ft.com/servlet/ContentServer?pagename=FT. com/WireFeed /WireFeed&c=WireFeed&cid=1074160683676& p=1014232938216 (viewed 13 February 2004)

16 Philps "Settlers Use Pigskin to Foil the Martyrs"

17 "State Senator Angers Muslims with Flier on Pig Entrails" *Associated Press* (27 June 2003), available at http://edition.cnn.com/2003/ALLPOLITICS /06/27/senator.pigentrails.ap/ (viewed 27 June 2003)

18 Hosenball, Mark and Michael Isikoff "Al Qaeda Strikes Again" in *Newsweek* (26 May – 2 June 2003) p.24

19 "Saudi Clerics Condemn Terrorism" *BBC News* (17 August 2003) http:// news.bbc.co.uk/go/pr/fr/-/1/hi/world/middle_east/3157493.stm

20 "Imam Fired For Praising Suicide Bombers" in *The Independent* (16 June 2003); Shirbon, Estelle "Rome Imam Suspended After Praising Suicide Bombers" Reuters (13 June 2003) available at http://www.reuters.com / newsArticle.jhtml?type=topNews&storyID=2928250

21 Björkman,W. "Shahid" in *E.J. Brill's First Encyclopaedia of Islam 1913-1936* (Leiden: E.J. Brill, 1993) Vol. VII p.261

22 Abshar-Abdalla, Ulil "Freshening Up Our Understanding of Islam" in *Kompas* (18 November 2002). Quotations are an English translation from the Indonesian original.

23   Zakaria, Fareed "Now, Saudis See the Enemy" in *Newsweek* (26 May – 2 June 2003) p.19

Chapter 10

1   Sun Tz˘u *The Art of War* with foreword by James Clavell (London: Hodder and Stoughton, 1981) p.26

2   Kaegi *Byzantium and the Early Islamic Conquests* p.274

3   Reported by Rood, Judith Mendelsohn "Why and How Should Christian Students Study World Religions?" in *CCCU Advance* (Spring 2003)

4   I am indebted to Daniel Pipes for his analysis pinpointing these four areas (understanding the enemy's motives, defining war goals, defining the enemy, defining the allies) in "Know Thy Terrorists" in *New York Post*, November 19, 2002

5   Speaking at the Royal United Services Institute, UK (21 November 2002)

6   al-Asi "Qur'anic Teaching on the Justification for Jihad and Qital" p.7

7   Haqqani, Hussain "Where's the Muslim Debate?" in *The Wall Street Journal* (22 May 2003)

8   A selection of extracts from the Saudi press are given in Zakaria "Now, Saudis See the Enemy"

9   "The Enemy Within", an editorial in the *Arab News* (an English language Saudi daily) quoted in Zakaria "Now, Saudis See the Enemy"

10   Qusti, Raid in the *Arab News*, quoted in Zakaria "Now, Saudis See the Enemy"

11   Al-Tarifi, Adel Zaid in *Al-Watan*, quoted in Zakaria "Now, Saudis See the Enemy"

12   This process starts at a young age. The Palestinian Authority Education Ministry set a children's letter-writing competition in which the themes were (1) Lod and Jaffa are Palestinian cities (2) Glorifying violence, hate, death for the sake of Allah – *shahada* (3) Hatred of America. Some of the winning entries were published in the daily newspaper *Al-Quds* (28 May 2003). English translation in *Palestinian Media Watch Bulletin* (1 June 2003)

13   General M. Zia-ul-Haq, Chief of the Army Staff, later president of Pakistan, writing in the foreword to Malik, Brigadier S.K. *The Quranic Concept of War* Indian edition (New Delhi: Himalayan Books. 1986) (no page number)

14   Ferguson *War and Peace in the World's Religions* p.132

15   TV interview for BBC World (screened approximately 23 April 2003)

16   For example, Eliza Manningham-Buller, the director-general of Britain's MI5, stated in a speech on 17 June 2003 that "Breaking the link between terrorism and religious ideology is difficult." ("MI5 Chief Fears Dirty Bomb is Inevitable" in *The Times* (18 June 2003))

17   Tibi, Bassam *Arab Nationalism: Between Islam and the Nation-State* 3rd edition (Basingstoke: Macmillan Press Ltd, 1997) pp.232-3

18   For example, as Kennedy records (Th*e Prophet and the Age of the Caliphates* p.35) the Muslim side at the Battle of Badr (624) is known to have consisted of 86 *muhajirun* and 230 *ansar*. The army was not described as a single force of 316 Muslims.

19   Sicker *The Islamic World in Ascendency* p.9

20   van Ess, Josef *Theologie und Gesellschaft im 2. und 3. Jahrhundert Hidschra. Eine Geschicthe des religiösen Denkens im frühen Islam* (Berlin: de Bruyter, 1991-5) Vol. 1 p.17

21   Quoted in Baljon, J.M.S. *The Reforms and Religious Ideas of Sir Sayyid Ahmad Khan* (Lahore: Shaikh Muhammad Ashraf, 1964) pp.117-9

22   Sciolino, Elaine "French Islam Wins Officially Recognized Voice" in *The New York Times* (14 April 2003)

23   Sciolino, Elaine "French Threat to Militant Muslims After Council Vote" in *The New York Times* (15 April 2004)

24   Private gathering attended by the author, London, 29 September 2003

Appendix 4

1   http://news.bbc.co.uk/1/hi/world/middle_east/3368957.stm (viewed 6 May 2004)

Bibliography

Abdelnasser, Walid M. *The Islamic Movement in Egypt* (London: Keegan Paul International, 1994)

Abd es-Salam, Kamal Boraiq'a "Responding to Dr Bat Ye'or" (23 August 2002) in *Religious News Service from the Arab World* (2 September 2002)

'Abdul Khaliq, Sheikh 'Abdul Rahman *Verdict on the Treaties of Compromise and Peace with the Jews* reproduced at http://www.islaam.com/articles/treaty.htm (viewed 18 September 2001)

Abedi, Mehdi and Gary Legenhausen (eds.) *Jihad and Shahadat: Struggle and Martyrdom in Islam* (Houston: Institute for Research and Islamic Studies, 1986)

Abshar-Abdalla, Ulil "Freshening Up Our Understanding of Islam" in *Kompas* (18 November 2002). Quotations are an English translation from the Indonesian original.

Abu Gheith, Suleiman, "In the Shadow of the Lances" from the Center for Islamic Research and Studies website (originally www.alneda.com then changed to http://66.34.191.223).Reported by MEMRI Special Dispatch Series No. 388 (12 June 2002)

Abu-Manneh, Butrus "The Naqshabandiyya-Mujaddidiyya in the Ottoman Lands in the Early 19th Century" in *Die Welt des Islams* Vol. 12 (1986) pp.1-36

Abu Yusuf, Ya'qub b. Ibrahim al-Ansari *Kitab al-Kharaj* (Cairo, 1933)

Abu Yusuf, Ya'qub b. Ibrahim al-Ansari *Kitab al-Radd 'ala Siyar al-Awza'i* ed. Abu al-Wafa al-Afghani (Cairo, 1938)

Abu Zahra, Muhammad *Al-'Alaqat al-Dawliyya fi l-Islam* (Cairo: al-Dar al-Qawmiyya li-l-Tiba'a wa-l-Nashr, 1964)

Ahmad, Hazrat Mirza Ghulam *Jesus in India: Jesus' Escape from Death on the Cross and Journey to India* (London: The London Mosque, 1978). English version of *Masih Hindustan mein* (1899)

Ahmad, Mirza Ghulam *Tohfah Golrviyah* (1902). Republished in vol. 17 of *Ruhani Khaza'in*, the collected works of Ghulam Mirza Ahmad (Rabwa, 1965)

Akbar, M.J. *The Shade of Swords: Jihad and Conflict between Islam and Christianity* (London: Routledge, 2002)

Alexander, Yonah and Michael S. Swetnam *Usama bin Laden's al-Qaida: Profile of a Terrorist Network* (Ardsley, USA: Transnational Publishers, Inc., 2001)

Ali, Abdullah Yusuf *The Holy Qur'an: Text, Translation and Commentary* (Leicester: The Islamic Foundation, 1975)

al-Ali, Hamid Abdullah "The Legality of Killing Jewish Women and Children in Palestine" in *Al-Watan* (31 August 2001). English translation by Shira Gutgold published in the *Jerusalem Post* (5 September 2001)

Almascaty, Dr Hilmy Bakar *Panduan Jihad Untuk Aktivis Gerakan Islam [A Manual for Jihad for Islamic Movement Activists]* (Jakarta: Gema Insani Press, May 2001)

Anderson, Sir Norman (ed.) *The World's Religions* 4th edition (Grand Rapids, Michigan: Eerdmans, 1975)

Anderson, Sir Norman *Islam in the Modern World: A Christian Perspective* (Leicester: Apollos, 1990)

al-Ansari, 'Abd al-Hamid "Landmarks in Rational and Constructive Dialogue with the 'Other'" in *Al-Hayat* (London) (31 May 2002). Extracts in English translation in MEMRI Special Dispatch Series No. 386 (5 June 2002)

Ansari, Sarah F.D. *Sufi Saints and State Power: The Pirs of Sind, 1843-1947* (Lahore: Vanguard Books, 1992) published by arrangement with Cambridge University Press

al-Ansari, Seif Al-Din writing in *Al-Ansar*, No. 16 (24 August 2002) www.jehad.net. Extracts in English translation in MEMRI Special Dispatch Series No. 418 (4 September 2002)

al-Aqqad, Abbas Mahmoud *Haqa'iq al-Islam wa Abatil Khusumih* (Cairo: Dar al-Hilal, 1957)

Ardabili *al-Anwar li-'Amal al-Abrar* (Cairo, no date)

Armanazi, Najib *L'Islam et le Droit International* (thesis) (Paris: Librairie Picart, 1929)

Armstrong, Karen *Holy War* (London and Basingstoke: Macmillan London Limited, 1988)

Ashburn, Kristen "The Suicide Bombers" in *Telegraph Magazine* (15 November 2003) pp.24-33

al-Asi, Imam Mohammed "Qur'anic Teaching on the Justification for Jihad and Qital" in *Crescent International* (1-15 June 2003) pp.7, 11

al-Azdi al-Basri, Muhammad b. 'Abdullah Abu Isma'il *Ta'rikh Futuh al-Sham* ed. 'Abd al-Mun'im 'Abdullah 'Amir (Cairo: Mu'assasat Sijill al-'Arab, 1970); ed. William Nassau Lees. Bibliotheca Indica (Calcutta, 1857)

Badawi, Zaki *Islam in Britain* (London: Taha Publishers, 1981)

al-Baghdadi, 'Abd al-Qahir *Mukhtasar Kitab al-Farq Bayn al-Firaq* ed. Philip Hitti (Cairo, 1924)

Baghdadi, Abu Mansur 'Abd al-Qahir ibn Tahir *Kitab Usul al-Din* (Istanbul, 1928)

al-Baladhuri, Ahmad b. Yahya *Futuh al-Buldan* [*Conquests of the Countries*] ed. M.J. De Goeje (Leiden: Brill, 1866)

Baljon, J.M.S. *The Reforms and Religious Ideas of Sir Sayyid Ahmad Khan* (Lahore: Shaikh Muhammad Ashraf, 1964)

Banerjee, Mukulika *The Pathan Unarmed: Opposition and Memory in the North West Frontier* (Karachi: Oxford University Press, 2000)

al-Banna, Hasan *Five Tracts of Hasan al-Banna (1906-1949): A Selection from the Majmu'at Rasa'il al-Imam al-Shahid* (Berkeley, California: University of California Press, 1978)

Barghuthy, Omar Saleh, "A Ministry of Propaganda under the Fatimids" in *Journal of the Middle East Society* (Spring 1947) pp. 57-9

Batrafi, Khaled Muhammad "Why do we hate the People of the Book?" in *Al-Hayat* (21 October 2001). Extracts in English translation quoted in MEMRI Special Dispatch Series No. 295 (1 November 2001)

Bat Ye'or *The Decline of Eastern Christianity under Islam: From Islam to Dhimmitude* (Cranbury, New Jersey / London: Farleigh Dickinson University Press and Associated University Presses, 1996)

Bayoumi, Dr Abdel-Mo'ti "Wrong Zionist Perceptions of Jihad in Islam via the Internet" in *Al-Musawwar* (23 August 2002). English translation in *Religious News Service from the Arab World* (2 September 2002)

Bilal, Abdul Rahman *Islamic Military Resurgence* (Lahore: Ferozsons (Pvt.) Ltd, 1991)

Bin Omar, Abdullah "The Striving Sheik: Abdullah Azzam" translated by Mohammed Saeed in *Nida'ul Islam*, Issue 14 (July-September 1996) http://www.islam.org.au/articles/14/AZZAM.HTM (viewed 28 September 2003)

Blair, John C. *The Sources of Islam: An Inquiry into the Sources of the Faith and the Practice of the Muhammadan Religion* (Madras: The Christian Literature Society for India, 1925)

Blankinship, Khalid Yahya *The End of the Jihad State: The Reign of Hisham Ibn 'Abd al-Malik and the Collapse of the Umayyads* (Albany: State University of New York Press, 1994)

Bos, Stefan J. "Christians Near Northern Iraq Persecuted" in *Assist News Service* (5 April 2003)

Bostom, Andrew G. "Muhammad, the Qurayza Massacre, and PBS" in *FrontPageMagazine.com* (20 December 2002)

Breydy, Michael *Corpus Scriptorum Christianorum Orientalium* Vol. 471-2 Scriptores Arabici T.44-5 (Louvain: E. Peeters, 1985)

Brock, S.P. "North Mesopotamia in the Late Seventh Century. Book XV of John Bar Penkaye's *Ris Melle*" in *Jerusalem Studies in Arabic and Islam* Vol. 9 (1987) pp.51-75

Brown, Judith M. *Modern India: The Origins of an Asian Democracy* 2nd edition, in The Short Oxford History of the Modern World series (Oxford: Oxford University Press, 1995)

al-Bukhari, al-Imam Abu Abdillah Muhammed, *Sahih Al-Bukhari*, ed. Shaikh Qasem al-Rifaie (Beirut: Dar Al-Qalam, 1987)

Carey, Andrew "Islam's Confused Identity" in *The Church of England Newspaper* (28 August 2003) p.8

Caroe, Olaf *The Pathans 550 B.C. – A.D. 1957* (London: Macmillan & Co. Ltd, 1965)

Cassese, A. (ed.) *The Current Legal Regulation of the Use of Force* (Dordrecht: Martinus Nijhoff, 1986)

Chen, Joanna "A Martyr or a Murderer" in *Newsweek* (23 February 2004)

Cook, David *Studies in Muslim Apocalyptic* Studies in Late Antiquity and Early Islam 21 (Princeton, New Jersey: The Darwin Press, 2002)

Corbin, Henri *En Islam Iranien* (Paris: Gallimard, 1971)

Cragg, Kenneth *The House of Islam* 2nd edition (California: Dickenson Publishing Co., 1978)

Cragg, Kenneth "A Tale of Two Cities: Helping the Heirs of Mecca to Transform Medina" in *Mission Frontiers* (December 2001)

Crumley, Bruce "Jihad's Hidden Victim" in *Time* (2 June 2003) p.48

al-Daqs, Kamil Salama *Ayat al-Jihad fi l-Qur'an al-Karim* (Kuwait: Dar al-Bayan, 1972)

Daraz, Muhammad 'Abd Allah "Mabadi' al-Qanun al-Dawli al-'Amm li-l-Islam" in *Risalat al-Islam* 2 (1950)

al-Dawalibi, Ma'ruf "Islam and Nationalistic and Secularistic Trends" in *Ash-Sharq al-Awsat* (31 December 1989) reprinted in Kharofa (1994) pp.1-17

Dawoud, Khaled "America's Most Wanted" in *Al-Ahram Weekly Online*, Issue No. 552 (20-26 September 2001)

Declaration of Jihad Against the Country's Tyrants, Military Series recovered by police in Manchester UK from the home of Nazihal Wadih Raghie, 10 May 2000

Delehaye, Hipployte "Passio sanctorum sexaginta martyrum" in *Analecta Bollandiana: A Journal of Critical Hagiography* Vol. 28 (1904) pp.289-307

Dentan, Robert C. (ed.) *Lectures of the Department of Near Eastern Languages and Literatures at Yale University* American Oriental Series No. 38 (New Haven, Connecticut: Yale University Press, 1955)

Doctrina Iacobi nuper baptizati ed. N. Bonwetsch *Abhandlungen der Königlichen. Gesellschaft der Wissenschaften zu Göttingen.* Philologisch-Historische Klasse. Neue Folge Vol.12, No. 3 (Berlin: Weidmannsche Buchh., 1910)

Donner, Fred M. "The Sources of Islamic Conceptions of War" in Kelsay and Johnson (1991) pp.31-69

Donohue, J.J. and J.L. Esposito (eds.) *Islam in Transition: Muslim Perspectives* (New York: Oxford University Press, 1982)

Dozy, R. *Histoire des Musulmans d'Espagne*, 4 vols (Leiden: Brill, 1861)

Drogin, Bob and Greg Miller "Spy Agencies Facing Questions of Tactics" in *Los Angeles Times* (29 October 2001)

E.J. *Brill's First Encyclopaedia of Islam 1913-1936* 9 vols (Leiden: E.J. Brill, 1993)

Ellis, Eric "Mahathir Tirade at 'Jews Ruling World'" in *Times Online* (17 October 2003) http://www.timesonline.co.uk/printFriendly/0,,1-3-857059,00.html (viewed 5 December 2003)

Enayat, Hamid *Modern Islamic Political Thought* (Austin: University of Texas Press, 1982)

The Encyclopaedia of Islam new edition 11 vols (Leiden: Brill, 1979 onwards)

Engineer, Ali Asghar "Islam and Non-violence" in Kumar (1995)

Esposito, John (ed.) *Voices of Resurgent Islam* (New York: Oxford University Press, 1983)

Esposito, John (ed.) *The Oxford History of Islam* (Oxford: Oxford University Press, 1999)

Esposito, John L. *Unholy War: Terror in the Name of Islam* (Oxford: Oxford University Press, 2002)

Eutychius *Das Annalenwerk des Eutychios von Alexandrien* ed. and transl. Michael Breydy *Corpus Scriptorum Christianorum Orientalium* Vol. 471-2 Scriptores Arabici T.44-5 (Louvain: E. Peeters, 1985)

el Fadl, Khaled Abou *Rebellion and Violence in Islamic Law* (Cambridge: Cambridge University Press, 2001)

al-Fagih, Saad "The War that Bin Laden is Winning" in *The Guardian* (13 May 2003)

Faraj, Muhammad 'Abd al-Salam *Al-Faridah al-Gha'ibah [The Neglected Duty].* English translation in Jansen, Johannes J. G. *The Neglected Duty: The Creed of Sadat's Assassins and Islamic Resurgence in the Middle East* (New York: Macmillan, 1986) pp.159-234

Fatoohi, Louay *Jihad in the Qur'an: The Truth from the Source* (Kuala Lumpur: A.S. Noordeen, 2002)

Ferguson, John *War and Peace in the World's Religions* (London: Sheldon Press, 1977)

Fighel, Jonathan "Sheikh Abdullah Azzam: Bin Laden's Spiritual Mentor" Institute for Counter Terrorism (27 September 2001) http://www.ict.org.il/articles/articledet.cfm?articleid=388 (viewed 28 September 2003)

Firestone, Reuven *Jihad: The Origin of Holy War in Islam* (New York: Oxford University Press, 1999)

Fredegarius *Chronicles* ed. Bruno Krusch (Hanover: MGH Scriptores Rerum Merovingicarum T.2, 1888, repr. 1984)

Friedman, Thomas L. "Defusing the Holy Bomb" in *The New York Times* (27 November 2002)

Gardner, Frank "Grand Sheikh Condemns Suicide Bombings" (BBC News, 4 December 2001). Available at www.bbc.co.uk/hi/english/world/middle_east/newsid_1690000/1690624.stm (viewed 5 December 2001)

al Ghunaimi, Mohammad Talaat *The Muslim Conception of International Law and the Western Approach* (The Hague: Martinus Nijhoff, 1968)

Gold, Dore *Hatred's Kingdom: How Saudi Arabia Supports the New Global Terrorism* (Washington DC: Regnery Publishing Inc., 2003)

Guillaume, Alfred *The Life of Muhammad: A Translation of Ibn Ishaq's Sirat Rasul Allah* (Karachi: Oxford University Press, 1955)

Gunaratna, Rohan *Inside Al Qaeda : Global Network of Terror* (London: Hurst & Company, 2002)

Haddad, Y.Y. "The Quranic Justification for an Islamic Revolution: The View of Sayyid Qutb" in *Middle East Journal* Vol. 37 No. 1 (Winter 1983)

Haddad, Y.Y. "Sayyid Qutb: Ideologue of Islamic Revival" in Esposito (1983) pp.67-98

Haleem, Harifyah Abdel, Oliver Ramsbotham, Saba Risaluddin and Brian Wicker (eds.) *The Crescent and the Cross: Muslim and Christian Approaches to War and Peace* (Basingstoke: Macmillan Press Ltd, 1998; New York: St Martin's Press, Inc., 1998)

Hamidullah, Muhammad *Documents sur la Diplomatie Musulmane à l'époque du Prophete et des Khalifes Orthodoxes* (Paris: Librarie Oriental et Americane, Thesis, University of Paris, 1935)

Hamidullah, Muhammad *Muslim Conduct of State* 3rd edition (Lahore: Sh. Muhammad Ashraf, 1953)

Hamidullah, Muhammad *The Battle Fields of the Prophet* (Lahore: Idra-e-Islamiat, 1993)

Haqqani, Hussain "Where's the Muslim Debate?" in *The Wall Street Journal* (22 May 2003)

Harnden, Toby "Video Games Attract Young to Hizbollah" in *The Daily Telegraph* (21 February 2004) p.18

al-Hawali, Sheikh Safar bin Abdur-Rahman *Open Letter to President Bush* (15 October 2001) Azzam Publications http://202.95.140.21/¬acom/fatwas/print_view.php?id=2 (viewed 4 June 2002)

The Hedaya : Commentary on the Islamic laws transl. Charles Hamilton (New Delhi: Kitab Bhavan, 1985). This is a facsimile of a book originally published in 1791.

Hider, James "Iraqis Drugged, Brainwashed and sent to die for Bin Laden" in *Times Online* (22 March 2004)

Higgins, Rosalyn "The Attitude of Western States towards Legal Aspects of the Use of Force" in Cassese (1986)

Holt, P.M. *A Modern History of the Sudan* 3rd edition (London: Weidenfeld and Nicolson, 1967)

Holt, P.M., Ann K.S. Lambton and Bernard Lewis (eds.) *The Cambridge History of Islam Vol. 1A The Central Islamic Lands from pre-Islamic Times to the First World War* (Cambridge: Cambridge University Press, 1970)

Hookway, James "How a Terrorist Proves his Faith" in *Far Eastern Economic Review* (14 November 2002)

Hooper, Charles *Civil Law of Palestine and Transjordan* (Jerusalem: Azriel, 1933-6)

Hopwood, Derek *Egypt: Politics and Society 1945-1990* (London: Harper Collins Academic, 1991)

Hosenball, Mark and Michael Isikoff "Al Qaeda Strikes Again" in *Newsweek* (26 May – 2 June 2003) pp.20-6

Hughes, Thomas Patrick *A Dictionary of Islam* (Lahore: Premier Book House, 1885)

Hulsman, Cornelis "Commenting on Bat Ye'or's article" in *Religious News Service from the Arab World* (28 August 2002)

Huntington, Samuel P. *The Clash of Civilisations and the Remaking of the World Order* (New York: Simon and Schuster, 1996)

Hurley, Victor *Jungle Patrol: The Story of the Philippine Constabulary* (New York: E.P. Dutton, 1938)

Ibn 'Abd-Allah, Hasan *Athar al-Uwal fi Tartib al-Duwal* (Cairo, 1878 or 1879). The original work dates from 1308 or 1309.

Ibn Abidin, Muhammad Amin *Radd al-Muhtar 'ala al-durr al-Mukhtar* 7 vols (Cairo, 1856 or 1857)

Ibn Abi Zayd al-Qayrawani, Abu Muhammad 'Abdullah *La Risâla (Epître sur les éléments du dogme et de la loi de l'Islam selon le rite mâlakite).* Arabic text with French translation by Leon Bercher, 4th edition (Algiers, 1951).

Ibn A'tham al-Kufi, Abu Muhammad Ahmad *Kitab al-Futuh* ed. Muhammad 'Ali al-'Abbasi and Sayyid 'Abd al-Wahhab Bukhari 8 vols, (Hyderabad: Da'irat al-Ma'arif al-'Uthmaniyya, 1968-75)

Ibn Baz, Abdul-Aziz, Abdul-Aziz Ibn Abdullah Al-Shaykh Abdullah, Salih Ibn Fawzan Al-Fawzan and Bakr Ibn Abdullah Abu Zaid (The Permanent Committee for Academic Research and Ifta) *Unification of Religions Fatwa* no. 19402 (2 June 1997) available at www.troid. org/articles/islaamicinfo/Islaamingeneral/whatisislaam/unificationofreligion (viewed 7 August 2003)

Ibn Baz, Shaykh and Shaykh Uthaymeen *Muslim Minorities: Fatawa Regarding Muslims Living as Minorities* (Hounslow: Message of Islam, 1998)

Ibn Hisham, 'Abd al-Malik *al-Sira al-Nabawiyya* ed. Heinrich Ferdinand Wüstenfeld *Sirat Rasul Allah [Das Leben Muhammeds]* 2 vols (Göttingen: Dieterischen Buchhandlung, 1858-60)

Ibn Khaldun *The Muqaddimah: An Introduction To History* transl. Franz Rosenthal 3 vols (London: Routledge & Kegan Paul, 1958)

Ibn Naqib al-Misri, Ahmad *Reliance of the Traveller: A Classic Manual of Sacred Islamic Law 'Umdat al-Salik* ed. and transl. Nuh Ha Mim Keller revised edition (Beltsville, Maryland: Amana Publications, 1997)

Ibn Qudama, Abu Muhammad 'Abd-Allah ibn Ahmad ibn Muhammad *Kitab al-Mughni* ed. M. Rashid Rida, 9 vols (Cairo, 1947 or 1948)

Ibn Rushd, Abu al-Walid Muhammad Ibn Muhammad (Averroes) *Bidyat al-Mujtahid wa-Nihayat al-Muqtasid [The Beginning for him who Interprets the Sources Independently and the End for him who Wishes to Limit Himself]* Chapter on jihad in English translation in Peters (1996) pp.29-42

Ibn Sa'd, Muhammad *Kitab al-Tabaqat al-Kabir* ed. Eduard Sachau et al. 9 vols (Leiden: Brill, 1904-40)

Ibn Sallam, Abu 'Ubayd al-Qasim *Kitab al-Amwal* ed. Muhammad Khalil Haras (Cairo, 1968)

Ibn Taymiyya, Taqi al-Din *Ahmad al-Siyasa al-Shar'iyya fi Islah al-Ra'i wa-al-Ra'iyya [Governance according to God's Law in Reforming both the Ruler and his Flock]*. Section on jihad reproduced in Peters (1996) pp.43-54

Ibn 'Uthaymeen, Sheikh *Riyaadhus-Saaliheen* Vol.1 pp.165-6. Available at www.fatwa-online.com/fataawa/worship/jihaad/jih004/0010915_1.htm (viewed 12 August 2003)

Ibrahim, Naajeh, Asim Abdul Majid and Esaam-ud-Deen Darbaalah *In Pursuit of Allah's Pleasure* (London: Al-Firdous Ltd, 1997)

Inalcik, Halil *The Ottoman Empire: the Classical Age 1300-1600* (London: Phoenix Press, 2000)

Iqbal, Anwar "Islamic schools create Pakistani dilemma" United Press International (17 August 2002)

Istanbuli, Yasin *Diplomacy and Diplomatic Practice in the Early Islamic Era* (Oxford: Oxford University Press, 2001)

Izutsu, Toshihiko *The Structure of the Ethical Terms in the Koran* (Tokyo: Keio Institute of Philological Studies, 1959)

Jaber, Hala and Uzi Mahnaimi "Suicide Bombing was a Family Affair" in *The Sunday Times* (18 January 2004)

Jameelah, Maryam *Islam and Modernism* (Sant Nagar, Lahore: Mohammad Yusuf Khan, 1968)

Jandora, John W. "Developments in Islamic Warfare: The Early Conquests" in *Studia Islamica* Vol. 64 (1986) pp.101-13

Jansen, Johannes J. G. *The Neglected Duty: The Creed of Sadat's Assassins and Islamic Resurgence in the Middle East* (New York: Macmillan, 1986)

John, Bishop of Nikiu *Chronicle* transl. R.H. Charles (London, Oxford, 1916)

John, Elizabeth and K.T. Chelvi "The Chilling Jemaah Islamiyah Goal" in *New Sunday Times* (19 January 2003)

John Bar Penkaye *Ris Melle*. See Brock (1987)

Johnson, James Turner "Historical Roots and Sources of Just War Tradition in Western Culture" in Kelsay and Johnson (1991) pp.3-30

Johnson, James Turner and John Kelsay (eds.) *Cross, Crescent and Sword: The Justification and Limitation of War in Western and Islamic Tradition* (Westport, Connecticut: Greenwood Press, 1990)

Johnson, Nels *Islam and the Politics of Meaning in Palestinian Nationalism* (London: Kegan Paul, 1982)

Johnson, Paul *The Birth of the Modern: World Society 1815-1830* (New York: Harper Collins, 1991)

Jukes, Worthington *Frontier Heroes: Reminiscences of Missionary Work in Amritsar 1872-1873 and on the Afghan Frontier in Peshawar 1873-1890* (manuscript dated Exmouth, 1925, re-typed Peshawar, 2000)

Juynboll, Gautier H.A. (transl.) *The History of Al-Tabari Vol. XIII: The Conquest of Iraq, Southwestern Persia, and Egypt* (Albany: State University of New York Press, 1989)

Kaegi, Walter E. *Byzantium and the Early Islamic Conquests* (Cambridge: Cambridge University Press, 1992)

al-Kalbbi, *Al-Hafz Al-Tasshel Fi Aleolom Al Tanzel [The Easiest Revelation of Theology]*

Kandhalvi, Muhammad Zakariyya "Stories of Sahabah" in *Tablighi Nisab* (Dewsbury: Anjuman-e-Islahul Muslemeen of U.K., no date but probably soon after 1938)

Kelsay, John and James Turner Johnson (eds.) *Just War and Jihad: Historical and Theoretical Perspectives on War and Peace in Western and Islamic Traditions* (Westport, Connecticut: Greenwood Press, 1991)

Kennedy, Hugh *The Prophet and the Age of the Caliphates: the Islamic Near East from the Sixth to the Eleventh Century* (Harlow: Pearson Education Limited (Longman), 1986)

Kepel, Gilles *Jihad: The Trail of Political Islam* transl. Anthony F. Roberts (London: I.B. Tauris, 2002)

Kepel, Gilles "The Origins and Development of the Jihadist Movement: From Anti-Communism to Terrorism" transl. Peter Clark in *Asian Affairs* Vol. 34 No. 2 (July 2003) pp.91-108

Khadduri, Majid *War and Peace in the Law of Islam* (Baltimore: The Johns Hopkins Press, 1955)

Khadduri, Majid (transl. and annotated) *The Islamic Law of Nations: Shaybani's Siyar* (Baltimore: The Johns Hopkins Press, 1966)

Khan, Majid Ali *The Pious Caliphs* (New Delhi: Millat Book Centre, 1976)

Khan, Sir Syed Ahmed in *The Pioneer* (23 November 1871) and in *Review on Dr Hunter's Indian Musulmans: Are They Bound in Conscience to Rebel Against the Queen?* (Benares: Medical Hall Press, 1872)

Kharofa, Ala'Eddin "Muhammad the Messenger of God (PBUH) and Westerners" in Kharofa (1994) pp.95-102

Kharofa, Ala'Eddin *Nationalism Secularism Apostasy and Usury in Islam* (Kuala Lumpur: A.S. Nordeen, 1994)

Khomeini, Ayatollah Ruhollah "Islamic Government" in Donohue and Esposito (1982) pp.314-22

Kister, M.J. "The Massacre of the Banu Qurayza: A Re-examination of a Tradition" in *Jerusalem Studies in Arabic and Islam* Vol. 8 (1986) pp.61-96. Also reproduced in Kister, M.J. *Society and Religion from Jahiliyya to Islam* (Aldershot: Variorum, 1990).

Klein, F.A. *The Religion of Islam* (London: Curzon Press Ltd and New York: Humanities Press Inc, 1906, reprinted 1971, 1979)

Kohlberg, Etan "The Development of the Imami Shi'i Doctrine of Jihad" in *Zeitschrift der Deutschen Morgenlaendischen Gesellschaft* Vol. 126 (1976)

Kraemer, Joel "Apostates, Rebels and Brigands" in *Israel Oriental Studies* Vol. 10 (1980) pp.34-73

Kramer, Martin *Islam Assembled: The Advent of the Muslim Congresses* (New York, Columbia University Press, 1986)

Kumar, R. (ed.) *Khan Abdul Gaffar Khan: A Centennial Tribute* (New Delhi: Nehru Memorial Museum and Library, Har-Anand Publications, 1995)

Lewis, Bernard *The Assassins: A Radical Sect in Islam* (London: Phoenix, 2003). First published 1967.

Lewis, Bernard *The Political Language of Islam* (Chicago and London: The University of Chicago Press, 1988)

Lewis, Bernard "The Revolt of Islam" in *The New Yorker* (19 November 2001)

MacAskill, Ewen and Ian Traynor "Saudis Consider Nuclear Bomb" in *The Guardian* (18 September 2003)

al-Mahmasani, Subhi *al-Nazariyya al 'Amma Li'l-Mujibat wa'l-'Uqud* (Beirut, 1948)

Mahmassani, Sobhi "International Law in the Light of Islamic Doctrine" in *Academie de Droit International, Recueil des Cours* Vol. 117 (1966)

Al-Majalla transl. Charles Hooper in *Civil Law of Palestine and Transjordan* Vol. 1 (Jerusalem: Azriel, 1933-6)

Malik, Brigadier S.K. *The Quranic Concept of War* Indian edition (New Delhi: Himalayan Books. 1986)

Mango, Andrew *Atatürk* (London: John Murray, 1999)

Mansour, Mu'aadh "The Importance of Military Preparedness in Shari'ah" in *Al-Battar Training Camp* issue 1 (December 2003 or January 2004?) www. hostinganime.com/battar/b1word.zip. Excerpts in English translation in MEMRI Special Dispatch Series No. 637 (6 January 2004)

Mansur, 'Ali 'Ali *Al-Shari'a al-Islamiyya wa-l-Qanun al-Dawli al'Amm* (Cairo: al-Majlis al-A'la li-l-Shu'un al-Islamiyya, 1971)

Marcus, Itamar "PA TV Glorifies First Woman Suicide Terrorist – Wafa Idris" in *Palestinian Media Watch Bulletin* (24 July 2003)

Marcus, Itamar "UN is Funding Summer Camps Honoring Terrorists" in *Palestinian Media Watch Bulletin* (25 July 2003)

Marty, Martin E. and Appleby, R. Scott (eds) *Fundamentalisms and the State: Remaking Polities, Economies and Militance* The Fundamentalism Project Vol. 3 (Chicago and London: University of Chicago Press, 1993)

al-Mawardi, Abu'l Hasan *The Ordinances of Government: al-Ahkam al-Sultaniyya w'al-Wilayat al-Diniyya* transl. Wafaa H. Wahba, The Centre for Muslim Contribution to Civilization (Reading: Garnet Publishing Ltd, 1996)

Mawdudi, Sayyid Abul A'la *Jihad fi Sabilillah (Jihad in Islam)*, transl. Kurshid Ahmad, ed. Huda Khattab (Birmingham: Islamic Mission Dawah Centre, 1997)

Mawlawi, Sheikh Faysal "Attacking US Bases in Arab Countries" (23 March 2003) www.islamonline.net/fatwa/english/FatwaDisplay. asp?hFatwaID=94843 (viewed 18 August 2003)

Mayer, Ann Elizabeth "War and Peace in the Islamic Tradition and International Law" in Kelsay and Johnson (1991) pp. 195-226

McGrory, Daniel and Sam Lister "Prophets of Hate Prey on Rootless Misfits" in *The Times* (31 January 2003)

MEMRI The Middle East Media Research Institute, P.O. Box 27837, Washington DC 20038-7837, USA http://memri.org

Michael the Syrian *Chronique* ed. and transl. J.-B. Chabot 4 vols (Paris: E. Leroux, 1899-1910)

Mikkelson, Barbara and David "Pershing the Thought" in Urban Legends Reference Pages at www.snopes.com/rumors/pershing.htm (26 February 2002) (viewed 11 December 2002)

Mishkat al-Masabih English translation with explanatory notes by James Robson 2 vols (Lahore: Sh. Muhammad Ashraf, 1990)

Moinuddin, Hasan *The Charter of the Islamic Conference and Legal Framework of Economic Co-operation among Its Member States* (Oxford: Clarendon Press, 1987)

Muir, Sir William *Mahomet and Islam* (London: The Religious Tract Society, 1895)

an-Nabhani, Taqiuddin *The Islamic State* (London: Al-Khilafah Publications, no date)

Nasif, Sheikh Mansur Ali *Al-Tajj al Jami lil-usul fi Ahadith al-Rasul* (Istanbul: Dar Ihya al-Kutub al-'Arabiyyah, 1961). Also published in Cairo by Matba'ah 'Isa al Babl al Halabi (no date).

Nettler, Ronald "A Modern Islamic Confession of Faith and Conception of Religion: Sayyid Qutb's Introduction to *tafsir, Fi Zilal al-Quran"* in *British Journal of Middle Eastern Studies* Vol. 21 No. 1 (1994)

Nicephorus *Short History* ed. C. Mango (Washington: Dumbarton Oaks, 1990)

Noth, Albrecht "Heiliger Kampf (Gihad) gegen die 'Franken': Zur Position der Kreuzzüge im Rahmen der Islamgeschichte" in *Saeculum* Vol. 37 (1986) pp.240-59

Obermann, Julian "Early Islam" in *Lectures of the Department of Near Eastern Langages and Literatures at Yale University* ed. Robert C. Dentan, American Oriental Series No. 38 (Yale University Press, 1954?)

Overy, Richard (ed.) *The Times History of the World* new edition (London: Times Books, Harper Collins Publishers, 1999)

Palestinian Media Watch bulletins http://www.pmw.org.il

Palmer, J.A.B. "The Origin of the Janissaries" in *Bulletin of the John Rylands Library*, Manchester, Vol. 35, No. 1 (September 1952) pp. 448-81

Pargoire, J. "Les LX Soldats Martyrs de Gaza" in *Echos d'Orient: Revue de Théologie, de Droit Canonique, de Liturgie, d'Archaelogie, d'Histoire et de Géographie Orientales* Vol. 8 (1905) pp.40-3

Parry, Richard Lloyd "Muslim nations defend use of suicide bombers" in *The Independent* (11 April 2002)

Paz, Reuven *The Heritage of the Sunni Militant Groups: An Islamic internacionale?* (4 January 2000) http://www.ict.org.il/articles/articledet. cfm?articleid=415 (viewed 5 December 2003)

Peters, Rudolph *Islam and Colonialism: The Doctrine of Jihad in Modern History* (The Hague: Mouton, 1979)

Peters, Rudolph *Jihad in Classical and Modern Islam: a Reader* (Princeton: Markus Wiener Publishers, 1996)

Phillipson, Coleman *The International Law and Custom of Ancient Greece and Rome* 2 vols (London: Macmillan & Co. Ltd, 1911)

Philps, Alan "Settlers Use Pigskin to Foil the Martyrs" www.telegraph.co.uk (26 February 2002) (viewed 5 December 2003)

Pipes, Daniel "Muslims Love Bin Laden" in *New York Post* (22 October 2001)

Pipes, Daniel "Know Thy Terrorists" in *New York Post* (19 November 2002)

Piscatori, James *Islam in a World of Nation States* (Cambridge: Cambridge University Press, 1986)

Price, Randall *Unholy War* (Eugene, Oregon: Harvest House Publishers, 2001)

Qutb, Sayyid *Fi Zilal al-Quran* (Beirut: Dar al-Shuruq, 1987)

Qutb, Sayyid *Islam and Peace* (Cairo: Dar al-Shuruq, 1988)

Qutb, Sayyid *Milestones* (Lahore: Qazi Publications, no date). Also *Milestones [Ma'alem Fil Tariq]* (Indianapolis: American Trust Publications, 1990)

Qutb, Sayyid *The Islamic Concept and its Characteristic* (Indianapolis: American Trust Publication, 1991)

Rahim, Abdur *The Principles of Muhammadan Jurisprudence* (London: Luzac, printed Madras 1911)

Rahman, Shaykh Omar Abdul *The Present Rulers and Islam. Are they Muslims or Not?* (London: Al-Firdous, 1990)

Rajaee, Farhang *Islamic Values and World View: Khomeyni on Man, the State and International Politics* (Lanham, Maryland: University Press of America, 1983)

al-Rajihi, Ahmad Naser "Heavenly Religions Encourage Legitimate War" in *Ash-Sharq al-Awsat* (28 January 1990) reprinted in Kharofa (1994) pp. 24-30

Rapoport, David C. "Comparing Militant Fundamentalist Movements and Groups" in Marty and Appleby (1993) pp.429-61

Rasheed, Asra *Death* (Birmingham: Al-Hidaayah Publishing and Distribution, 2001)

Reeve, Simon *The New Jackals: Ramzi Yousef, Osama bin Laden and the Future of Terrorism* (London: André Deutsch, 1999)

Reynalds, Jeremy "Radical Islamic Group Threatens Britain After Police Raid" in *Assist News Service* (30 July 2003)

Roberts, Tom (writer and director) *Witness: Inside the Mind of the Suicide Bomber* (Channel 4, 10 November 2003)

Rogerson, Barnaby *The Prophet Muhammad* (London: Little, Brown, 2003)

Rood, Judith Mendelsohn "Why and How Should Christian Students Study World Religions?" in *CCCU Advance* (Spring 2003)

Sachedina, Abdulaziz "The Development of Jihad in Islamic Revelation and History" in Johnson and Kelsay (1990)

Sachedina, Abdulaziz "Justification for Violence in Islam" in *Journal of Lutheran Ethics* (19 February 2003)

al-Saidi, 'Abd al-Muta'ali *Fi Maydan al-Ijtihad* (Helwan: Jam'iyyat al-thaqafa al-Islamiyya, no date)

Salibi, Kamal S. *Syria Under Islam: Empire on Trial 634-1097* (Delmar, New York: Caravan Books, 1977)

Schacht, Joseph *The Origins of Muhammadan Jursiprudence* (Oxford: Oxford University Press, 1950)

Sciolino, Elaine "French Islam Wins Officially Recognized Voice" in *The New York Times* (14 April 2003)

Sciolino, Elaine "French Threat to Militant Muslims After Council Vote" in *The New York Times* (15 April 2004)

Sebeos *Histoire d'Héraclius* transl. F. Macler (Paris: E. Leroux, 1904)

Sebeos *History* transl. Robert Bedrosian (New York: Sources of the Armenian Tradition, 1985)

Shahid, Irfan "Asrar al-nasr al-'arabi fi futuh al-Sham" in *Bildad al Sham Proceedings* (1985)

Shahrastani, Abu al-Fath Muhammad ibn 'Abd al-Karim *Kitab al-Milal wa al-Nihal* ed. Cureton (London, 1846)

Shaltut, Mahmud *Al-Qur'an wa al-Qital [The Qur'an and Fighting]* (Matba'at al-Nasr and Maktab Ittihad al-Sharq, 1948). English translation in Peters (1996) pp.60-101

Shaltut, Mahmud *The Muslim Conception of International Law and the Western Approach* (The Hague: Martinus Nijhof, 1968)

Shariati, Ali *On the Sociology of Islam* transl. Hamid Algar (Berkeley: Mizan Press, 1979)

Shariati, Ali "Intizar: The Religion of Protest and the Return to Self" in Donohue and Esposito (1982) pp.298-304

Shawkani, Abu al-Fath Muhammad ibn 'Abd al-Karim *Nayl al-Awtar* 8 vols, 2nd edition (Cairo, 1952)

Shaybani, Muhammad ibn al-Hasan *Sharh Kitab al-Siyar al-Kabir* with commentary by Shams al-Din Muhammad b.Ahmad b. Sahl Sarakhsi, 4 vols (Hyderabad, 1916-17)

Shaybani *Siyar* translated with an introduction, notes and appendices by Majid Khadduri as *The Islamic Law of Nations: Shaybani's Siyar* (Baltimore: The Johns Hopkins Press, 1966)

Shemesh, A. Ben *Taxation in Islam* Vol. 2 (Leiden: Brill, London: Luzac & Co. Ltd, 1965)

Shirbon, Estelle "Rome Imam Suspended After Praising Suicide Bombers" Reuters (13 June 2003). Available at http://www.reuters.com/newsArticle.jht ml?typetopNews&storyID=2928250 (viewed 19 June 2003)

Sicker, Martin *The Islamic World in Ascendancy: From the Arab Conquests to the Siege of Vienna* (Westport, Connecticut: Praeger Publishers, 2000)

Simpson, John "Why Tourists are Now the Ideal Targets" in *The Sunday Telegraph* (1 December 2002) p.21

Sirriyeh, Elizabeth *Sufis and Anti-Sufis: The Defence, Rethinking and Rejection of Sufism in the Modern World* (Richmond: Curzon Press, 1999)

Smith, Jane Idleman and Yvonne Yazbeck Haddad *The Islamic Understanding of Death and Resurrection* (Albany: State University of New York Press, 1981)

Solihin, S.M. *Studies on Sayyid Qutb's Fi Zilal al-Quran* (unpublished thesis, Department of Theology, University of Birmingham, 1993)

Sophronius, *Sermones*. PG 87.3: 3201-364 in "Weihnachspredigt des Sophronios" ed. H. Usener *Rheinisches Museum für Philologie* n.s. 41 (1886) pp.500-16

Stalinksy, Steven "Saudi Policy Statements on Support to the Palestinians" MEMRI Special Report No. 17 (3 July 2003)

St Clair-Tisdall, W. *The Sources of Islam: A Persian Treatise* transl. and abridged by Sir William Muir (Birmingham: Birmingham Bible Institute, 197?)

Suleiman, Mustafa "The Rector of the Azhar University asks Arabs to Obtain Mass Destruction Weapons" in *Al-Usboa* (21 April 2003). English translation in *Arab-West Report* (17-23 April 2003)

Sun Tzŭ *The Art of War* Foreword by James Clavell (London: Hodder and Stoughton, 1981)

al-Syowty, JaLal al-Deen *Al-Atkon Fee Alom Al-Qur'an [The perfection of Qur'anic theology]* al-Tabari, Abu Ja'far Muhammad ibn Jarir *Ta'rikh al-rusul wa'l-muluk (Annales)* ed. M.J. De Goeje et al. 15 vols (Leiden: Brill, 1879-1901)

al-Tabari, Abu Ja'far Muhammad ibn Jarir *Kitab al-Jihad wa Kitab al-Jizya wa Ahkam al-Muharibin min Kitab Ikhtilaf al-Fuqaha* ed. J. Schacht (Leiden: Brill, 1933)

Taha, Mahmoud Mohamed *The Second Message of Islam* transl. Abdullah Ahmed An-Na'im (Syracuse, New York: Syracuse University Press, 1987)

Taheri, Amir "Tantawi's Tantrum" in *National Review Online* (16 May 2003)

Tantawi, Sheikh Muhammad Sayyid – a summary of his teachings can be found at http://www.sunnah.org/history/Scholars/mashaykh_azhar.htm (viewed 25 January 2002)

Thalib, Ahlus Sunnah wal Jama'ah Ustadzjaf ar Umar, address broadcast on Radio SPMM [The voice of struggle of the Maluku Muslims] (1-3 May 2002). Excerpts at www.persecution.org/news/report2002-05-15.html (viewed 20 May 2002)

Theophanes *Theophanis Chronographia* ed. C. De Boor 2 vols (Leipzig, 1883-5)

Tibi, Bassam *Arab Nationalism: Between Islam and the Nation-State* 3rd edition (Basingstoke: Macmillan Press Ltd, 1997)

Tibi, Bassam *Conflict and War in the Middle East: From Interstate War to New Security* 2nd edition (Basingstoke and London: Macmillan Press Ltd, 1998)

van Ess, Josef *Theologie und Gesellschaft im 2. und 3. Jahrhundert Hidschra. Eine Geschicthe des religiösen Denkens im frühen Islam* 6 vols (Berlin: de Bruyter, 1991-5)

Vasiliev, A.A. *A History of the Byzantine Empire* 2 vols (Madison: University of Wisconsin Press, 1958)

Waddy, Charis *The Muslim Mind* 2nd edition (Longmans, 1976)

Walsh, Duncan "Boys Rescued from Kenya's Islamic School of Torture" in *The Times* (30 January 2003)

Waqidi, Abu 'Abd-Allah Muhammad ibn 'Umar *Kitab al-Maghazi* ed. Alfred von Kremer (Calcutta, 1856)

Watt, W. Montgomery *Muhammad Prophet and Statesman* (Oxford: Oxford University Press, 1961)

Watt, William Montgomery *The Formative Period of Islamic Thought* (Oxford: Oneworld Publication, 1998)

Wood, Rick "Wahhabism: Out of Control?" in *Mission Frontiers* (December 2001)

Woolacott, Martin "The Bali Bomb may Deal a Fatal Blow to the Islamists" in *The Guardian* (18 October 2002)

al-Ya'qubi, Ahmad b. Abi Ya'qub *Ta'riqh* ed. M. Th. Houtsma 2 vols, (Leiden: Brill, 1883)

al-Yassini, Ayman *Religion and State in the Kingdom of Saudi Arabia* (Boulder, Colorado: Westview Press, 1985)

Zakaria, Fareed "Now, Saudis See the Enemy" in *Newsweek* (26 May – 2 June 2003) p.19

Zakaria, Fareed "Suicide Bombers Can be Stopped" in *Newsweek* (25 August – 1 September 2003) p.15

az-Zubaidi, Al-Imam Zain-ud-Din Ahmad bin Abdul-Lateef (compiler) *The Translation of the Meanings of summarized Sahih Al-Bukhari Arabic-English*, transl. Dr Muhammad Muhsin Khan (Riyadh: Maktaba Dar-us-Salam Publishers, 1994)

Zuhayli, Wahba *Athar al-Harb fi al-Fiqh al-Islami. Dirasa muqarina.* (Beirut: Dar al-Fikr, 1965)

Zwemer, S.M. *Arabia: The Cradle of Islam* (Edinburgh and London: Oliphant Anderson and Ferrier, 1900)

Index of Qur'an References

Note: Verse numbers vary slightly between different translations of the Qur'an, so it may be necessary to search in the verses just preceding or just following the verse numbers given here to find the relevant text in any given translation.

Index of *Hadith* References

Index